Essentials *of*
Development
Economics

*This was probably the best textbook
I have ever read and probably the ONLY
textbook that I have read completely.*
　　　　　—Maybo Li, UC Davis student

Essentials *of*

Development

Economics

J. EDWARD TAYLOR

with Travis Lybbert

 REBEL TEXT

Berkeley, California

You can order this and other books at rebeltext.org

Problems, programs, and data sets are available at rebeltext.org

■ ■ ■

RebelText logo by Peri Fletcher

Cover and book design, typesetting, and file preparation by Jan Camp
www.jcampstudio.com • www.arclightbooks.com

ISBN: 978-0-9771037-7-5

Manufactured in the USA.
Published by Arc Light Books / RebelText
Berkeley, California
www.rebeltext.org

Contents

Preface

It was Winter Quarter 2012. The memory of pepper spray still permeated the air above the UC Davis quad. I gritted my teeth and told the campus bookstore to order up 125 copies of an undergraduate econometrics textbook at $150 a shot. (That's a gross of $18,750 just from my class.)

Over dinner that night, my 20-year-old son, Sebastian, just back from occupying the Port of Oakland, said he spent $180 on a new edition calculus text required for his course. My 16-year-old son, Julian, exclaimed: "That's obscene." Sebastian responded, "You're right. Basic calculus hasn't changed in decades. You don't need new editions to learn calculus."

Before dinner was over, my two kids ambushed me and made me promise never, ever, to assign an expensive textbook to my students again.

"So, what do you want me to do then, write one?" I asked them.

"Exactly," they answered in unison.

"And get a good title for it," my wife, Peri, added.

The next day, RebelText was born. Its first creation was *RebelText: Essentials of Econometrics*. That seemed like a big enough project, but then Rich Sexton, my department chair, assigned me to teach our enormous undergraduate development economics course. Naturally, I had to write a book for that one, too. That's how *RebelText: Essentials of Development Economics* became the second member of the RebelText line.

What's RebelText?

First, it's affordable. It costs as little as one-fifth the price of a normal textbook. Second, it's concise. It covers what I can hope to get through in a quarter-long course (but wish I had a semester to do). Third, it's compact. Being both affordable and compact, you can carry it around with you. Write in it. Don't worry about keeping the pages clean, because at this price there's no need to resell it after the class is through (or worry about whether there will still be a market for your edition).

The price of a RebelText covers the costs of printing and student assistants and research to keep the series going. That's why it's so low. No mega-profits for presses, always pushing for a new edition to spoil the resale market. This RebelText will naturally evolve as needed to keep pace with the field, but there will never, ever, be a new edition just for profits' sake.

Who Should Have this Book?

When I sat down to write *Essentials of Development Economics*, I wanted a compact book for an upper-division undergraduate development economics class. That is primarily what this is. The undergraduate development textbooks out there not only are very expensive; I have found them not to be particularly good teaching tools. They tend to be a smorgasbord of topics instead of providing students with the essential idea and tool kit for doing development economics. Every year students complain about this in their evaluations. The knowledge in this book should poise any undergraduate for further study or to venture out into the real world with the essential economic development concepts and tools under her belt, and then some.

There's a striking disconnect between development textbooks and journal articles. Specialized journal articles really are what shape the way we think about development economics problems and research. They were not written for undergraduate courses. Nevertheless, the topics they cover, research approaches they use, and critical findings they present are essential to understanding development economics, and they *can* be made accessible. Journal articles are highlighted in boxes throughout this book.

QR (Quick Reference) codes link readers with online materials, including images and video clips of some of the most influential leaders in development economics presenting their ideas about material in the book. You will find several of these scattered throughout the book. If you do not have a tablet or smart phone, don't worry—the links are also available as urls in the "Resources" area of rebeltext.org.

As the book took shape my vision for it got bigger. I found myself wishing I'd had something like it while I was a graduate student, to put all those journal articles into perspective. Writing *RebelText* forced me to sit down and think hard about what the *essentials* of development economics are. This is much harder to do for development economics than, say, econometrics, in which a single general model (the classical regression model) is the launching pad for a whole course.

That's where Travis came in.

Travis is a quickly rising star in the development economics world. Less than a decade out of graduate school, he has research projects underway on three continents, dozens of publications that include top economics and development economics journals, and numerous awards, including the best article of the year in the *American Journal of Agricultural Economics* and teaching awards at both UC Davis and Cornell. In short, Travis is out there reshaping the field, and he knows how to teach it.

The result of all this hard thinking is a more structured and comprehensive approach as well as a fresh take on what development economics is about. *RebelText: Essentials of Development Economics* takes the most exciting discoveries and critical methods in the field and makes them accessible to students in a way that they have not been before.

How to Use RebelText

RebelText was created to make learning and teaching as efficient as possible. Students need to learn the essentials of the subject. They do not want to wade through thick textbooks in order to locate what they need, constantly wondering what will and won't be on the next test. Because it is so concise, there is no reason not to read and study every word of

RebelText: Essentials of Development Economics. All of it could be on the test. Master it, and you will be well positioned to go out and do development work in the real world. You can think of this book as presenting the "best practices" and state-of-the-art methods for doing development economics. By mastering it, you'll also have the conceptual and intuitive grounding you need in order to move on to higher-level development economics courses. You'll probably find yourself referring back to it from time to time, so keep it on your shelf!

RebelText comes with its own "living" website: rebeltext.org. There, you'll find data sets included in this book, interesting links, and other items of interest. Updated homework questions often are used as an excuse for printing new editions of textbooks. The way we see it, that's what websites are for. When my colleagues and I use RebelText, this website becomes a center of class activity.

If you are teaching with RebelText, consider contributing your ideas about novel uses of our book and website, interesting data sets, programs, and projects. To find out how, visit rebeltext.org and click on "contributing to RebelText."

About the Authors

Ed loves teaching economics, especially microeconomics, econometrics, and economic development. He's been doing it for about 25 years now at UC Davis, where he is a professor in the Agricultural and Resource Economics Department. He's also done a lot of economics research; at last count he had published about 136 articles, book chapters, and books on topics ranging from international trade reforms to ecotourism, immigration, and rural poverty. He's in *Who's Who in Economics*, the list of the world's most cited economists, and he is editor of the *American Journal of Agricultural Economics*. He has worked on projects with the United Nations, the World Bank, the Organization for Economic Cooperation and Development, and the Inter-American Development

Bank, as well as with foreign governments, including those of Mexico, Honduras, Canada, and China. He is working on a book called *Beyond Experiments: Simulation Methods for Impact Evaluation*, which will present a new approach to doing impact evaluation and cost-benefit analysis. You can learn more about Ed at his website: jetaylor.ucdavis.edu.

Travis Lybbert was initially torn between Environmental Studies and Landscape Architecture as an undergraduate major at Utah State University. A class on Environmental and Resource Economics convinced him that economics offered a powerful lens through which to understand social problems, dilemmas and potential solutions. After graduating with an Economics major (and French and Environmental Studies minors), he lived in Morocco for a year as a Fulbright student. The experience prompted him to pursue graduate work in economic development at Cornell University. After teaching for two years at the Honors College at Florida Atlantic University, he arrived at UC Davis where he is currently Associate Professor in the Agricultural and Resource Economics Department. Travis has worked in Africa, India, and at the World Trade Organization. His current projects include: assessing drought risk, coping and vulnerability in Morocco and Burkina Faso; risk and poverty dynamics among Kenyan pastoralists; micronutrient supplements and household welfare in Malawi, Burkina Faso and Ghana; and cell phones and adult literacy in Niger. Travis teaches both graduate and undergraduate courses in economic development and applied economics. To learn more about him, visit his faculty website: tlybbert.ucdavis.edu.

Acknowledgements

This is the second book in the RebelText series. Neither one would have happened without my family and students. Special thanks go to Sebastian and Julian, who shamed me into writing it; to Peri, who has supported this project from the start; to Steve Boucher and Michael Carter for all the inputs they provided for chapters 10–11; and to my cutting-edge team of graduate student assistants, including: Michael Castelhano, Mateusz Filipski, Justin Kagin, Dale Manning, Karen Thome, and Abbie Turiansky, all of whom provided valuable research assistance and advice at various stages of this project.

-J. Edward Taylor
Berkeley, California
2012

1.

What Development Economics Is All About

Malawi is one of the poorest countries in the world. The average person living there had an annual income of $330 in 2010. That is not even a dollar a day. Even when we adjust for a low cost of living, the average Malawian lived off what in the United States would be the equivalent of around $850 per year.[1]

What is the solution to Malawi's pervasive poverty?

Like other less-developed countries (LDCs), Malawi has tried a number of different strategies to stimulate development and raise the welfare of its people. It made the growth of smallholder production a cornerstone of its development and poverty-alleviation strategy, by focusing on improving smallholders' access to agricultural input and output markets. Eighty-one percent of Malawi's population is rural, and smallholders make up about 90% of the poor. Food production is a major source of livelihood for most rural households. Productivity and, in particular, fertilizer use are low. Only 67% of agricultural households used fertilizer in 2004.[2]

Before 1998, Malawi relied on market price supports to transfer income to farm households. (Next door in Zambia, where per-capita income was $1,400 in 2010, the government continues paying farmers prices well above market levels for their maize.[3]) In recent years, fertilizer subsidies were the primary method of transferring income to rural Malawi households. Government payments for farmers' inputs is expensive and controversial. More than 50% of the Ministry of Agriculture's budget has gone toward paying for these subsidies.[4]

Most recently, the country has taken a new line of attack by introducing a Social Cash Transfer Scheme (SCTS) that targets ultra-poor households (those living on less than $0.10 per day) whose members are unable to work due to disability, age, illness or a high dependency ratio (too many people to take care of at home). Rather than specifically targeting agricultural production like the price supports or fertilizer subsidies, cash transfers raise incomes directly, allowing households to increase consumption or to invest in production activities. The government and researchers hope these transfers will stimulate production in other ways, while creating positive spillovers that benefit other households in the economy.

Studies to test the effectiveness of the SCTS are in the field. Similar programs are being implemented throughout the continent, in Ethiopia, Ghana, Kenya, Zambia, Zimbabwe, Lesotho, and other poor countries. The United Nations (UNICEF and the Food and Agricultural Organization-FAO), in conjunction with several universities and agencies, have launched an ambitious project to document the impacts of these transfer programs on a range of outcomes, from crop production to AIDS prevention.[5]

Development economists are on the front line of this effort, helping to design and evaluate SCT programs. On a micro level, this is a good example of the sorts of things development economists do. A whole chapter later in this book (Chapter 11: What Works and What Doesn't?) is dedicated to project impact evaluation.

Development Economics involves much more than this, though.

What Is Development Economics?

Usually, a development economics class is a potpourri of special topics. It's hard for it not to be, because economic development involves so many different things:

- It's income growth. How can we have development without growth in countries whose per-capita incomes now hover around $1-2 per day?

- It's welfare economics, including the study of poverty and inequality.

- It's agricultural economics. How to make agriculture more productive is a big question in countries where most of the population is rural and agricultural.

- It's economic demography, the study of population growth in a world with more than 7 billion people, and population distribution in a world with more than a quarter of a billion international migrants and many more internal ones. (China will have about that many internal migrants in the near future, if it doesn't already.)

- It's labor economics: education, health, conditions in the workplace.

- It's the study of markets for goods, services, inputs, outputs, credit, insurance, without which whole economies can grind to a standstill.

- It's public economics, including the provision of public goods from roads and communications to utilities and waste treatment, and it's about managing the macro economy, too.

- Development is about natural resources and the environment: energy, water, deforestation, pollution, climate change, sustainability.

What is economic development *not* about, you might ask?

Lurking behind this question is another one, which lies at the heart of why I wrote this book: Why is there a field of development economics? After all, most economics departments have courses in each one of the above areas—and more.

Wikipedia defines development economics as "a branch of economics which deals with economic aspects of the development process in low-income countries." This implies that there must be something different about studying economics in low-income countries.

Clearly there is. Economic development entails far-reaching changes in the structure of economies, technologies, societies, and political systems. Development economics is the study of economies that do not fit many of the basic assumptions underpinning economic analysis in high-income countries, including well-functioning markets, perfect information, and low transaction costs. When these assumptions break down, so do the most basic welfare and policy conclusions of economics.

This book, like other development economics texts, touches on many different topics. However, its focus is on the fundamental things that distinguish rich and poor countries and the methods we use to analyze critical development economics issues. After reading and studying it, you should have both a tool kit for doing economic development research and an idea set to help you understand why poor countries are different and what this means for the theory and practice of development economics.

The Evolution of Development Economics

Economics classes rarely spend much time on history. But the brief history of development economics is instructive. Studying the process economists have gone through to discover what economic development is helps *us* understand the various approaches people have taken over time and how we got to the ideas that are popular now. What we *thought* development meant at the beginnings of our field's history is quite different from the way we see it today.

The origins of modern development economics are not found in low-income countries, but rather in relatively developed countries devastated by war. In the aftermath of World War II, there was a need for economic theories and policies to support the rebuilding of war-torn Europe and Japan. The United States adopted the Marshall Plan to help rebuild European economies. This was a massive program: $13 billion over four years was a lot of money back then!

In the 1950s and 1960s, economists turned their attention from Europe to the economic problems of Africa, Asia and Latin America. Lessons learned in Europe did not transfer easily to those settings; it quickly became clear that poor countries faced fundamentally different challenges.

Early development economists focused on growth, often blurring the lines between growth and development. In poor countries, major structural transformations were needed to achieve growth. By comparing different countries' growth experiences (including the past experiences of the more developed countries), economists tried to uncover the conditions that determine successful development and economic growth.

Taking Off

Seminal work during this early period of development economics includes Walter Rostow's treatise on the stages of economic growth: the traditional society, the pre-conditions for take-off, the take-off, the drive to maturity, and the age of high mass-consumption.[6] Nobel laureate Simon Kuznets (whom we shall revisit later in this chapter) countered this simplistic view that all countries go through a similar linear set of stages in their economic history. He argued instead that key characteristics of today's poor countries are fundamentally different from those of high-income countries before they developed.

The Anatomy of Growth

Economists recognized the need to understand how the growth process works. Growth is so important that we will devote a whole chapter to it in this book. There, we'll focus on modern growth theory, but growth models have played an important role since the start of development economics.

A simple aggregate growth model developed by Sir Roy F. Harrod and Evsey Domar became part of the basic creed of development economists in the 1950s and 1960s.[7] The Harrod–Domar model's main implication was that investment is the key driver of economic growth. It focused economists' and policy makers' attention on generating the savings required to support higher growth rates in poor countries. Although simplistic, this was a precursor to models used to analyze economic growth in developing countries today.

Nobel Laureate W. Arthur Lewis viewed growth through a higher-resolution lens. His famed work, *Economic Development with Unlimited Supplies of Labor*, shifted attention from aggregate growth to structural transformation.[8] Lewis introduced the dual sector model, demonstrating that the expansion of the modern (industrial or capitalist) sector depends on drawing labor from the traditional (agricultural or subsistence) sector. He focused on poor, labor-rich countries, in which a labor surplus in the subsistence sector could be a valuable resource for industrial growth: industry could expand without putting upward pressure on wages. Implicit in the Lewis model is a simple, demand-driven model of migration: as urban industry expands, people move off the farm to fill the new jobs. Whether or not workers really can be moved out of agriculture without losing crop production is an empirical question that some economists still try to answer today.

Lewis was criticized for largely ignoring agriculture. His work was extended and formalized by Gustav Ranis and John Fei, who demonstrated that industrial growth depends on agricultural growth as well as industrial profits.[9] If agricultural production does not keep up, food prices rise, and this forces urban wages up, squeezing profits and investment in industry. The growth of industry, then, depends on agriculture. Recognition that different sectors of the economy are linked in critical ways was an important contribution of dual-economy models and is a basis for more sophisticated economy-wide models today.

The assumption that there is surplus labor in the traditional sector (that is, that the marginal product of labor there is zero) was questioned by another Nobel laureate, Theodore Schultz.[10] He pointed out evidence of labor shortages during peak harvest periods even in economies like India and China, where a labor surplus existed at other times of the year. Thus, he argued, one cannot assume that countries can move labor out of agriculture without suffering a drop in crop production—unless they adopt new agricultural technologies. Schultz emphasized the importance of technological innovation and revolutionized economists' thinking by putting forth the thesis that farmers in less-developed countries are "efficient but poor." That is, while they might appear to be inefficient (compared, say, to commercial farmers in rich countries), poor farmers optimize given the severe resource constraints they face, including traditional technologies and limited human capital. The efficient-but-poor hypothesis continues to shape the way development economists think about and model poor rural economies. Nevertheless, recent work questions whether production, land tenancy (e.g., sharecropping), and other institutions in poor countries really are efficient in an economic sense.

The burgeoning early development economics literature produced far too many works to catalogue here, but two others deserve special mention because of the far-reaching impact they had on economic thinking and, more importantly, policies.

Import-substitution Industrialization

In 1950, Raul Prebisch and Hans Singer independently observed that the terms-of-trade, or the ratio of prices, between primary (agricultural, resource extraction) and manufactured products erodes over time.[11] As people's income increases, the share of income they spend on manufactures increases, while the share spent on primary goods falls. This happens globally as well as locally. Prebisch and Singer argued that this drives up the prices of manufactured goods relative to primary goods. Poor countries that continue to specialize in primary-goods production lose out compared to countries that protect and promote their industries.

Prebisch and Singer's work was enormously influential in promoting protectionist trade policies, shielding infant industries in poor countries from international competition. Its policy prescriptions ran soundly against the doctrine that countries should follow their comparative advantage in trade. In retrospect, countries that followed this advice did not fare as well as countries like the "Asian Tigers" (Hong Kong, Singapore, South Korea and Taiwan) that followed more outward (trade)-oriented development models.

Linkages

Albert Hirschman, another early pioneer in development economics, put forth the interesting and influential argument that imbalances between demand and supply in less-developed economies can be good: they create pressures that stimulate economic growth. Hirschman was instrumental in creating a focus on economic linkages, which pervade economy-wide modeling, a staple of development policy analysis today. By promoting investments in industries with many linkages to other firms, governments can have a multiplier effect on economic growth; the effects of a policy spread to industries linked to the targeted industry. Backward linkages transmit growth effects from an input-demanding activity (e.g., textiles) to input suppliers (cotton mills or wool producers). Forward linkages stimulate the growth of activities ahead of firms, as when investment in an electricity generator facilitates the growth of electricity-using industries.

Hirschman argued that agriculture generated few linkages with the rest of the economy. This, particularly when combined with the Prebisch-Singer hypothesis, contributed to the sense among policy makers that agriculture is unimportant and countries ought to use their scarce resources to promote industrial, not agricultural, growth. John Mellor countered this argument in his seminal work, *The New Economics of Growth*, which documented the importance of consumption linkages between rural households and urban industries. If most of a country's population is rural, where will the demand for new industrial production be if not in rural households? Rising agricultural incomes, then, provide a critical market for manufactures, thereby stimulating industrial growth.

Development economists had begun to take more of a systems view of poor economies, recognizing the linkages among production sectors and between firms and households that are important in shaping economic growth. They would soon rethink their emphasis on growth, though.

Rethinking Growth: Inequality and Poverty

The United Nations declared the 1960s to be the decade of development. In 1961, it:

> "...called on all member states to intensify their efforts to mobilize support for measures required to accelerate progress toward self-sustaining economic growth and social advancement in the developing countries."

Each developing country set its own target, but the overall goal was to achieve a minimum annual growth rate of 5% in aggregate national income by the end of the decade.[12] The world came close to realizing the UN's goal. Less-developed countries achieved an average annual growth rate of 4.6% from 1960-1967. However, their population also increased. As a result, their per capita gross product (income divided by population) rose only about 2%.

When the UN Development Decade ended in 1970, the gap between rich and poor countries had widened: two-thirds of the world's population had less than one-sixth of the world's income. This raised new questions about the meaning of development. Evidently, a tide of rising world income did not lift all—or even most—boats. The U.N. General Assembly concluded that one of the reasons for the slow progress was the absence of a clear international development strategy.

The problem of rising inequality made development economists rethink their focus on growth. Before then, the key work linking growth and inequality was Simon Kuznets' "inverted U" hypothesis. It stated that economic growth decreases inequality in rich countries but increases it in poor countries.[14] It tended to create a sense of complacency about inequality: sure, inequality increases for awhile as poor countries grow, but eventually countries "outgrow" it and become more equal. At least, that's what Kuznets saw when he used cross-section data to compare rich and poor countries. (Cross section data are data on different countries at the same point in time. It would have been nice to track the same countries over time to see if inequality first increases then decreases as economies grow, but we didn't have the data to do that back when Kuznets put forth his novel theory.)

As panel data became available to track individual countries' growth and inequality, the inverted-U theory has been challenged repeatedly in the development economics literature, though it seems to fit some countries well. (Panel data provide information on the same units (here, countries) over time.) Today, China is growing fast, and inequality there is increasing. Brazil and Mexico have much higher per-capita incomes than China, and inequality there is going down. Then there's the United States, where inequality fell through the 1970s but is rising again now.

Development economics shifted its attention from income growth to income inequality. In 1974, Hollis Chenery, head of the World Bank's economic research department, published an influential book called *Redistribution with Growth*. It demonstrated that when assets (such as land) are distributed unequally, economic growth creates an unequal distribution of benefits. Around the same time (1973), Irma Adelman and Cynthia Taft Morris published a book called *Economic Growth and Social Equity in Developing Countries*. They found that as incomes grew, not only did inequality increase, but the *absolute* position of the poor *worsened*. At the early stages of a country's economic growth, the poorest segment of society may be harmed, as traditional economic relationships in subsistence economies are displaced by emerging commercial ones. Growth was more equitable in countries that redistributed assets, like land and human capital (education), *before* the growth happened.

Robert McNamara, the World Bank's president, presented Chenery's findings at a 1972 UN Conference in Santiago, Chile. The new position of the World Bank and development economics profession was that growth is not enough. McNamara and many development economists recommended redistribution before growth; for example, land reforms and other measures to raise the productivity of small farmers and widespread rural education programs.

The development economics mantra had shifted from "growth" to "inequality," "poverty," "basic needs," and "broad-based economic growth." National planning offices cropped up around the world, often with "five-year plans" inspired by the Soviet Union's planning models but not necessarily socialistic in nature. While I was an undergraduate student I worked for a year with the National Planning Office in Costa Rica, which hardly was a communist state! This period saw the advent of economy-wide models as a tool for development planning and policy. These models were designed to simulate the complex impacts that policies have on whole economies as well as on particular social groups. They continue to be a staple of development economics research and policy design.

The 1970s marked the beginning of what has become an ongoing friction between direct government involvement in the development process and market-led development. The traditional neoclassical economic view, inspired by Adam Smith's "invisible hand," is that individuals and firms, in the pursuit of their self-interest, are led as if by an invisible hand to economic efficiency. For example, competition among profit-maximizing firms drives down prices for selfish, utility-maximizing consumers. However, the invisible hand does not typically lead to fair outcomes, so government intervention can often play a role in promoting social objectives other than efficiency, such as equality or protection of domestic industries.

The 1960s and 1970s witnessed increasing government involvement in markets: setting prices, controlling trade, and creating "para-statal" enterprises that did everything from buying and selling crops to drilling for oil. Much of the focus of these efforts was on stimulating industrial growth; however, most of the population in poor countries—especially the very poor—depended heavily on agriculture. In many countries, import-substitution industrialization policies created severe biases against agriculture, in three ways:

- "Cheap food policies" directly harmed agriculture while helping to keep urban wages low.

- Steep tariffs and quotas on imported industrial goods and direct subsidies were used to promote industrialization. This increased the profitability of industrial compared to agricultural production.

- Macroeconomic policies like over-valued exchange rates made imported industrial inputs and technologies (as well as food) cheaper. This created yet another bias against agriculture, by making traded goods (food) less profitable than non-traded goods (manufactures, which were protected from trade competition).

Trusting Markets

The 1980s saw the beginning of a backlash against too much state involvement in the economy. This was the era of Ronald Reagan and Margaret Thatcher, in which we recognized the inefficiencies of state-planned economic systems like in the Soviet Union and China compared with the more laissez-fair political systems in the west. Meanwhile, it became clear that the countries that were experiencing the most rapid and broad-based growth were *not* the inward-oriented countries following import-substitution industrialization, like Kenya, Mexico and Brazil. Instead, they were the outward (export)-oriented economies, particularly the Asian Tigers. In those countries, governments were involved, sometimes heavily, in the economy, but opening up to market competition made it possible to become competitive on a world scale.

In the 1970s and 1980s, the world economy went into a recession as oil prices soared. Debt crises struck many LDCs (particularly in Latin America), forcing them to rethink their development policies—often as part of "structural adjustment" programs required by the International Monetary Fund (IMF) as a condition for restructuring their debt.

The World Bank's 1984 *World Development Report* was somewhat of a watershed. It called for removing distortions created by governments' over-involvement in agricultural markets. Almost overnight, governments began to withdraw from markets, dismantling import-substitution industrialization policies and opening up to trade. Less-developed countries around the world entered into free-trade agreements (see box, "Major Free-trade Agreements").

Major Free-Trade Agreements by Year

- ASEAN Free Trade Area (AFTA), 1992
- Asia-Pacific Trade Agreement (APTA), 1975
- Central American Integration System (SICA), 1993
- Central European Free Trade Agreement (CEFTA), 2006
- Common Market for Eastern and Southern Africa (COMESA), 1994
- G-3 Free Trade Agreement (G-3), 1995
- Greater Arab Free Trade Area (GAFTA), 1957
- Gulf Cooperation Council (GCC), 1981
- North American Free Trade Agreement (NAFTA), 1995
- South Asia Free Trade Agreement (SAFTA), 2004
- Southern African Development Community (SADC), 1992
- Southern Common Market (MERCOSUR), 1991
- Trans-Pacific Strategic Economic Partnership (TPP), 2005
- U.S.-Central American Free-Trade Agreement (CAFTA), 2006

Not (Quite) Trusting Markets

The market liberalization movement continued into the 1990s; however, the enthusiasm for free trade became tempered by a realization that market liberalization does not necessarily improve people's economic welfare if markets do not work properly. This produced a surge of research documenting market failures in LDCs as well as their underlying causes. (Markets and market failures are the subject of Chapter 9.)

Joseph Stiglitz, who received the 2001 Nobel Prize in Economics, along with other economists, demonstrated that markets are rarely efficient. He attributed this largely to imperfect information, which creates high transaction costs that lead to widespread market failures, particularly in poor countries. When markets do not work well, government involvement in the economy can often improve welfare. Development economists have been careful to warn that market failures do not necessarily warrant broad state intervention in the economy: there are government failures as well as market failures. However, the scope for the state to raise welfare by intervening in markets, it seems, is much larger than previously thought.

The Experimental Revolution

Today, much of the focus of development economics has shifted to the micro, project-evaluation level. Increasingly, development economics research involves using experiments to learn about people's economic behavior and evaluate the impacts of policy interventions on welfare outcomes. When experiments are not possible, economists use other methods, including econometrics and simulation modeling, to try to identify the impacts of policies and programs. The social cash transfer programs mentioned at the start of this chapter are an example. Today, if you work for an NGO, international development agency, or even LDC government, there is a good chance you'll be dealing with experimental economics. Experiments have become such an important part of development economics that we devote an entire chapter (Chapter 11: "What Works and What Doesn't?") to them in this book.

What Is Economic Development, Then?

Economic development has different meanings in different contexts. In rich countries, it is pretty much equated with growth. Picture the urban developer who makes skyscrapers sprout from vacant lots in a blighted city core. Politically, development projects in high-income countries often are motivated by some of the same goals that inspire development projects in poor countries, particularly the creation of new jobs, incomes, and tax revenues. Their ultimate aim, however, is likely to be growth.

Most development economists today would say that economic development is not equivalent to growth, although it is difficult to achieve development goals without growth. Development projects around the world focus on concrete outcomes related to poverty, malnutrition, inequality, and health. Development is about satisfaction of basic physical needs like nutrition, shelter, and clothing, and about the development of the mind (and of course people's earnings potential), through education. Projects also focus on the environment, conservation, and sustainable resource use; on human rights, gender and ethnic equity, and even government corruption.

All of these questions can be vital not only to determining who reaps the benefits of economic growth, but also to growth itself. Herein lies a fundamental difference in the way we tend to look at economics and politics in rich and poor countries. In high-income countries (not to mention our micro-economic courses!), economic efficiency and equity tend to be viewed as separate questions. The efficient allocation of resources is critical to ensure that economies produce the biggest possible economic pie, given the constraints they face (i.e., limited resources and technologies). Efficiency is the primary focus of the vast majority of our economics classes.

What about equity? How the pie gets distributed usually is an afterthought. It is sometimes thought of as being more the domain of politics than economics. Think about the economics courses you've taken. The textbook view is that efficiency and equity are sequential, or recursive, problems: First grow the pie, and once that's done, think about how it gets distributed (or step back and let the market decide).

Clearly, there's an important separability assumption here: that efficiency can be achieved regardless of how income is distributed. Is this a reasonable assumption? In a competitive market equilibrium, there will be different outcomes depending upon what the initial distribution of wealth looks like. But provided the basic assumptions of the competitive model (which you learned in your introductory economics courses) hold, all will be efficient in the Pareto sense: you cannot make anyone better off without making someone else worse off. If you ever studied an Edgeworth Box, you've seen how economists show this.

The separability of equity and efficiency was reinforced by the Nobel Laureate Ronald Coase, who argued that bargaining will lead to an efficient outcome regardless of the initial allocation of property rights, even in the case of externalities (a cost or benefit not reflected in prices, like pollution). According to Coase it doesn't matter whether you have the right to smoke or I have the right to breath clean air. Once we have finished bargaining with each other, the amount of smoke in the air will be the same. This view has achieved the status of a theorem: Coase's Theorem.

If efficiency and equity are truly separate issues, then there is not much room for economic policy, nor much reason for efficiency-minded economists to worry about equity. (Of course, even economists might worry about equity for other (i.e., humanitarian) reasons.)

It might surprise you, then, that a great deal of development economists' effort goes into discovering how equity and efficiency are intertwined, especially in poor countries. How assets are distributed clearly affects efficiency if:

- Banks are unwilling to loan money to small farmers
- Poor people cannot get insurance to protect themselves against crop loss or sickness
- Poverty and malnutrition prevent kids from growing up to become productive adults
- Access to markets for the stuff people produce, the inputs they use, and the goods they demand is different for the poor and rich
- The ability to get a job depends on who you are, not on how productive you are

In these and many other cases, the separability of equity and efficiency breaks down. A person's capacity to produce (or even consume) efficiently depends upon how wealth is distributed to start out with because the basic assumptions of competitive markets often don't hold for the poorest members of society. A rich farmer can produce where the market price equals the marginal cost of producing corn, the basic requirement for profit maximization and efficiency. But if a poor farmer lacks the cash to buy fertilizer, and no bank will lend to her, she will not be able to produce as efficiently as the large farmer. Efficiency then depends on how income is distributed to begin with.

The conditions under which equity affects efficiency are many, and they permeate the economies and societies of poor countries. Development economics, more than anything else perhaps, is the study of economies in which equity and efficiency are closely interrelated. This opens up a whole realm of possibilities for policy and project interventions to increase economic efficiency as well as equity. More often than not, equity and efficiency are not only complementary; they are inseparable.

The Millennium Development Goals (MDGs)

Eradicating extreme poverty continues to be one of the main chal-lenges of our time, and is a major concern of the international com-munity. Ending this scourge will require the combined efforts of all, governments, civil society organizations and the private sector, in the context of a stronger and more effective global partnership for development. The Millennium Development Goals set timebound targets, by which progress in reducing income poverty, hunger, disease, lack of adequate shelter and exclusion—while promoting gender equality, health, education and environmental sustainabil-ity—can be measured. They also embody basic human rights—the rights of each person on the planet to health, education, shelter and security. The Goals are ambitious but feasible and, together with the comprehensive United Nations development agenda, set the course for the world's efforts to alleviate extreme poverty by 2015.

—United Nations Secretary-General BAN Ki-moon

In September 2000 189 nations came together at United Nations Head-quarters in New York and adopted the United Nations Millennium Declaration. In it, they committed to creating a new global partnership to reduce extreme poverty and achieve a set of specific development targets by 2015. These targets (see Appendix at the end of this chap-ter), which range from health to environment to gender equality, have become known as the Millennium Development Goals (MDGs).[14] Set-ting goals like these and monitoring our progress towards achieving them requires tremendous amounts of data, measurement methods, and above all, commitment.

If you attend almost any international development meeting, you almost certainly will hear the MDGs come up. The MDGs are often used by governments and international development agencies to motivate and justify specific development projects. They have galvanized efforts to meet the needs of people in the world's poorest countries.

The UN Secretary General explains the Millennium Development Goals.

The Organization of this Book

This book was written to provide students with the essential tools and concepts of development economics. Most development texts are written around topics: money, labor, population, and so on. The chapters in this book are less about topics than providing a window into how developing economies are different and what this means for the way we study them. Most of the cutting-edge research by economists is found in journal articles that are beyond the reach of most undergraduate students. Text boxes scattered throughout the book try to make this research available, summarizing the questions it asks, the methods it uses, key findings, and why they are important. By the end of this book, our hope is that students will have a new understanding of what economists bring to development research and policy and be conversant in many of the approaches they employ.

The rest of this book is all about seeking answers to big questions.

Chapters 2 through 5 are about understanding, measuring, and analyzing the four key elements of economic development: Income (Chapter 2), Poverty (Chapter 3), Inequality (Chapter 4), and Human Development (Chapter 5).

A theme that emerges from the first five chapters is that income growth is an important, though by no means sufficient, condition for achieving economic development. How can countries, regions, and households make their incomes grow? Chapter 6 ("Growth") gives an introduction to aggregate (national) growth theory and concludes by asking whether poor countries, regions, and households are "catching up," and whether income growth alone will enable countries to reach the Millennium Development Goals.

Agriculture still dominates the economies of many countries in terms of income and employment. Chapter 7 ("Agriculture") presents the key tools economists have come up with to analyze agricultural economies, with an eye towards understanding a wide array of impacts, from agricultural policies to trade and climate change. This chapter begins with the agricultural household model, the staple of microeconomic analysis of agricultural and rural economies. It concludes with village and rural economy-wide models, which let us see how households are connected with each other and transmit impacts of policy, market, and environmental shocks.

Most of the world's poverty is in rural areas. Rural economies, though, are becoming less agricultural over time, as households get an increasing share of their income from non-agricultural activities. For a growing number of people, getting out of poverty means moving off the farm. Chapter 8 ("Transformation") looks at the far-reaching transformations of rural and national economies that accompany economic growth and what this means for how we do economic analysis and design development policies.

Markets and trade are vital for countries to grow and spread the benefits of this growth across a broad population. However, markets fail for many people, and others find themselves unable to compete in an increasingly global economy. In Chapters 9 ("Markets, Information, and Trade") and 10 ("Credit and Risk"), we see why economists think markets are so important to economic development, why markets fail for many people, how globalization creates both winners and losers, and what this all means for development policies.

As households and individuals seek out livelihoods in increasingly complex and global economies, governments, international development agencies, and development banks carry out a wide diversity of development projects. Evaluating the impacts of these programs is the focus of a new generation of development economists, inspired by experimental methods. Chapter 11 ("What Works and What Doesn't") looks at why economists do experiments, what the limitations of experiments are, and how projects and policies affect non-beneficiaries as well as beneficiaries.

Appendix

The Eight Millennium Development Goals

MDG 1: End poverty and hunger

Target 1.A: Halve, between 1990 and 2015, the proportion of people whose income is less than $1 a day

Target 1.B: Achieve full and productive employment and decent work for all, including women and young people

Target 1.C: Halve, between 1990 and 2015, the proportion of people who suffer from hunger

MDG 2: Universal Education

Ensure that, by 2015, children everywhere, boys and girls alike, will be able to complete a full course of primary schooling

MDG 3: Gender Equity

Eliminate gender disparity in primary and secondary education, preferably by 2005, and in all levels of education no later than 2015

MDG 4: Child Health

Reduce by two thirds, between 1990 and 2015, the under-five mortality rate

MDG 5: Maternal Health

Target 5.A:

Reduce by three quarters the maternal mortality ratio

Target 5.B:

Achieve universal access to reproductive health

MDG 6: Combat HIV/AIDS
Target 6.A:
> Have halted by 2015 and begun to reverse the spread of HIV/AIDS

Target 6.B:
> Achieve, by 2010, universal access to treatment for HIV/AIDS for all those who need it

Target 6.C:
> Have halted by 2015 and begun to reverse the incidence of malaria and other major diseases

MGD 7: Environmental Sustainability
Target 7.A:
> Integrate the principles of sustainable development into country policies and programmes and reverse the loss of environmental resources

Target 7.B:
> Reduce biodiversity loss, achieving, by 2010, a significant reduction in the rate of loss

Target 7.C:
> Halve, by 2015, the proportion of the population without sustainable access to safe drinking water and basic sanitation

Target 7.D:
> By 2020, to have achieved a significant improvement in the lives of at least 100 million slum dwellers

MDG 8: Develop a Global Partnership for Development
Target 8.A:
> Develop further an open, rule-based, predictable, non-discriminatory trading and financial system

Target 8.B:
    Address the special needs of least developed countries
Target 8.C:
    Address the special needs of landlocked developing countries
    and small island developing States
Target 8.D:
    Deal comprehensively with the debt problems of developing
    countries
Target 8.E:
    In cooperation with pharmaceutical companies, provide access
    to affordable essential drugs in developing countries
Target 8.F:
    In cooperation with the private sector, make available benefits of
    new technologies, especially information and communications

Learn more about the Millennium Development Goals at: http://www.
un.org/millenniumgoals/bkgd.shtml

Additional Reading

Each year, The World Bank publishes its World Development Report with its own special topic (not to mention a great source of data on an array of development indicators). As you can see, they cover an enormous array of topics. These reports are available online.[15]

World Development Reports, 2000-2012

WDR 2012: Gender Equality and Development The 2012 World Development Report on Gender Equality and Development finds that women's lives around the world have improved dramatically, but gaps remain in many areas. The authors use a conceptual framework to examine progress to date, and then recommend policy actions.

WDR 2011: Conflict, Security, and Development Conflict causes human misery, destroys communities and infrastructure, and can cripple economic prospects. The goal of this World Development Report is to contribute concrete, practical suggestions to the debate on how to address and overcome violent conflict and fragility.

WDR 2010: Development and Climate Change The main message of the report is that a "climate-smart" world is possible if we act now, act together, and act differently.

WDR 2009: Reshaping Economic Geography Places do well when they promote transformations along the dimensions of economic geography: higher densities as cities grow; shorter distances as workers and businesses migrate closer to density; and fewer divisions as nations lower their economic borders and enter world markets to take advantage of scale and trade in specialized products. WDR 2009 concludes that the transformations along these three dimensions of density, distance, and division are essential for development and should be encouraged.

WDR 2008: Agriculture for Development In the 21st century, agriculture continues to be a fundamental instrument for sustainable development and poverty reduction. WDR 2008 concludes that agriculture alone will not be enough to massively reduce poverty, but it is an essential component of effective development strategies for most developing countries.

WDR 2007: Development and the Next Generation Developing countries which invest in better education, healthcare, and job training for their record numbers of young people between the ages of 12 and 24 years of age, could produce surging economic growth and sharply reduced poverty, according to this report.

WDR 2006: Equity and Development Inequality of opportunity, both within and among nations, sustains extreme deprivation, results in wasted human potential and often weakens prospects for overall prosperity and economic growth, concludes this report.

WDR 2005: A Better Investment Climate for Everyone Accelerating growth and poverty reduction requires governments to reduce the policy risks, costs, and barriers to competition facing firms of all types—from farmers and micro-entrepreneurs to local manufacturing companies and multinationals—concludes this report.

WDR 2004: Making Services Work for Poor People This report warns that broad improvements in human welfare will not occur unless poor people receive wider access to affordable, better quality services in health, education, water, sanitation, and electricity. Without such improvements, freedom from illness and from illiteracy—two of the most important ways poor people can escape poverty—will remain elusive to many.

WDR 2003: Sustainable Development in a Dynamic World Without better policies and institutions, social and environmental strains may derail development progress, leading to higher poverty levels and a decline in the quality of life for everybody, according to this report.

WDR 2002: Building Institutions for Markets Weak institutions--tangled laws, corrupt courts, deeply biased credit systems, and elaborate business registration requirements--hurt poor people and hinder development, according to this report.

WDR 2000-2001: Attacking Poverty This report focuses on the dimensions of poverty, and how to create a better world, free of poverty. The analysis explores the nature, and evolution of poverty, and its causes, to present a framework for action.

Chapter One Notes

1. The true cost of living is difficult to compare across countries. Here we use the purchasing power parity method. Even income can be hard to measure in a country where most crop production is for home consumption. These issues will be addressed later in this book.

2. Mateusz Filipski and J. Edward Taylor. 2012. "A Simulation Impact Evaluation of Rural Income Transfers in Malawi and Ghana." *Journal of Development Effectiveness,* Vol. 4, Issue 1, pp. 109-129.

3. Chewe Nkonde, Nicole M. Mason, Nicholas J. Sitko and T.S. Jayne. "Who Gained and Who Lost from Zambia's 2010 Maize Marketing Policies?" Working Paper No. 49, Food Security Rresearch Project, Lusaka, Zambia, January 2011 (http://www.aec.msu.edu/fs2/zambia/wp49.pdf).

4. http://web.worldbank.org/WBSITE/EXTERNAL/COUNTRIES/AFRICAEXT/MALAWIEXTN/0,,contentMDK:21575335~pagePK:141137~piPK:141127~theSitePK:355870,00.html

5. You can read about some of these programs at the Transfer Project website, housed at the University of North Carolina, Chapel Hill; http://www.cpc.unc.edu/projects/transfer.

6. Walter W. Rostow, *The Stages of Economic Growth: A Non-Communist Manifesto,* Cambridge: Cambridge University Press, 1960.

7. Roy F. Harrod, 'An Essay in Dynamic Theory' (1939), *Economic Journal* 49:14–33.

8. Lewis, W. Arthur (1954). "Economic Development with Unlimited Supplies of Labor,". *Manchester School of Economic and Social Studies,* Vol. 22, pp. 139-91.

9. Gustav Ranis and John C. Fei. 1961. "A Theory of Economic Development." *American Economic Review* (September) 51:533-58.

10. Theodore W. Schultz. 1964. *Transforming Traditional Agriculture.* New Haven: Yale University Press.

11. Raúl Prebisch, "Commercial Policy in the Underdeveloped Countries," *American Economic Review* 49 (May 1959): 251–273.

12. United Nations, Encyclopedia of the Nations. http://www.nationsen-cyclopedia.com/United-Nations/Economic-and-Social-Development-FIRST-UN-DEVELOPMENT-DECADE.html

13. Kuznets, Simon. 1955. Economic Growth and Income Inequality. *American Economic Review* 45 (March): 1-28

14. See http://www.un.org/millenniumgoals/bkgd.shtml

15. http://econ.worldbank.org/WBSITE/EXTERNAL/EXTDEC/EXTRESEARCH/EXTWDRS/0,,contentMDK:20227703~pagePK:478093~piPK:477627~theSitePK:477624,00.html

2.

Income

Economic development entails many different sorts of outcomes: income growth, poverty, inequality, human welfare. These outcomes are interrelated. As we shall see, they can shape one another in complex and important ways. Before we learn how to study these outcomes and consider ways to influence them with policies and projects, we need to know how to measure them. This chapter is about measuring income. That might sound boring and straightforward, but read on...you'll be surprised by how interesting, challenging, and controversial income can be.

Measuring Income

Income is a basic development indicator and important input into achieving economic development outcomes, for a simple reason: Poor countries have fewer resources available to accomplish their development goals.

Before going any further, we should agree on how to measure income. The most basic measure of a country's income is the gross domestic product (GDP). There is a fundamental identity in economics: In all economic activities, total income must always equal total expenditures. Every dollar of sales by a shirt factory (income) either goes towards purchasing the inputs used to produce the shirts or gets paid out as profit (expenditures). Thus, we can calculate a country's GDP in either of two ways.

First, we can add up the value of all *final* goods and services *produced within the country and then sold*. By final, we mean goods and services that are *not* inputs into the production of some other good. For example, cotton is rarely a final good; it is an input into the production of cloth. Cloth, in turn, is an input into producing clothes. Clothes are almost always a final good—we buy and wear them, rather than using them to produce something else.

You can see the potential for double-counting here. The price of a shirt includes the cost of the cotton fabric to the garment factory as well as the cost of the cotton to the textile mill. If we added the value of the cotton, fabric, and shirt together to calculate GDP, we would significantly overestimate the value of what was produced in our economy. We also want to be careful not to count the value of inputs produced in foreign countries. If the buttons on our shirts were produced in Mexico, they are part of Mexico's GDP, not ours. In short, calculating national income is a lot harder than it sounds.

How do we value all of these final goods? We use market prices. This gives us the GDP at market prices.

The second way is to add up the cost of all factor inputs (capital, labor, land), or value-added. Any economic activity takes intermediate inputs (cotton fabric, thread, buttons) and uses factors of production (labor and capital) to turn these inputs into a product (shirts). The income the shirt factory creates is the difference between the value of the shirts it sells and the cost of the cotton fabric, thread, buttons, and other intermediate inputs it buys to produce the shirts. This is the value that the shirt factory adds to the cotton fabric and other intermediate inputs once it has turned them into shirts. Value-added is the factory's payments to labor and capital. Adding this up gives us the GDP at factor cost without running the risk of double-counting.

To make the difference between these two approaches crystal clear, let's introduce a new concept: Income accounting. Table 2.1 is an input-output table for a simple economy consisting of only three production sectors: Agriculture, Industry, and Services. Agriculture produces a total output of $920, and Industry and Services produce $1425 and $567, respectively. You'll notice that these numbers appear twice, as both the row and column total for each sector.

The columns show the expenditures of each sector, that is, where all the money went. In order to produce its output, Agriculture bought $225 in intermediate inputs from itself (e.g., seed), $320 from the industrial sector (e.g., chemical fertilizer), and $75 from services (e.g., contractors and accountants). It spent $100 in wages and purchased $50 in imported inputs. Finally, the agricultural sector generated $150 in profits, for an expenditure total of $920.

The total expenditures must equal the total value of agricultural production. The Agriculture row tells us where this production went, or in other words, who paid money to farms. Reading across the first row you can see that $225 of the value of agricultural output was sold back to agriculture, as intermediate inputs (e.g., seeds), $75 to industry (e.g., as wheat to flour mills), and $2 to services (e.g., food to schools). The difference between the total agricultural production ($920) and these intermediate uses of agricultural goods ($225+$75+$2=$302) is the final demand for agricultural output ($618).

Table 2.1: An Input-Output Table

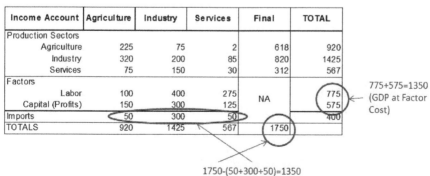

Income Account	Agriculture	Industry	Services	Final	TOTAL
Production Sectors					
Agriculture	225	75	2	618	920
Industry	320	200	85	820	1425
Services	75	150	30	312	567
Factors					
Labor	100	400	275	NA	775
Capital (Profits)	150	300	125		575
Imports	50	300	50		400
TOTALS	920	1425	567	1750	

775+575=1350
← (GDP at Factor Cost)

1750-(50+300+50)=1350
(GDP at Market Prices)

You can interpret the Industry and Service accounts in exactly the same way.

It is easy to calculate GDP from the input-output table, using either of the two methods. GDP at market prices is the sum of the total final demand ($618+$820+$312) minus imported inputs ($50+$300+$50), or $1350. GDP at factor cost is just the sum of payments to factors (labor and capital), or value-added: $775+$575=$1350. As you can see, it doesn't matter which way we do it—we end up with the same GDP.

Now you've not only learned how to calculate GDP but a little bit about input-output (IO) accounting, too. IO was the basis for centralized planning in the former Soviet Union and other countries. Today, it is the starting point for doing any kind of economy-wide analysis. Computable general-equilibrium (CGE) models and other types of economy-wide analysis are largely beyond the scope of this book, but we will refer to them from time to time, and when we do, you can remember this simple IO example. IO tables can be constructed for any economy or activity, from countries or groups of countries (even the entire world!) to villages or agricultural households. With the right data, you could make one for your university, student union, or student farm.

You will run across a couple of other names for national income. The gross national product (GNP), also known as gross national income (GNI), is the same as GDP, but it includes the value of goods and services produced by citizens abroad. For example, Mexican migrant workers in the United States send home, or remit, more than $25 billion annually. This is value produced by Mexicans abroad, so it is counted in Mexico's GNP (but not in its GDP). It is removed from the US GDP when calculating the US GNP. For the most part, there is little difference between GNP and GDP, so the two are often used almost interchangeably. This is not technically correct, though, and in a few cases it matters. For example, in a Mexican village, counting the remittances that flow in makes a big difference when calculating village income (the gross village product).

What's Not in GDP

Now that we know what's in GDP, let's ask ourselves what isn't. This might seem technical, but it really matters, especially in poor countries where a lot of what's produced never gets sold and a lot of what goes into production never gets bought.

Look at our IO table. Everything is in value terms. The GDP at market prices is the value of all *final* goods and services *produced* in a country then *sold*. The GDP at factor cost also was calculated based on goods sold and inputs purchased.

Most staple production in poor countries is for subsistence: It isn't sold. We'll discuss subsistence production and its ramifications in detail in a later chapter. For now, what matters is that, unless a crop is sold, it may not be counted as part of national income. To count subsistence production, we would need not only to expand our definition of national income to include it but also find a way to place an economic value on a non-marketed good. Some countries try to do this more than others.

The same applies to family inputs. Most labor on small farms is not hired but supplied by the family itself. No wage is paid for this labor, yet clearly it is part of the value-added produced by agriculture.

What about barter? Labor exchanges? Forget it—they aren't in the GDP.

We can take special steps to count these non-market activities in our income calculations, but it won't be easy. For starters, how do we value family labor? Or labor exchanged? Do we use the market wage? I might have to monitor my hired workers to make sure they give me the same value product per day as my own labor does (see Chapter 9, "Markets, Information, and Trade"). You can bet that I have knowhow about my farming operation that my hired workers do not. A day of my labor is likely more productive than a day of hired or exchanged labor, and therefore worth more than the market wage.

What about the value of subsistence production? Is the price of a traditional variety of maize grown by an indigenous farmer in Oaxaca the same as the price of corn in a market? (As we shall see in Chapter 9, it turns out to be higher.) How do we value bartered goods?

Even in rich countries controversy surrounds national income accounting. The same work may or may not contribute to national income, depending on who does it. Last night, my wife and I made a nice teriyaki chicken dinner. The value we produced cooking at home obviously didn't get counted in the GDP. However, if we had hired a cook to do the same thing, it would have. I can hire a carpenter to fix my house or do it myself (that's what Home Depot is for). In the first case, GDP goes up, in the second, it does not. All the time we spend raising our children doesn't count in the U.S. GDP. If we hired a nanny, it would.

These questions strike right at the heart of gender in development. In many settings, women are more involved in non-market activities than men are; thus, the fruits of women's work are under-counted in the GDP.

Then there is the underground economy, which generally does not get counted in the GDP yet in some cases might include a significant part of the economy. In 2010, California voters considered legalization of marijuana under Proposition 19. Imagine how much Mendocino County's GDP would have risen if that proposition had passed!

I bet you never thought measuring national income could be so interesting...and controversial! Just a few weeks before he was assassinated in 1968, as part of a speech he made at the University of Kansas, Robert Kennedy gave what might be the most emotionally moving account ever of what's in the GNP—and what isn't.[1]

Per-capita Income

Once we know gross national income, we can convert it to per-capita income simply by dividing by the country's population. This is very important if we wish to compare standards of living across countries.

China's gross GDP (in nominal terms; see below) was $5.8 trillion in 2010. The U.S. GDP was $14.6 trillion. Yet with a little more than 1.3 billion people (compared to 308 million in the U.S.), China's per-capita income was $4,260, while the U.S's was $47,140!

Exchange Rates and Purchasing Power Parity

How did we come up with this income figure for China? After all, they don't use dollars much over there; the currency in China is the *renmin bi* (also called the Chinese *yuan*). To convert to dollars, we divided the China GDP in *renmin bi* by the nominal exchange rate, which in 2010 was 6.62.

This isn't a fair comparison, you might say, because $4,260 goes a lot further in China than in the U.S., where the cost of living is higher. You're right—about 78% further, according to the World Bank.[2] If we add this additional "purchasing power" to the per-capita income of China, we get: 1.78*$4,260=$7,570. We call this the purchasing power parity (PPP) – adjusted per-capita income. PPP adjustments are essential if we wish to compare incomes and understand differences in standards of living across countries.

Price Deflating

We also want to be able to compare incomes in the same countries over time. When we do that, we need to adjust for changes in prices over time. Here's an example. Between 2009 and 2010, the GDP of the Democratic Republic of the Congo (DRC) rose a hefty 31%, from $12.2 billion to $16.1 billion. Of course, it didn't really grow that much (that is, not in real terms). Inflation in 2010 was 22%, which makes the 2010 GDP look higher than it really was. To get the real (inflation-adjusted) GDP growth, we have to take the 2010 GDP and divide it by one plus the rate of inflation: GDP(real)=GDP(nominal)/(1.22). This gives us a 2010 real GDP of $13.1 billion and a (still respectable) real GDP growth rate of (13.1/12.2)-1=0.07, or 7%. The DRC had an unusually high inflation rate, by international standards. In all countries, though, when comparing incomes over time, it is crucial to adjust for inflation.

Green Accounting and Externalities

Yet another thing missing from national accounts is the environmental cost of producing countries' incomes. Remember that anything not bought and sold in an economy is not counted as part of GDP. This includes the clean air and water that get "used up" when factories belch smoke into the atmosphere and sludge into a river. We call these *environmental externalities*. The GDP may miss the depletion of natural resources if the cost of these resources is not properly reflected in market prices. Does the rising world price of oil reflect the fact that we are nearing "peak production?" It can be argued that the cost of natural resource depletion is already factored into rising resource prices. Climate change takes the stakes of not taking environmental costs into account to a whole new, global level.

To the extent environmental costs are not reflected in the GDP, the methods described above may overstate income. The economist Robert Repetto and co-authors wrote that ignoring environmental costs in our GDP calculations:

> "...Reinforces the false dichotomy between the economy and 'the environment' that leads policy makers to ignore or destroy the latter in the name of economic development."[3]

The economist Peter Wood proposed a way to deal with environmental costs in GDP calculations. He called it "Green Accounting." If we know what the environmental costs of production are, we can include them in our input-output table by adding an "environment account" as in Table 2.2.

Table 2.2: An Input-Output Table with Green Accounting.

Income Account	Agriculture	Industry	Services	Final	TOTAL
Production Sectors					
Agriculture	225	75	2	618	920
Industry	320	200	85	820	1425
Services	75	150	30	312	567
Factors					
Labor	90	360	247.5	NA	697.5
Capital (Profits)	135	270	112.5		517.5
Imports	50	300	50		400
Environment	25	70	40		135
TOTALS	920	1425	567	1750	

Notice the new row, labeled "Environment." Think of it as environmental inputs (like clean air) that get used to produce stuff. Now, producing $920 in agricultural output incurs a $25 environmental cost. The environmental costs associated with industrial and service production are $70 and $40, respectively. These environmental costs decrease our GDP from $1,350 to $1,215.

To include this environmental account in our table, I assumed that 10% of value-added in each activity was at the expense of "using up" environmental inputs for which there are no market transactions. This might seem arbitrary, and it is: We do not really know what the true environmental costs of production are (though they're not likely to be zero). This is the greatest challenge to green accounting, though substantial research is going into estimating the environmental costs of various economic activities. If we can figure out a way to create markets for environmental goods, our green accounting problem will be solved.

Environmental costs are not the only externalities we might want to think about. Obesity, for example, increases the GDP: the more food people consume, the higher GDP becomes. Over-consumption comes at a cost, though: The World Health Organization estimates that 1.5 billion adults 20 and older were overweight in 2008. Sixty-five percent of the world's population lived in countries where being overweight killed more people than being underweight.[4] The health consequences of over-consumption are not reflected in our GDP calculations except, ironically, as a benefit: higher value-added in the health industry! So should we include the negative health consequences of obesity as externalities in our GDP calculations? If so, then where do we stop and call it a day?

Where Do We Stack Up? Making an Index

Earlier in this chapter we considered how to compare economies in terms of income. In coming chapters we will also compare countries with respect to other outcomes, including poverty, inequality, and human welfare. With 196 countries in the world, that's a lot of outcomes. It gets more complex still when we look at data from surveys of thousands of households within countries. We need efficient, easy-to-understand ways of making sense of all those data. Often, a good way to start is to make an index.

To make an index, we take a variable of interest (say, income, poverty, inequality, or even a composite of different things) and normalize it to have a common starting point or range. You will run across a wide variety of indices in this book. For most of these indices, we will take the variable of interest, which typically takes on a wide range of values, and transform it into a measure that ranges from zero to one. This can be an incredibly useful tool to make sense of complex data, as we shall see.

Here's a simple example of how to make an index of country per-capita income. It will convey the intuition behind an index, and is the basis for constructing part of the Human Development Index in Chapter 5. Let Y_i be the PPP adjusted per-capita income of country i, Y_{min} be the lowest per-capita income of all countries, and Y_{max} be the highest. In 2010, PPP adjusted per-capita incomes in the world ranged from US$409 (Burundi) to $86,899 (Luxembourg).[5] Egypt had a PPP-adjusted per-capita income of $6,180. Is this high or low? Clearly, it is a lot lower than Luxembourg's, which other countries could never aspire to. Yet it is considerably higher than Burundi's.

One way of comparing country incomes would be to rank them from poorest to richest. An income ranking would place Egypt 60th from the poorest among the 167 countries for which per-capita income was available from the World Bank in 2010. We could divide Egypt's rank by the total number of countries, and we would have the share of countries with income at or below Egypt's. This turns out to be:

$$60/167 = 0.359$$

Doing this for all countries gives us the cumulative distribution function of per-capita incomes, which we often refer to as $F(Y_i)$. We shall use this to calculate the Gini index of inequality in the next chapter.

A drawback of an index based on rankings instead of actual incomes is that it does not tell us *how much* higher or lower one country's income is than that of other countries. Being the 60th from the poorest country doesn't tell us much if we don't know what the distribution of incomes looks like.

We can make an index sensitive to income levels for any country i as follows: Take the difference between country i's income and that of the poorest country (Burundi), and divide this by the difference between the highest (Luxembourg) and lowest (Burundi) income:

$$I_Y(i) = \frac{Y_i - Y_{min}}{Y_{max} - Y_{min}}$$

This index will range from zero (for the poorest country, the numerator is zero) to one (for the richest country, the numerator is the same as the denominator). It has other nice properties. For example, if country i's income stays the same, while the richest country's income increases, country i's income position as measured by this index will decrease. It turns out that the same thing will happen if country i stays put, but the poorest country's income increases.

For Egypt, the value of our index is:

$$I_Y(\text{Egypt}) = (6{,}180 - 409) / (86{,}899 - 409) = 0.067$$

As you can see, Egypt looks much worse off using this index than the one based only on rankings (0.067, compared with 0.359). Many countries are much richer than Egypt. It turns out that Egypt's income makes it more similar to the countries below it than to those above it in terms of income. The last index gives us a better sense of where Egypt finds itself in the global income spectrum.

The average per-capita income is one way of measuring welfare. In a micro-economics course we measure consumer welfare using a utility function, in which utility depends on consumption. Consumption, in turn, is constrained by income. Thus, rising income translates into higher utility for consumers (assuming the budget constraint is binding, which has always been my family's experience!). Nevertheless, the average per-capita income does not tell us anything about how income is distributed: a very equal or unequal income distribution can have the same average per-capita income. In Chapter 4 we will see how to consider income inequality when measuring social welfare.

A Useful Typology

Many different terms have been used over the years to classify countries in terms of their level of development.

"Third World" has been used to refer to low-income countries, but it is largely out of use these days. It was a product of the Cold War years, in which the world was divvied up geo-political-economically into three groups of countries: the "First World" (high-income western countries: Western Europe, the United States and Canada, and Japan); the "Second World" (a little-used label referring to the USSR, China, and Eastern Europe); and the "Third World" (low and middle income countries, which sadly were often the theater in which conflicts between First and Second World countries played out).

"Less Developed," "Underdeveloped," and "Developing" are terms often heard at international forums. The first, being comparative, is a broad classification containing any country not included among the "More Developed" or "Developed" countries. The second has a somewhat pessimistic connotation, implying that the country is less developed than it ought to be, while the third has a more optimistic twist, implying that countries in this group are, indeed, developing.

The rapidly growing economies of Asia, Latin America and Eastern Europe are sometimes referred to as "Emerging Economies." China is a clear example from this group in Asia, Brazil in Latin America.

High-income economies sometimes are called "Industrialized;" however, this term is antiquated given that rich countries exist in a post-industrial world, in which the biggest share of the economy is services, not industry.

"Transitional Economies" are those that once were in the "Second World" but are transitioning towards becoming open-market economies. This term most often is used in reference to Eastern Europe and the former Soviet republics.

"North" and "South" sometimes are used as synonyms for "Developed" and "Less-developed." This typology is rather imprecise, though, because there are relatively high-income countries in the South (e.g., Australia and New Zealand) and relatively low-income countries in the North, depending upon where the line between "North" and "South" is drawn. (Indeed, most of the world's land mass is "North" if one uses the Equator as the geographic delineator.)

As you can see these are very broad, imprecise, and somewhat value-laden categories. We need a more objective typology to work with. The World Bank's country classification is based on an objective measure, income, and includes four broad categories: low, lower middle, upper middle, and high income. More than simply a descriptive typology, this designation is used in the Bank's operations to determine which countries are entitled to receive assistance under different lending terms and which are entitled to different programs. The low-income and middle-income economies are also classified by region. The World Bank recognizes that a country's income classification does not necessarily reflect its development status. Nevertheless, its classification is widely used. In 2010, the per-capita gross national income (defined below) defining each group were:

- Low Income: $1,005 or less
- Lower Middle Income: $1,006 – $3,975
- Upper Middle Income: $3,976 – $12,275
- High Income: $12,276 or more

The table that follows shows a listing of selected countries classified according to the 2010 World Bank standard. African countries dominate the "Low Income" category. Haiti is the only country from the Americas in this category, and Afghanistan, Myanmar, and Bangladesh are the only Asian ones.

As we move up to the "Lower-middle-income" countries, two European economies creep in: Albania and the Ukraine. We see the countries of Central America and one South American one, Paraguay. India, Iraq, Philippines, Pakistan, and Vietnam are in this category, along with a few African countries, including Egypt, Morocco, Sudan, Ghana, and Zambia.

By the time we get to the "Upper-middle-income" countries, Africa is barely represented. Here we find South Africa, Libya, Angola, and Tunisia. A number of eastern European and middle eastern countries are found here, along with most of South America, including Brazil, Chile, and Argentina. Mexico straddles the line between "Upper Middle Income" and "High Income." China, Malaysia, and Thailand are the major Asian countries in this category.

At the top tier we do not find any African or Latin American countries. Western Europe dominates this category, along with Canada, the United States, the "Asian Tigers," and a few oil exporters, including Saudi Arabia, Qatar, and the United Arab Emirates.

From a practical perspective, the World Bank's classification is useful because it gives us precise definitions of which countries belong in which group. As we shall see, income is an important correlate with other development outcomes.

Poverty, Income Inequality, and Human Welfare

Consider these three statements:

- In 2010, just under 1.3 billion people—22.4% of the world's population—lived on less than $1.25 a day (PPP adjusted).[6]

- The low-income countries contained 12.5% of the world's population but controlled less than 1% of its income, while the high-income countries had a little over 16% of its population and 72% of its income.[7]

- In the poorest 10% of countries, those with GDP per capita less than $1,123, life expectancy averaged 54.4 years (compared to 80 in the richest 10%), and years of schooling averaged 3.2 years (compared to 10.5 years).[8]

They present a lot of striking numbers, but they tell us very different things. The first sentence is about poverty, the second is about inequality, and the third is about human welfare. How are they related to one another and to what constitutes economic development? Are they just different sides of the same story? Does inequality imply poverty? Is it sufficient to focus our attention on poverty if our ultimate goal is to improve human welfare? Is income growth sufficient to deal with all these concerns?

In the next three chapters we'll learn how development economists study poverty, inequality, and human welfare and their relationship to income.

World Bank Country Classification (Partial Listing)[9]

Low-income economies

Haiti	Afghanistan	Bangladesh
Myanmar	Eritrea	Tanzania
Burkina Faso	Burundi	Malawi
Ethiopia	Mali	Zimbabwe
Rwanda	Kenya	Uganda

Lower-middle-income economies

Albania	Ukraine	West Bank and Gaza
El Salvador	Guatemala	Honduras
Nicaragua	Paraguay	Indonesia
India	Iraq	Yemen, Rep.
Philippines	Pakistan	Vietnam
Tonga	Congo, Rep.	Egypt, Arab Rep.
Senegal	Lesotho	Sudan
Ghana	Morocco	Zambia

Upper-middle-income economies

Russian Federation	Azerbaijan	Serbia
Belarus	Kazakhstan	Macedonia, FYR
Bulgaria	Jordan	Lebanon
Turkey	Iran, Islamic Rep.	Brazil
Chile	Ecuador	Peru
Argentina	Jamaica	Panama
Colombia	Costa Rica	Mexico
Dominican Republic	Venezuela, RB	Uruguay
Cuba	China	Malaysia
Thailand	Angola	Algeria
Tunisia	Libya	South Africa

High-income economies

Australia	Germany	Portugal
Austria	Greece	Poland
Belgium	Hungary	Ireland
Italy	Israel	Spain
Czech Republic	Switzerland	Sweden
Finland	Norway	United Kingdom
France	Netherlands	Canada
United States	Qatar	United Arab Emirates
Saudi Arabia	Japan	Hong Kong SAR, China
New Zealand	Korea, Rep.	Singapore

Chapter Two Notes

1. Address, University of Kansas, Lawrence, Kansas, March 18, 1968. Robert F. Kennedy describes what's in the GNP—and what isn't.

2. http://siteresources.worldbank.org/DATASTATISTICS/Resources/GNIPC.pdf

3. Repetto, R., Magrath, W., Wells, M., Beer, C., and Rossini, F., 1989, *Wasting Assets. Natural Resources in the National Accounts,* World Resources Institute, Washington.

4. http://www.who.int/mediacentre/factsheets/fs311/en/

5. You can see all the countries' PPP adjusted GDPs at the World Bank website http://data.worldbank.org/indicator/NY.GDP.PCAP.PP.CD

6. http://povertydata.worldbank.org/poverty/home/; Unless otherwise specified, you can assume that per-capita incomes mentioned in this chapter are PPP adjusted.

7. The World Bank, *2011 World Development Report* (http://wdr2011.worldbank.org/fulltext).

8. United Nations Human Development Report, 2011; http://hdr.undp.org/en/statistics/hdi/

9. Source: The World Bank. For a complete listing, see:

   http://data.worldbank.org/about/country-classifications/country-and-lending-groups#Lower_middle_income

3.

Poverty

Hear how poverty feels to a
poor woman in rural India.

Alleviating poverty is the biggest single concern confronting development economics. Before we can tackle the challenges of addressing poverty, we have to agree on how to measure it.

Everybody knows how to make a poverty index. Count how many people are below the poverty line, divide by the total population, and you've got the share of people in poverty. If there are q people with income below the per-capita poverty level and N people in the total population, our index is:

$$P_H = \frac{q}{N}$$

We call this the "poverty headcount index." Because N is always greater than q, the headcount measure will always be less than one, and it will be zero only if nobody is below the poverty line. This makes it a good index. Counting heads is all you need to do to make a headcount index.

Or is it? Suppose we have to construct a poverty index for some population (a country, region, or village) starting from scratch. That problem comes up a lot in development economics. The first question we face is: "What's the poverty line?"

Finding the Poverty Line

Every country has its own poverty line. Often there are separate ones for urban and rural populations, reflecting differences in the cost of living between the two. Politics invariably play some role in deciding where the poverty line *is* drawn, but where the poverty line *should* be drawn is fundamentally an economics problem.

Where do we start? Let's think about food poverty. How much does it cost to meet a person's minimum food requirements? A nutritionist's answer would be: "It depends." There are online calorie calculators by gender, weight, height, and activity level. The World Health Organization (WHO) establishes nutritional guidelines for different countries. As this passage from the WHO website suggests, it is not an easy task:

> The [WHO] Department of Nutrition for Health and Development…continually reviews new research and information from around the world on human nutrient requirements and recommended nutrient intakes. This is a vast and never-ending task, given the large number of essential human nutrients. These nutrients include protein, energy, carbohydrates, fats and lipids, a range of vitamins, and a host of minerals and trace elements.[1]

Suppose we agree on the minimum nutrient intake for an average individual in our study area. We could find all the baskets of foods available that can give us this nutrient level, price each one, choose the cheapest basket, and call this the food poverty line. This food poverty line would be the minimum amount of money needed for a person to meet his or her nutrient requirements.[2]

The trouble is that people do not live on food alone. We have other essential needs: clothing, shelter, cooking fuel and other energy, health care, and if we want our children someday to escape from poverty, education, too. Where we draw the poverty line will depend on the costs of these things as well as food.

Now our job is getting more complicated. Is there a reasonable way out of this?

Actually, there might be. Suppose we survey a large sample of people in the population, asking people what foods they consume (a one or two-week recall is commonly used for this), how much they consume, the prices they pay for each food item, and what their income is. Surveys like this have been done for nearly every country, thanks largely to the Living Standards Measurement Survey (LSMS) initiative by The World Bank.[3]

We could take all the food combinations from the survey and convert them into the amounts of nutrients consumed, using conversion coefficients available from the WHO. Then we could graph nutrient demand ($C(Y)$, on the vertical axis) against income (Y, on the horizontal axis), in Figure 2.1.

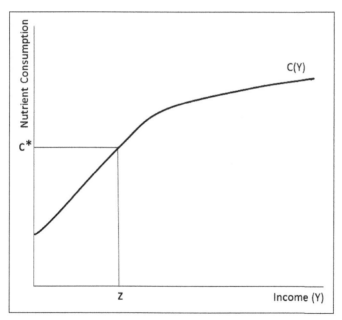

Figure 2.1: The poverty line, z, is the income required to reach the minimum level of nutrient consumption, given households' spending patterns.

Once we have this graph, we can find c^*, the minimum nutrient requirement, and bounce a line off our nutrient demand curve to get the minimum level of income needed to meet the food requirement. This minimum income (z in our figure) would take into account the fact that people spend income on things other than food, so it can be our poverty line.[4]

You might argue that z is too high, because some people spend too much of their income on non-nutritious stuff. For example, if people spend money on alcohol, cigarettes, or fancy clothes instead of food, their income will have to be higher in order to reach a nutrient intake of c^*. On the other hand, one also can argue that at very low incomes people do not spend *enough* income on essentials like health, shelter, or education. In that case z will be too low; people really need more money to satisfy their nonfood basic needs. On balance, our figure probably gives a reasonable approximation to the poverty line. In practice, economists construct poverty lines in different ways, but the basic theory for how it is done is like what's in our figure.

The common international poverty line since 2008 has been set by the World Bank at $1.25 in PPP-adjusted 2005 dollars. However, the official poverty line is much higher in rich than poor countries. For example, the U.S. poverty income for a family of 4 in 2012 was $23,050 per year, or $15.79 per person per day.[5]

More than Counting Heads

Most people think of the incidence of poverty, or headcount index, when they think about quantifying "poverty." The headcount measure is useful, but it doesn't tell us all we need to know in order to analyze poverty and design policies to alleviate it. In practice, we need to know *how poor* people are, not just *whether* they are poor. That is, we need to know the depth of poverty. We could easily imagine two countries with the same poverty headcount but with the poor clustered just below the poverty line in one country and far below the poverty line in the other. A cash transfer to eliminate poverty would have to be larger in the second country, where poor people tend to be very poor instead of a little poor.

The difference between a person's income and the per-capita poverty line is called the "poverty gap." If we know poor person i's income (Y_i) and the poverty line (z), we can easily calculate the person's poverty gap; it is $z - Y_i$. The total cost of eliminating poverty is the sum of all poor people's poverty gaps. Summing the gap across all q poor people in our population, we get the total poverty gap: $\sum_{i=1}^{q}(z - Y_i)$. The total poverty gap is critical to know for poverty alleviation programs, because it is the cost of bringing everyone up to the poverty line.

The poverty gap gives us more information than the headcount, allowing us to measure the impacts of programs on poverty more accurately. For example, a program might raise a poor person's income but not by enough to get her above the poverty line. A reasonable person would say the program reduced poverty. The poverty gap would decrease as a result of the program, even though the headcount measure would not change.

The Severity of Poverty

Does the poverty gap give us all the information we need? Consider this scenario: Program A reduces the total poverty gap by providing a cash transfer to people just below the poverty line. Program B reduces the poverty gap by the same amount, but it does this by targeting the transfer to the very poorest people in society, that is, people in extreme poverty. The poverty gap does not let us distinguish between the effects of these two programs, because it changes by the same amount no matter which poor person gets the cash.

How can we make our poverty measure sensitive to whom gets the cash, that is, the severity of poverty?

The easiest way is to square the poverty gap. If we measure poverty using $(Y_i - z)^2$, our index will increase disproportionately as the poverty gap increases. For example, if the gap is \$2, the gap squared is \$4, but if the gap is \$4, the gap squared is \$16. Based on this index, a program is more effective at reducing poverty if it raises income of extremely poor households.

The economists Erik Thorbecke and his students Joel Greer and James Foster proposed a single index that embodies all three of these measures as special cases. The Foster-Greer-Thorbecke measure is the most widely used poverty index in economics. Its formula is:

$$FGT_\alpha = \frac{1}{Nz^\alpha} \sum_{i=1}^{q} \left(z - Y_i\right)^\alpha$$

where we set α depending on the kind of index we want. You can see the poverty gap, $z - Y_i$, to the right of the summation. When $\alpha=0$, the term in the summation equals one for every poor person. We sum up the ones over the q poor people and divide by N (since z^α also equals 1 when $\alpha=0$). This yields the headcount measure. That is, $FGT_{\alpha=0} = \frac{q}{N}$. It is a useful index, because $0 \le FGT_{\alpha=0} \le 1$.

When $\alpha=1$, the index equals:

$$FGT_{\alpha=1} = \frac{1}{Nz} \sum_{i=1}^{q} \left(z - Y_i\right)$$

The right-most term, $\sum_{i=1}^{q} \left(z - Y_i\right)$, is the total poverty gap, or the cost of bringing all poor people just up to the poverty line. To make an index, we have to divide this by the largest value the total poverty gap could have. Nz, the total population times the poverty line, is what the total poverty gap would be if everyone in the population had zero income. The total poverty gap divided by Nz, like the headcount index, lies between zero (nobody is in poverty) and one (everyone is in poverty and no one has any income at all).

To analyze the severity of poverty, we set $\alpha=2$. In this case, the index becomes:

$$FGT_{\alpha=2} = \frac{1}{Nz^2} \sum_{i=1}^{q} \left(z - Y_i\right)^2$$

In this version of the FGT index, people in extreme poverty will be weighted more than people just below the poverty line. You can see that this, too, is bounded by zero (nobody is in poverty) and one (everybody is in poverty and no one has any income at all). In the latter case, the term in parentheses becomes Nz^2, so the quotient becomes one.

Often, when we perform poverty analyses we report all three versions of the FGT index. The second ($\alpha=1$) and third ($\alpha=2$) versions decrease whenever the income of a poor person increases. The third version decreases more if the poor person whose income goes up is extremely poor. The first ($\alpha=0$) version decreases only if the income gain pops the poor person above the poverty line. Together, the three versions of the FGT provide a comprehensive picture of changes in poverty due to a policy or some other exogenous shock.

Calculating an FGT Index: A Simple Example

Suppose we survey a small village consisting of only ten people, with a poverty line of $z = 28$. We find their incomes to be as shown in Table 3.1.

Table 3.1: Incomes and Poverty Measures for a Hypothetical Village

Person	Income	1 if in Poverty, 0 Otherwise	Poverty Gap	Poverty Gap-squared
1	5	1	23	529
2	12	1	16	256
3	22	1	6	36
4	24	1	4	16
5	30	0	0	0
6	40	0	0	0
7	50	0	0	0
8	70	0	0	0
9	80	0	0	0
10	100	0	0	0
Sum		4	49	837
z	28			

Using the data in the table, we can calculate the three versions of the FGT index:

$$FGT_{\alpha=0} = 4/10 = 0.4$$

$$FGT_{\alpha=1} = \frac{49}{10(28)} = 0.35$$

$$FGT_{\alpha=2} = \frac{837}{10(28^2)} = 0.43$$

Now let's check the sensitivity of our measures to different cash transfers. Suppose we transfer $5 to person three, bringing her income up to $27. This is still (just) below the poverty line, so the headcount doesn't change. The poverty gap measure falls by four points, from .35 to .31. The gap-squared falls less, from 0.43 to 0.41.

Now what if we gave the $5 to the poorest household instead? The change in the poverty gap is the same as before, because it is insensitive to which poor person gets the cash. However, the gap-squared measure falls all the way to 0.32.

Because of its sensitivity to changes in extreme poverty, the third measure is the one Mexico uses to measure poverty impacts. In fact, ($\alpha=2$) is in the Mexican constitution!

Drought, Poverty, and Inequality: The Sahel

The Sahel is a ribbon of land running east-west across Africa and separating the Sahara desert to the North from the savannas in the south. The contrast between it and the sands of the Sahara are what give this zone its name, which means "coast" in Arabic.

As a transition zone, the Sahel is also a high-risk zone from an agroecological point of view. In 1984 a severe drought struck the Sahelian zone of Burkina Faso in West Africa. It was a human tragedy, but its timing was a researcher's dream, because it hit during a multi-year household survey being carried out by the International Food Policy Institute (IFPRI). IFPRI had just finished surveying households in a normal year, 1983-84. They surveyed the same households again the next year, after the drought struck. Households in this region practice rain fed agro pastoralism. The Sahel has extremely variable rainfall, a fragile environment, and poor agro climate. The people living there have learned how to adapt to their environment, doing their best to diversify their incomes beyond crop production.

Nothing prepared them for this drought, though.

The IFPRI data give us a unique insight into the impacts of agroclimatic shocks on poor households. Crop income was by far the largest source of income for households in the normal year, constituting 53% of the total. It fell 64% when the drought hit. All of the other income sources increased during the drought, though. Table 3.2 reveals how households scrambled to make up for their lost crop income. They sold off livestock: livestock accounted for just 14% of the normal-year's income, but animal sales increased 154% during the drought. Local non-farm income, mostly from wages, rose 26%; remittances from migrant work increased 54%; and transfers among households, while very small (1% in the base year), increased 58%.

Table 3.2: The Impact of Drought on Household Incomes in Burkina Faso

Income Source	Share in Normal-year Income	Percentage Change in Drought Year
Crop	0.53	-63.55
Livestock	0.14	154.34
Local Non-farm	0.22	25.91
Migration	0.09	53.87
Transfers	0.01	57.7
Total Income	**1.00**	**-25.12**

Source: Thomas Reardon and J. Edward Taylor, "Agroclimatic Shock, Income Inequality, and Poverty: Evidence from Burkina Faso," *World Development* 24(5):901-914, 1996.

It comes as no surprise that poverty rose sharply in the drought year. The headcount index shows that the poverty rate more than doubled, from .20 to .51. The severity of poverty increased by a factor of more than 8, from 0.02 to 0.19. The FGT index paints a stark picture of the human toll of drought in the Sahel.

Poverty Dynamics

Supposed you're a poor family farmer in the Sahel, with kids to feed. In a normal year, you can get enough out of your grain crop to cover your family's needs, provided you sell an animal or two to supplement your farm income. With a herd of six, including some decent breeding stock, you can do this every year.

One year the rains don't come. Your crop fails. You've got half a year until planting season. How do you keep food on your table?

You sell an animal. Then another, and another. As you plant your next crop, you're down to three animals. The seeds begin to germinate, the rain comes, but your money runs out. You sell another animal, and now you're down to two. With two months to go before harvest, your money runs out again.

What do you do? If you sell your last two animals, your breeding stock, how will you ever rebuild your herd?

Recent research by economists Travis Lybbert and Michael Carter at UC Davis and Chris Barrett at Cornell suggests that, in all likelihood, you won't sell those last few animals. If you do, you know you might never get out of poverty—you'll be caught in a "poverty trap."

…But if you don't sell those last two animals, your family goes hungry. You might survive alright, and so might your spouse and oldest kids. But what about your two-year-old girl? Your newborn baby boy, still un-weaned? By preserving your herd in the short run, might you be stunting your children's growth and jeopardizing their potential to lead a productive life in the future?[6]

Poor people around the world face these sorts of cruel choices daily. This highlights a very important point about poverty: It is not just that some people are poor and others are not. Poverty is dynamic, meaning that it changes over time. Some people are never poor. Others seem always to be poor, caught in a "poverty trap." Still others find themselves on the very cusp of poverty, and all it takes is a single adverse event to tip them into a poverty from which there may be no coming back.

Figure 2.2 illustrates this. Income depends on assets. This is true for livestock: the larger the herd, the greater the income you can make from it. It's also true for human capital: the healthier you are and the more education and skills you have, the more productive you can be and thus the higher the earnings you can get. As we saw in the example above, families can "consume" their assets, selling them off to get through a hard time, but that leaves them with less in the next period. They can also lose human capital if, for example, kids go hungry or don't go to school. Human capital can go down if malnutrition impairs children's development and learning. This, too, leaves households with less income in the future.

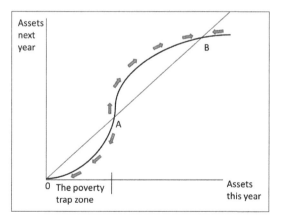

Figure 2.2: To the right of point A assets grow larger in the next period, driving the household to a favorable steady state at point B. To the left of point A assets decrease, driving the household into a poverty trap.

The horizontal axis measures a person's assets this year. The vertical axis measures his assets next year. Along the diagonal line, assets next year are the same as assets this year.

The S-shaped curve illustrates a different situation. Between points 0 and A, income is so low that people have to sell off their assets just to survive, like the pastoralist who sells off the last few animals in his herd. This means income in the next period will be lower than income in the current period, because assets will be lower. In the next period he will have to sell off even more assets, making income the period after that lower still. You can see where the dynamics will take him: once assets drop below A, they end up at zero, where they are the same tomorrow as today. Zero, then, is what we call a "steady state." Once you're there, you tend to stay there. The region from 0 to A in the diagram is the *poverty trap zone*.

There's another steady state in this diagram, though. Between points A and B, assets next year are higher than this year. The herd grows. People make enough income to invest some, increasing their income potential in the next period. The period after that, assets are higher still. Beyond a point, diminishing returns set in, when, for example, your herd gets too big for the land you can graze it on. The S-curve starts to flatten out. If you start out with a herd larger than A, the dynamics will push you up to B, on the diagonal line again. Beyond B, the herd is too large, and the dynamics push you back to B. Thus, B is a steady state too.

Shocks like a drought can take a household that is near point A and knock it into a poverty trap, possibly driving its assets all the way to zero. Adverse shocks can also knock households off point B, but if we've got the dynamics right, they will recover and return to the favorable steady state.

The 2003 Mexico National Rural Household Survey (Spanish acronym ENHRUM) found that 47% of the rural population had income below the poverty line. In 2008, the same households were surveyed again. This made it possible to look at the dynamics of poverty by tracking the same households' poverty status over time. In the five years between these two surveys, poverty in rural Mexico fell. The Mexican government has three different poverty lines, one for food (the food poverty line), another that adds in the cost of health and basic education (the capacities poverty line), and a third that adds in clothing, housing, and energy costs (the asset poverty line). By all three measures, the head-count rate fell by between 3.6% and 4.0%. The other two components of the FGT measure, the poverty gap and severity (gap-squared), also fell, as shown in Table 3.3.

This all seems like good news—and it is. But it masks the fact that many rural Mexicans were worse off in 2008 than in 2003. The table below takes all the rural Mexicans who were in poverty in 2003 and shows what percentage were still in poverty in 2008. It does the same for those who were *not* in poverty in 2003. Table 3.4 reveals some interesting—and troubling—poverty dynamics.

Table 3.3: Poverty Dynamics in Rural Mexico

FGT Index	Food Poverty Line			Table 3.4: Capacities Poverty Line (Adds Food, Health, Basic Education)			Asset Poverty Line (Adds Clothes, Housing, Energy)		
	2002	2007	% Change	2002	2007	% Change	2002	2007	% Change
Headcount (Alpha=0)	0.47	0.44	-3.6%	0.54	0.50	-3.9%	0.70	0.66	-4.0%
Depth (Alpha=1)	0.24	0.21	-2.2%	0.27	0.25	-2.5%	0.39	0.35	-3.4%
Severity (Alpha=2)	0.16	0.15	-1.3%	0.19	0.17	-1.6%	0.27	0.25	-2.4%

Headcount: Share of population in households with income below the poverty line

Depth: Also reflects how far below the poverty line poor individuals find themselves

Severity: Places greater weight on the poorest of the poor when calculating the poverty index

Source: Analysis of Mexico National Rural Household Survey data, 2003-2008.

Table 3.4: A Transition Matrix of Poverty Dynamics in Rural Mexico

	Poor in 2008	Not Poor in 2008
Poor in 2003 (47%)	51%	49%
Not Poor in 2003 (53%)	30%	70%

Source: Analysis of Mexico National Rural Household Survey data, 2003-2008.

Of the people who were in poverty in 2003, 51% were still in poverty in 2008. Let's call this "Group A." These people—around 24% (47%*51%) of the rural Mexican population—seem to be in a state of persistent poverty (though we would need to track them longer to be sure). At the other extreme, most of those who were *not* in poverty in 2003 (70%) were still not in poverty in 2008. This group, which we can call "Group B," appears as though it might be persistently *out* of poverty.

The good news is that 49% of the people who were *in* poverty in 2003 were *above* the poverty line in 2008. These people transitioned out of poverty during the five-year period, which is the reason why poverty in rural Mexico fell.

The bad news is that 30% of those who were *not* poor in 2003 *were* poor in 2008. These people transitioned *into* poverty.

Let's call these two transitional poverty groups "Group C." They might not be so different from one another.

Why are poverty dynamics important? First, just because people transition out of poverty doesn't mean their poverty problem is solved. Our challenge is not simply to get people out of poverty; it is also to keep them there, as well as to keep others from slipping into poverty.

Second, it is almost certain that different anti-poverty policies are needed for each one of these groups. For Group A, we need to have policies to enable people to extricate themselves from what might be poverty traps. For group B, we need policies that will create opportunities to stay out of poverty.

For Group C, those at the margins of poverty, for whom things can go either way, we need policies that can prevent adverse shocks from pushing people into potential poverty traps, and keep them out. The Sahelian farmer-pastoralist in our example above is a good illustration of the kinds of people likely found in this group. If we somehow could devise an insurance scheme that could enable people at the fringes of poverty to feed their children *and* preserve their productive assets at times of adversity, we might have a big impact on poverty and on preventing people from falling into poverty traps over time.

The economist Jeffrey Sachs argues that herein lies a critical role for international aid. Countries where many people find themselves caught in a poverty trap must invest to raise their physical and human capital assets above the critical level in our diagram above. But you can see that there's a vicious circle here, because poor countries lack the resources to do this. Sachs argues that aid from rich countries is needed to make these investments and set poor countries, and the poor people within them, on a path towards a new steady state where they are not poor. This is the idea between the United Nations Millennium Project, which Sachs directs (http://www.unmillenniumproject.org/).

Chapter Three Notes

1. See http://www.who.int/nutrition/topics/nutrecomm/en/index.html.
2. Some nutrients are easier to get from cheap foods than others. The most costly essential nutrients would have a relatively large impact on the cost of this poverty food basket.
3. The Development Research Group at the World Bank established the LSMS in order "to foster increased use of household data as a basis for policy decisionmaking." See http://econ.worldbank.org/WBSITE/EXTERNAL/EXTDEC/EXTRESEARCH/EXTLSMS/0,,contentMDK:

21610833~pagePK:64168427~piPK:64168435~theSitePK:3358997,00.
html

4. This is the approach proposed by Joel Greer and Erik Thorbecke, "Food Poverty Profile Applied to Kenyan Smallholders," *Economic Development and Cultural Change* 35:115-141, 1986.

5. This figure is for the 48 contiguous states plus the District of Columbia. The poverty lines are higher in Alaska and Hawaii.

6. The seminal article on poverty and asset dynamics is: Travis J. Lybbert, Christopher B. Barrett, Solomon Desta and D. Layne Coppock, Stochastic Wealth Dynamics and Risk Management among a Poor Population, *The Economic Journal*, 114 (October), 750–777, 2002.

4.

Inequality

There is no question that inequality matters to people. It was at the heart of the Occupy Movement, which struck cities around the world in the fall of 2011 with the rallying call "We are the 99 percent!"

There are several reasons why inequality is important from an economic (or political-economic) point of view, including:

- *Social justice.* Many people believe it is unfair for the benefits of economic growth to be concentrated among a select few.

- *Relative deprivation.* Economists usually assume people optimize by maximizing what they have: Firms maximize profits, households maximize utility from consuming more goods. But sociologists have long recognized that being deprived of goods that others have can make people unhappy. Suppose you live in a poor village and your income does not change while your neighbor's does. You see him remodel his house, his kids start dressing well, and a parabolic TV dish sprouts from his rooftop. Can you say you are just as well off as before?

- *Achieving the Millennium Development Goals.* Many countries have per-capita incomes dangerously close to, or even below, the World Bank's $1 and $2 a day poverty lines. How can those countries hope to achieve the Millennium Development Goals if their income distributions are highly unequal, and if the benefits of income growth do not reach the poor? Improving human development outcomes without growth in poor countries requires redistribution.

- *The structure of economies.* Different income groups have different spending patterns, and how income gets spent can help shape the structure of economies. (This is less the case in countries that open up to trade, as we shall see in Chapter 8.) Research from India, Mexico, and other countries reveals that poor and middle-income households are more likely to spend their income on goods and services produced within their country and that stimulate local employment. Rich households are more likely to use their income to buy imports, to buy goods produced in more capital-intensive industries, or to save abroad. Changes in the distribution of income can thus have important effects on production and employment in poor countries.

- *Economic efficiency.* Last but not least, economic efficiency is likely to depend on how income is distributed in poor countries, where assumptions about perfectly functioning markets break down. If there is no bank willing to loan money to the poor, then their ability to buy fertilizer probably depends on whether or not they have the liquidity (cash) to "self-finance" their production. If you have the cash, you use the optimal amount of fertilizer. If you don't, your efficiency will suffer. The inseparability of efficiency from equity is an ongoing theme in this book.

You might think inequality matters because the more unequally income is distributed the more people are poor. That's simply not true, though: Inequality is different from poverty. A society could have an unequal distribution of income with no one living below the poverty line, or a very equal distribution with everyone living in poverty.

There is only one instance in which there is a clear link between inequality and poverty. Imagine a society with just enough income to maintain everyone in the population *right at* the poverty line. In this case, *any* inequality would imply poverty. In real life there is not a *theoretical* connection between changes in inequality and poverty. The relationship is *empirical*, positive in some cases, negative in others. Later on in this chapter we'll see how, when drought struck the Sahel region of Burkina Faso, poverty increased but income got more equal. In short, we need to be very careful when making poverty or welfare conclusions from changes in inequality, and we need ways to empirically measure all three of these concepts.

Measuring Inequality

When we compared the index of per-capita income with income rankings in Chapter 2, we saw that the distribution of global income is very unequal. Can we use what we've learned to construct a useful index of income inequality?

Inequality can be measured in different ways. However, only a few are really useful for comparing inequality across countries or in the same country over time.

Here are a few ways of measuring inequality:

Frequency Distributions
We could just eyeball the distribution of income in a country. To do this, you can rank everyone in the country from poorest to richest, group them into income groups, and make a bar chart showing the percentage of the population in each income group. This would be a frequency distribution for income.

Figure 4.1 shows frequency distributions for Albania, Nicaragua, Tanzania and Vietnam.Looking at frequency distributions of different countries like the ones shown in the graph can give you a sense of differences in income inequality, but we typically want a more precise way to compare income inequality across countries.

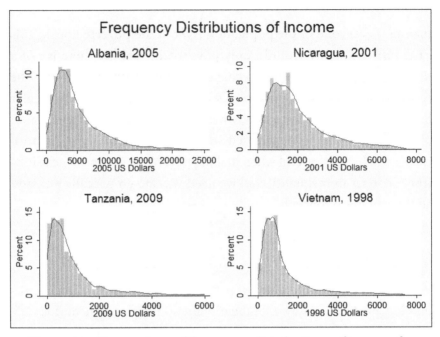

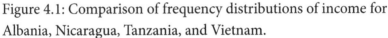

Figure 4.1: Comparison of frequency distributions of income for Albania, Nicaragua, Tanzania, and Vietnam.

A first step towards comparing income distributions is to group the population into equal parts along the horizontal axis. Figure 4.2 compares frequency distributions of income for Sweden (top) and Mexico (bottom), in which the population has been divided into 10 equal parts, or deciles.[1]

You can see in the picture that the poorest decile of Mexico's population received a small fraction of the income: The height of the smallest bar is 1.2, telling us that the poorest 10% of the population gets 1.2% of the income. None of the bottom 7 deciles gets anywhere near its proportional share (10%) of income. At the other extreme, the richest 10% get 42.2% of the income.

A nice thing about frequency distributions is that they give us a snapshot of inequality. In a perfectly equal income distribution, all the bars would be the same height. This clearly is not anywhere near the case in Mexico. It is not even the case in Sweden, which has the world's most equal income distribution.[2]

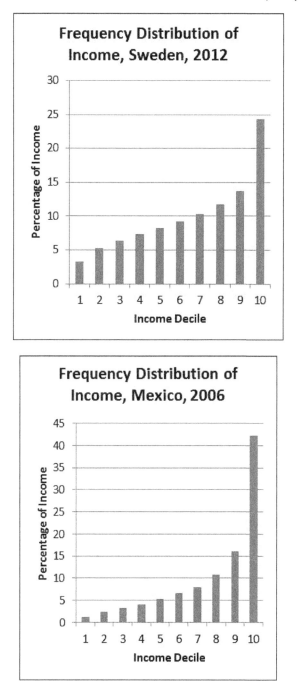

Figure 4.2: Decile frequency distributions of income
for Sweden (top) and Mexico (bottom).

Sweden's distribution seems more equal than Mexico's, but how much more equal is it? Is Mexico's more or less equal than, say, Tanzania's? How can we track changes in income inequality in the same countries over time?

We need an index of inequality. If you've taken statistics you might already know some measures of dispersion: the variance, standard deviation, coefficient of variation. It turns out that these are not very good indices, though. The variance has no bounds, and it is sensitive to the units we use to measure income. For example, suppose we calculated the variance of China's income. We could do this either in yuan or, using the current exchange rate of 6.3 yuan per US dollar, in dollars. Either way, it would be a huge number. If we calculated the variance of China's income in yuan instead of dollars, it would come out 6.3^2 or 39.69 times larger!

The standard deviation (SD) is the square root of the variance. It has the same problems as the variance for comparing dispersion or inequality across countries. Sometimes we try to normalize the SD of a variable like income by dividing by the variable's mean. This gives us the coefficient of variation (CV). It doesn't solve the problem, either: the CV can take on any value.

In short, these conventional statistical measures of variance don't help us compare inequality across countries (or in the same country over time).

Gini in a Nutshell

The most commonly used measure of inequality is the Gini Coefficient. Not only is it a neat index, with values between zero and one, but it satisfies all five properties that an inequality index should have:

1. Pigou-Dalton principle: Inequality, as measured by the index, should increase when income is transferred from a low-income household to a high-income household.

2. Symmetry: The measured level of inequality does not change when individuals trade places in the income distribution.

3. Independence of income scale: A proportional change in all incomes (like measuring income in dollars instead of yuan) does not alter inequality.

4. Homogeneity: A change in the size of the population will not affect measured inequality.

5. Decomposability: We would like to be able to use our index to understand how income from different sources (wages, profits) affects inequality. This means we should be able to decompose it with respect to income sources.

Several measures of inequality satisfy these given assumptions. The Gini coefficient is probably the most intuitive among them, as we shall see. It is also a measure of dispersion, like the variance. In fact, it has been argued that we should use it instead of the variance for portfolio analysis and other types of research.

Recipe for Making a Gini Coefficient

Here's how to make a Gini coefficient: First, remember in Chapter 2 when we lined everyone in the country up from poorest to richest? Let's do that again and make everyone stand on top of a horizontal axis (specially designed to support their weight!), like in Figure 4.3.

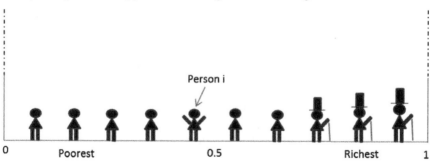

Figure 4.3: Ranking of population from poorest to richest.

Pick a person—say, person *i*. Starting at the far left, add up how many people are to the left of person i. That's how many people are poorer than person i. Add 1 and divide by the country's total population and you get the share of people with income at or below that of person i. Do this for every person and you have the cumulative population share from poorest to richest. For person i in our figure you can see that the share is 0.5, and for the far-right (richest) person it is 1.0.

Now figure out what share of the country's income each of these people has. To get the cumulative income shares, add up the income shares, starting at the far left, for each person in the population. Plot the cumulative income shares above each person as in Figure 4.4.

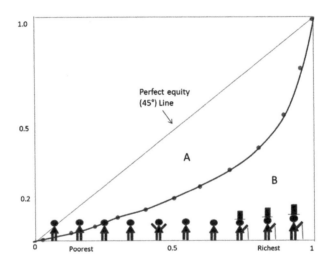

Figure 4.4: The Lorenz Curve relates population shares (horizontal axis) to cumulative income shares (vertical axis). The Gini coefficient of income inequality is the area between the perfect equity (45°) line and the Lorenz curve (area A) divided by the area of the triangle below the perfect equity line (area A+B).

For person i, the cumulative income share is 0.2. In other words, one-half of the population has income at or below person i's, but those people control only 20% of the country's total income. By the time we get to the very richest person, we have 100% of the country's population and income.

Connecting the dots, we get what is called the Lorenz Curve (LC). It shows what share of income each cumulative population share controls, from poorest to richest.

The more unequal the country's income distribution, the more bowed the LC will be towards the southeast corner of the unit box. The possibilities are bracketed by two extremes:

Perfect Equity. No society has it, but perfect equity means that each population share would have an equal share of total income: the poorest 20% would have 20% of the income, the poorest 50%, would have 50%, and so on. (Really, they wouldn't be the poorest 50%, because everyone would have the same income.) The "perfect equity line" is just the diagonal running from the origin to the top right corner of the box.

Perfect Inequality. No society has this, either, because all but one person would starve to death. In a world of perfect inequality, no one has anything except for the richest person, who has it all. The "line of perfect inequality," is just the outside border running across the horizontal axis and up the right-hand side of our box.

Now look at the area in between the LC and the perfect equity line (Area A) and the area between the LC and the perfect inequality line (Area B). Add them together and you get a triangle forming the southeast half of the box. The ratio:

$$\frac{A}{A+B}$$

... is the Gini index (or coefficient) of inequality. The Gini index always lies between zero and one. It equals zero only if there is perfect equity, so that the LC is the perfect-equity line (Area A is nil). It equals 1.0 only if there is perfect inequality, so the LC is the outside border of the box (Area B is zero).

Because $0 \leq G \leq 1$, the Gini coefficient is a useful way of measuring inequality, not only of income but of other things, as well, including wealth and assets. For example, a high Gini coefficient of land tells us that land is unequally distributed, and a low Gini for land indicates the opposite. Still, it is important to keep in mind that, like per-capita income, the Gini coefficient is an aggregate measure, a summary statistic.

It does not tell us everything we might want to know about the distribution of whatever it measures. Many different distributions can give the same Gini coefficient. In fact, the same Gini can come from an infinite number of different Lorenz curves! To illustrate this, look at Figure 4.5. Low-income households have a smaller share of total income in the economy depicted by the Lorenz curve that starts out lower. Yet these two Lorenz curves give the same Gini coefficient: the ratio A/(A+B) is the same for both.

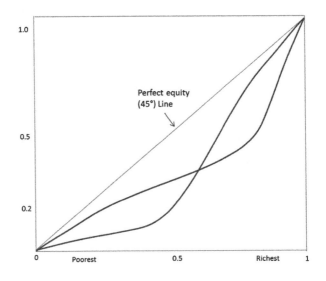

Figure 4.5: With intersecting Lorenz curves, different income distributions can give the same Gini coefficient.

With Gini Coefficients, we can get an idea of how different countries stack up in terms of inequality. It might seem hard to calculate the area between the Lorenz Curve and perfect equity line, but there's an easy way: after ranking everyone, just take the covariance between income and the cumulative population share, double it, and divide by mean income. For example, take a little economy with 10 people and incomes as in Table 4.1

Table 4.1: A Hypothetical Income Distribution

Person	Income (Y)	F(Y)
1	79.6	0.1
2	128.7	0.2
3	153.1	0.3
4	177.8	0.4
5	200.3	0.5
6	223.6	0.6
7	249.4	0.7
8	284.2	0.8
9	332.8	0.9
10	587.9	1

Cov(Y,F(Y))	34.485
Mean Income	241.74
Gini Coefficient	0.285307

The first column ranks people from poorest (1) to richest (10). The second column gives each person's income. The third gives the cumulative population share. If we take the covariance between the last two columns (34.485), double it, then divide by mean income (241.74), we get the Gini coefficient.[3]

What's Unequal? International Comparison of Inequality

In our little example, the Gini coefficient is very low: 0.28. That's around where the Gini for Sweden is, which is not surprising, because for our example I took the income deciles for Sweden and pretended they were people. This actually gives us a rough approximation of the Swedish income Gini. It isn't a very efficient use of our formula, though, because we lose a lot of information by lumping everybody into deciles. We'd be better off having a row in our data table for every single Swede! (A random sample of Swedes would do.)

Sweden is pretty much the lower bound on the world's Gini coefficients, because it has about the most equal income distribution on the planet. The U.S. Gini is a lot higher—around 0.45. If we grew the Swedish economy by one-third and gave *all* the new income to the richest decile, we'd get a Gini coefficient like that of the United States. (To do this in our example, just increase the top decile's income by 798.) Or we could grow the economy by 50% and split it between the top two deciles. Or we could just take away 70% of the poorest three deciles' income, and give it *all* to the richest decile. There are many ways to transform Sweden's income distribution and end up with the same Gini as the United States has, but any one of them would be a huge redistribution in favor of the rich.

Table 4.2 lists some Gini coefficients from other countries. It shows a wide range of Gini coefficients around the world, from below 0.30 for the most equitable countries to as high as 0.71 for the countries with the most unequal income distributions.

Table 4.2: Gini Coefficients for Selected Countries

Country	Source	Year	GINI index	Country	Source	Year	GINI index
Very Low Inequality				*Medium Inequality*			
Serbia	WB	2008	28.16	Thailand	WB	2009	40.02
Kazakhstan	WB	2009	29.04	Russian Federation	WB	2009	40.11
Pakistan	WB	2008	30.02	Philippines	WB	2009	42.98
Egypt, Arab Rep.	WB	2008	30.77	Argentina	WB	2010	44.49
Bangladesh	WB	2010	32.12	United States	CIA	2007	45.00
Low Inequality				*High Inequality*			
Poland	WB	2009	34.07	Mexico	WB	2008	48.28
Niger	WB	2008	34.55	Costa Rica	WB	2009	50.73
Sudan	WB	2009	35.29	Chile	WB	2009	52.06
Vietnam	WB	2008	35.57	Brazil	WB	2009	54.69
Japan	CIA	2008	37.60	*Very High Inequality*			
Turkey	WB	2008	38.95	South Africa	WB	2009	63.14
Burkina Faso	WB	2009	39.79	Namibia	CIA	2003	70.70

Sources: The World Bank (http://data.worldbank.org/indicator/ SI.POV.GINI) and the CIA (https://www.cia.gov/library/publications/ the-world-factbook/fields/2172.html)

You might wonder what the Gini coefficient for *the whole world* is. Would it be higher or lower than most country Ginis? Think about it: world income inequality includes both inequality within countries (which is what we have in our table) and inequality among countries, which is big: just look at the range of average per-capita incomes we saw in Chapter 2. A recent study put the global income Gini coefficient at around 0.62, which would put the world in our "Very High Inequality" category.[4]

Inequality and Poverty
In the last chapter we saw how a severe drought in the Sahel affected poverty. The poverty rate increased significantly, regardless of whether we measure it using the headcount or the severity measure. What happened to inequality? Was rising poverty in the Sahel accompanied by rising inequality?

Table 4.3 compares the impacts of the drought on poverty, as measured by two variants of the FGT measure, and on income inequality, using the Gini index.

Table 4.3: Impacts of Drought on Household Income Inequality and Poverty in Burkina Faso

Year	Poverty		Gini
	Headcount	Severity	
Normal Year	0.20	0.02	0.34
Drought Year	0.51	0.19	0.31

Source: Thomas Reardon and J. Edward Taylor, "Agroclimatic Shock, Income Inequality, and Poverty: Evidence from Burkina Faso," *World Development* 24(5):901-914, 1996.

It might come as a surprise that the drought had an equalizing impact on household incomes. The Gini coefficient for this region fell slightly, from 0.34 to 0.31.

Virtually all households were hard-hit by the drought. As the head-count shows, many households fell into poverty, while the severity index reveals that many poor people became much poorer. In relative terms, though, high-income households took a bigger hit. This explains why the Gini coefficient fell. These findings illustrate the lack of a clear relationship between poverty and inequality. When poverty increases, inequality may either increase or decrease.

Inequality and Social Welfare

At the end of Chapter 2 we noted that the average per-capita income often is used as an indicator of social welfare; however, it is a rough indicator, because it does not take into account how income is distributed. One way to bring income inequality into a social welfare function is to use the Gini coefficient of income inequality (G):

$$W = pcy(1 - G)$$

...where W represents social welfare and pcy is the average per-capita income in the economy (country, region, village, or whatever level we want to carry out the welfare analysis on).[5] This social welfare function has the properties that either an increase in income of any member of society or a transfer of income from a rich to a less-rich person will increase social welfare, no matter what the original income distribution looks like.[6]

Using this welfare function instead of per-capita income makes a big difference when measuring the impacts of income changes on welfare. For example, let's take the economy in Table 4.1 and give 30 units of income (an amount equal to 5% of the richest decile's income) first to the poorest then to the richest decile (leaving all other deciles unchanged). The results are shown in Table 4.4. In both cases, adding an amount equal to 5% of the richest decile's income raises average household income by 1.2%. However, the Gini coefficient falls when this income goes to the poorest decile, and it increases if the cash goes to the richest decile.

Welfare increases 3.2%—more than the percentage increase in average income—if the cash goes to the poorest decile. It goes up by only 0.2% if the same income goes to the richest decile. With this welfare measure, adding new income to an economy will not make welfare decrease, even if there is a negative effect on inequality; however, a negative effect on inequality drags down the measured welfare impact.

Table 4.4: Impacts of an Income Increase on Per-Capita Income, Inequality, and Welfare in a Hypothetical Economy

Impact on Per-capita Income, Inequality, and Welfare	Transfer of $30 (5% of Richest Decile's Income) to:	
	The Poorest Decile	The Richest Decile
Change in Average Per-Capita Income	1.2%	1.2%
Change in Gini	-5.0%	2.6%
Change in Welfare (W=pcy(1-G))	3.2%	0.2%

Gender Inequality and "The Girl Effect"

One of the greatest sources of inequality in poor countries is not among households but between the genders, including between men and women in the same households. Women are less likely to go to school, less likely to work, less likely to earn the same wage for comparable work, more likely to be in poverty, and less likely to hold political positions. In many countries they lack basic legal rights, like the right to own property or even travel without their husband's permission. And many women are actually missing. The female share of the world's population is lower than it would be if women had access to the same resources as men and if parents did not practice selective abortion. Amartya Sen coined the term "missing women," and Esther Duflo called it "the starkest manifestation of the lack of gender equality... Most of these missing women are not actively killed," she writes. "They die from cumulative neglect."[7]

How to reduce inequality between men and women is a major concern in development economics. On one hand, economic development can reduce gender inequality. For example, if poor couples are less likely to value girls, rising incomes should favor more gender equality. On the other hand, discrimination against women hinders development. A key theme of this book is that it generally is not possible to separate issues of equity and efficiency in poor countries. When women lack the same legal protections and access to resources as men, they are not as productive. Gender inequality thus hinders economic development as well as being hindered by underdevelopment.

The Girl Effect Factsheet.

Chapter Four Notes

1. This figure was constructed from data presented in Gerardo Esquivel's paper, "The Dynamics of Income Inequality in Mexico Since NAFTA," El Colegio de Mexico, December 2008 (http://www.cid.harvard.edu/Economia/GEsquivel.pdf).

2. Swedish disposable income data are from Statistics Sweden (http://www.scb.se/Pages/TableAndChart____226030.aspx)

3. If you aren't statistically inclined, don't worry: Excel will take the covariance for you. Just pick a cell, insert "=covar(array1, array2)" where array1 is the data in the second column and array2 is the data in the third column.

4. Postscript to the article 'World inequality and globalization' (*Oxford Review of Economic Policy*, Spring 2004). Bob Sutcliffe, April 2007, http://siteresources.worldbank.org/INTDECINEQ/Resources/PSBSutcliffe.pdf

5. This social welfare function was proposed by Shlomo Yitzhaki, "Stochastic Dominance, Mean Variance and Gini's Mean Difference," *American Economic Review*, vol. 72, pp. 178-85, 1982.

6. In calculus terms, the derivative of W with respect to income is positive (since $G < 1$), and the derivative with respect to G is negative.

7. Esther Duflo, Gender Equality in Development, Massachusetts Institute of Technology (http://economics.mit.edu/files/799), accessed December 2012; Amartya Sen, "More Than 100 Million Women Are Missing," *The New York Review of Books* 37(20), 1999.

5.

Human Development

Poverty is about income. Economic development ultimately is about people. In 1990, the Pakistani economist Mahbub ul Haq began urging the United Nations Development Program (UNDP) to create a broader measure of development that focused on human outcomes. He felt this was necessary in order "to shift the focus of development economics from national income accounting to people-centered policies."

The measure Haq proposed had to be simple to understand, and it had to encompass both economics and human wellbeing. Above all, it had to be an *index*, which would make it possible to compare improvements in wellbeing across countries. The Nobel laureate Amartya Sen provided the conceptual framework for this project. Actually, Sen initially opposed the idea, worrying that it would be too difficult to capture the full complexity of human development in a single index. In the end, Haq swayed Sen, by persuading him that only a holistic development index could shift policy-makers' and researchers' attention from economics to human wellbeing. That is how the Human Development Index (HDI) was born.

After considerable discussion and debate, the UNDP decided on an index that included the following economic and human outcomes:

Life expectancy at birth (years; LE). Because it is measured at birth, this index is affected by high infant mortality rates in some countries.

Education, composed of two separate measures: expected years of schooling for children (EYSC), and mean years of schooling for adults (MYSA). By having a separate measure for expected education of children, this index can reflect improvements in low-education countries that invest in expanding educational opportunities for kids. Mean years of schooling for adults would reflect such improvements only after many years have elapsed.

Income, measured as the gross national income (GNI) per capita, PPP adjusted to take into account cost of living differences among countries.

Table 5.1 shows the highest and lowest outcomes for each of these variables across the globe in 2010:

Table 5.1: The Two Ends of the Human Development Spectrum

Min/max and Country	Life expectancy at birth (LE, years)	Expected Years of Schooling (of children) (EYSC, years)	Mean years of schooling (of adults) (MYSA, years)	GNI per capita in PPP terms (constant 2005 international $)
Mininum	47.4	2.4	1.2	260
Country	Sierra Leone	Somolia	Mozambique	Liberia
Maximum	83.2	18	12.6	93383
Country	Japan	Australia	Norway	Qatar

Source: UN Development Program (UNDP) Human Development Reports;
http://hdr.undp.org/en/statistics/hdi/

The table shows massive disparities in human development indicators. People in the highest-ranked countries live more than 75% longer, have more than ten times more schooling, and make more than 350 times more income, on average, than people in the lowest-ranked countries.

We can argue about whether these variables are sufficient to capture the most critical differences across countries in terms of their human development. Surely, you can think of other variables that might be included in a HDI. A good index does not have to include every human outcome we can think of, though. A few well-chosen ones should do, as long as they are correlated with the other important outcomes that get left out. For example, access to health care is an essential part of development. But because life expectancy is closely related to health care, we do not necessarily have to include both life expectancy and health care in our index.

Constructing the HDI

Creating the HDI raised a challenging technical question: How do you construct an index from such qualitatively different outcomes as income, education, and life expectancy? The HDI is an index of indexes, one for each outcome. The outcomes in it are diverse, are measured in different units, and take on a very wide range of values.

Actually, we've already learned pretty much everything we need to make the HDI. At the end of Chapter 2 we constructed an income index. We calculate our gross national income index to include in the HDI for each country i, which we can call $I(GNI_i)$, as follows:

$$I(GNI_i) = \frac{Ln(GNI_i) - Ln(GNI_{min})}{Ln(GNI_{max}) - Ln(GNI_{min})}$$

This is just like the income index in Chapter 2 except that it takes the natural log of each GNI. There is a good reason to do this. We just saw that the country per-capita incomes for the 2010 HDI ranged from \$260 (Liberia) to \$93,383 (Qatar). That's a big range. We would expect that an increase in income in rich countries won't affect human development as much as the same increase in poor countries. Taking the natural log of each country's income accomplishes this. It compresses the income range, since Ln(260) = 5.56 and Ln(93,383) = 11.44.

Notice how we've used the highest and lowest GNIs to construct this index. The UN uses the highest and lowest incomes any country had between 1980 and 2010 ($163 and $108,211, respectively). We can use the same method to construct indexes for life expectancy at birth and the two education variables. For life expectancy, the UN uses a minimum value of 20, which from a practical point of view is about the lowest a society could have and still reproduce itself. The maximum *LE* is 83.2 (Japan in 2010). For the mean years of schooling for adults, it uses a maximum of 13.2 (the United States in 2002), and a minimum of zero (since, in theory, a society could survive with zero schooling). For expected years of schooling for children, the maximum is 20.6 (Australia in 2002), and the minimum, like for the other education variable, is zero.

In all these indexes, a country with an outcome equal to the minimum gets a value of zero, while a country with an outcome equal to the maximum gets a value of one. All other countries have values between zero and one.

The last step is to combine these four indices to make the HDI. We could just take the average of the four. The problem with that approach is that a country could do well on one component but miserably fail on another and still come out looking alright. If a country really fails on one human development dimension, we want our index to reflect this.

The UN opted for using geometric means. The geometric mean of *N* variables is the Nth root of the product of the three. This sounds pretty mathematical, but as the box ("The Math of Human Development") explains, the math we choose depends on what we want our index to say about society.

Here's how to make the HDI: First, the two educational indexes are combined, using a geometric mean, to make a single educational index, which we can call $I(E_i)$. It is computed as:

$$I(E_i) = \sqrt{I(EYSC_i) * I(MYSA_i)}$$

The HDI is calculated by taking the geometric mean of the three indexes, $I(GNI_i)$, $I(LE_i)$, and $I(E_i)$:

$$HDI_i = \sqrt[3]{I(GNI_i) * I(LE_i) * I(E_i)}$$

(Notice that this is the cubed root, since we are dealing with three indexes.) The HDI, like each of its components, ranges from zero to one. It is zero if a country has a zero for any of the three component indexes. It can only equal one if a country maxes out on all three indices.

The Math of Human Development

Choosing between the average and geometric mean might seem technical, but really it's about what we care about in development. Should a country that does well on one dimension but poorly on another have the same HDI as a country that does reasonably well on both? If all three indexes are the same (say, ½), the average and geometric mean will be the same:

$$\sqrt[3]{(1/2)^3} = 1/2$$

$$(1/2 + 1/2 + 1/2)/3 = 1/2$$

Otherwise, they will be different: for example if the indexes are ¼, ½, and ¾, the average is still ½ but the geometric mean is only 0.45. Suppose two countries have the same education level, but one has moderate income and moderate life expectancy, while the other has high income and low life expectancy. Even if the average of the three indexes is the same for the two countries, the second one will have a lower HDI using the geometric mean. The geometric mean penalizes countries that do well on one component but poorly on another.

We can take all 187 countries for which we have data, sort them from lowest to highest HDI, and divide them into quintiles (fifths). Table 5.2 shows the HDI ranges for each quintile:

Table 5.2: Country HIDs, by Per-Capita Income Quintile

Quintile		HDI Range	
		Low	High
Richer↓	1	0.22	0.44
	2	0.45	0.61
	3	0.61	0.69
	4	0.70	0.78
	5	0.78	0.91

Source: UN Development Program (UNDP) Human Development Reports; http://hdr.undp.org/en/statistics/hdi/

 A complete listing of HDIs and their components for the countries for which we have them in 2010 appears in the online appendix to this chapter and at the UN Human Development Index. You'll see the lowest quintile is dominated by African countries; in fact, with only a handful of exceptions (Afghanistan, Haiti, Nepal), all of the countries in the lowest quintile are African. With the exception of a couple of oil-producing and Asian countries, all in the top quintile are European or North American. In between is a diverse group of countries, including some that do well on one or two HDI components but not on the other one or two.

Income and Human Development

Does income explain human development, or do countries at similar income levels have different human development outcomes? There is clearly a built-in relationship between income and the HDI because one of the HDI's components is income. There is also almost certainly a relationship between income and both life expectancy and educational attainment. We can see evidence for this in Figure 5.1, which graphs different countries' HDIs (vertical axis) against their per-capita GNIs (horizontal axis).

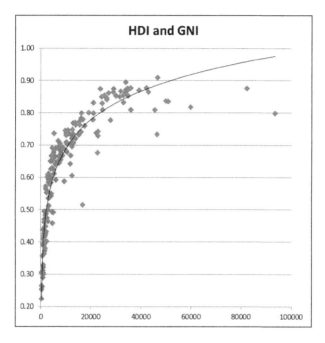

Figure 5.1: The HDI increases sharply with per-capita income then tapers off.

It is clear that the HDI rises sharply with per-capita income. Nevertheless, there are some wide variations in human development outcomes among countries even at the same income levels.

Let's dig more deeply into the UNDP data and look for countries in which the connection between income and human development is not so clear. This might offer us some insights into why some countries have managed to do a better job of meeting their human development challenges than others. One way to do this is to rank countries first in terms of per-capita GNI, then in terms of HDI, and then take the difference between the two rankings. A positive difference means that a country was ranked relatively high in terms of income but low in terms of the HDI. You can think of these as the under-performers: They seem to have gotten disproportionately little human development out of their incomes. If the rank difference is negative, a country over-performed: It was ranked higher in HDI than income.

Table 5.3 shows the countries with the biggest rank differences, positive or negative. You could draw the line on what "biggest" means wherever you wish; I chose countries that have a rank difference of more than 25 (positive in the top panel, negative in the bottom).

Look at Equatorial Guinea. Its income rank is very high: it had the 44th highest income among the 187 countries in our data. It is the richest country in Africa in terms of per-capita income, with a PPP-adjusted per-capita income of $16,908. You'd think it would score highly on life expectancy and education, the other two components of the HDI, but it doesn't. Its average life expectancy is a dismal 50.8 years, and the average adult has only 5.4 years of schooling.

What's the story in Equatorial Guinea? It is one of the largest oil producers in Africa, but its considerable oil wealth is in the hands of relatively few people. Most of the population lives in rural areas, where subsistence production predominates. (We will look at subsistence production in Chapter 7). Getting quality data on Equatorial Guinea is problematic. A Gini coefficient for income is not available from The World Bank or the CIA. However, the Vision of Humanity's Global Peace Index estimates a Gini of 0.65, making Equatorial Guinea one of the most unequal countries in the world.[1]

It might seem surprising that a country with so much oil wealth would have a relatively poor record in terms of the HDI, but Equatorial Guinea is not the only one. The United Arab Emirates, Kuwait, Angola, and Qatar are among the top twenty oil exporters in the world, and all are of them are on our "under-performers" list. So are Gabon and Trinidad and Tobago, two other oil exporters. Having oil riches does not seem to be enough to bring about human development.

The World Bank's Data Visualizer makes it possible to visualize the evolution of countries over time with regard to income and various human development indicators:

The World Bank Data Visualizer.

Another standout on the worst performers' list is South Africa. It has the largest economy in Africa, and the World Bank ranks it as an upper-middle income country. But it also has one of the world's most unequal income distributions (a Gini of 63.14, according to the World Bank), and an alarmingly high HIV infection rate (on the order of 20%). You can see in the table that South Africa does relatively well in terms of education, but its life expectancy at birth is only 52.2 years.

It is harder to find countries that significantly over perform in terms of human development. The world's greatest over-performer is Cuba, ranking 47 places higher in terms of human development than income. This is a country where the PPP-adjusted per-capita income is $5253, about half of South Africa's and less than a third of Equatorial Guinea's. Yet Cuba has one of the highest life expectancies in the world (79 years). The average Cuban child can expect to end up with 17.5 years of schooling, more than the average U.S. child (16 years). Overall, there are only six countries whose HDI ranking beats their GNI ranking by more than 25 places, but there are eleven in which the HDI ranking is 25 places lower than the GNI ranking.

Table 5.3: Over- and Under-performers in Human Development

Country	LE: Life expectancy at birth (years)		EYSC: Expected Years of Schooling (of children) (years)		MYSA: Mean years of schooling (of adults) (years)		GNI: Per capita GNI in PPP terms (constant 2005 inter-national $) (Constant 2005 international $)		HDI	GNI Rank (Lowest to Highest)	HDI Rank (Lowest to Highest)	GNI Rank - HDI Rank
	Level	Index	Level	Index	Level	Index	Level	Index				
Worst Performers:												
Equatorial Guinea	50.8	0.49	7.7	0.37	5.4	0.41	16908	0.71	0.51	143	54	89
Kuwait	74.5	0.86	12.3	0.60	6.1	0.46	46428	0.87	0.73	181	129	52
Botswana	53.3	0.53	12.2	0.59	8.9	0.67	12479	0.67	0.61	124	74	50
Oman	72.8	0.84	11.8	0.57	5.5	0.42	22633	0.76	0.68	150	100	50
South Africa	52.2	0.51	13.1	0.64	8.5	0.64	9257	0.62	0.59	109	66	43
Angola	50.7	0.49	9.1	0.44	4.4	0.33	4659	0.52	0.46	79	40	39
Gabon	62.3	0.67	13.1	0.64	7.5	0.57	11771	0.66	0.64	121	83	38
Qatar	78.2	0.92	12	0.58	7.3	0.55	93383	0.98	0.80	187	153	34
Bhutan	66.8	0.74	11	0.53	2.3	0.17	5060	0.53	0.49	82	49	33
United Arab Emirates	76.4	0.89	13.3	0.65	9.3	0.70	59819	0.91	0.82	185	158	27
Trinidad and Tobago	69.9	0.79	12.3	0.60	9.2	0.70	22979	0.76	0.73	151	125	26
Average, Worst	*64.35*	*0.70*	*11.63*	*0.56*	*6.76*	*0.51*	*27761*	*0.73*	*0.64*	*137*	*94*	*44*
Best Performers:												
Cuba	79	0.93	17.5	0.85	9.9	0.75	5253	0.53	0.74	84	131	-47
Georgia	73.5	0.85	13.1	0.64	12.1	0.92	4535	0.51	0.69	76	111	-35
Grenada	75.8	0.88	16	0.78	8.6	0.65	6914	0.58	0.71	93	121	-28
Palau	71.5	0.81	14.7	0.71	12.1	0.92	9617	0.63	0.75	110	138	-28
New Zealand	80.5	0.96	18	0.87	12.5	0.95	23776	0.77	0.87	153	180	-27
Madagascar	66.5	0.74	10.7	0.52	5.2	0.39	840	0.25	0.44	11	37	-26
Average, Best	*74.47*	*0.86*	*15.00*	*0.73*	*10.07*	*0.76*	*8489*	*0.54*	*0.70*	*88*	*120*	*-32*

Source: Analysis of data from the UNDP Human Development Report; http://hdr.undp.org/en/statistics/data/

In short, there are large variations in human development outcomes among countries. There are also large discrepancies within countries; in particular, human development outcomes tend to be most dismal in rural areas of poor countries, where most of the world's poverty is found. Still, there's no denying that income appears to be a key correlate of human development. Income growth is a key for improving human wellbeing in the world's poorest countries, and it is the topic of our next chapter.

Chapter Five Notes

1. You can read about the Global Peace Index at http://www.visionofhumanity.org/gpi-data/#/2011/conf/

6.

Growth

The average per-capita GDP in 2000 was $35,082 in the United States, $450 in India, and $256 in Uganda.

Why were they so different?

For one thing, workers were a lot more productive in the United States than in India, and they were more productive in India than in Uganda. The average worker in the United States produced $70,102 of income (GDP) in 2000. By contrast, the average worker in India produced $1,211, and in Uganda, $611.

Why was worker productivity so different?

For one thing, U.S. workers had a lot more capital to work with than Indian workers, and Indian workers had a lot more than Ugandan workers. The average U.S. worker had about $146,640 worth of capital to work with. The average worker in India had $6,848, and in Uganda, $536.[1] There is no question that capital makes workers more productive.[2]

Does this mean that capital is the key to development?

As we saw in Chapter 1, many early development economists thought so. They confounded economic development and growth, and they saw investment in capital as the key to growth. We have seen that income is an important ingredient in what we think of as economic development (though not the only one). Without economic growth, achieving the millennium development goals becomes difficult or insurmountable.

If (helped, perhaps, by massive international aid) countries could just accumulate capital, would they grow faster?

In this chapter, we'll learn what the best-known growth economist, Nobel Laureate Robert Solow, thinks. ("No.") We'll explore the basics of neoclassical growth theory, which Solow pioneered five decades ago; the relatively recent field of endogenous growth; and theoretical versus empirical growth models. The big questions we want to answer here are: "What makes economic growth happen?" and "Why do some countries grow so much faster than others?"

Lurking behind these questions is another, perhaps bigger one. If the economic returns to capital are so high, why isn't there more capital? Why do some countries invest so much in capital, while others invest so little?

What a Difference a Century Makes

Imagine a country where the life expectancy at birth is 47.8 years. Out of every 1000 babies born, 150 die within their first year of life. Ten percent of the population is completely illiterate, and only 7% ever graduate from high school. One-third of homes have running water, 15% have flush toilets, and only 3% are lit by electricity. Women comprise only 18% of the paid workforce. Flu and pneumonia are common causes of death. The average per-capita income is around $14.30 per day.

Is this country real? It might strike you as bizarre. For one thing, a per-capita income of $14.30 per day (about like China's) is high for a country with such poor human development outcomes.

It is real, though—or more accurately, it was. The country described above is the United States in the year 1900.[3]

How did we get from then to now? Why do some countries grow quickly, while others do not? Answering questions like this one is the great challenge of modern growth theory.

The Neoclassical Growth Model

To analyze why incomes grow over time, we need a model of how income gets "produced." In other words, we need an *income production function*. Income production functions take many forms and are estimated on different levels, from countries to households. Here we'll learn about the aggregate growth model, which is what most people think about when they hear the word "growth." First, though, let's go out to the farm and learn what a production function is.

The Production Function

A *production function* in economics summarizes the technological relationship between inputs and outputs. You can think of it as taking different combinations of inputs and determining the maximum level of output attainable with those inputs. Alternatively, you can think of it as telling us the minimum combinations of inputs required to produce a given level of output.

Figure 6.1 shows a simple production function for a firm (e.g., a farm) that produces an output, Q (say, kilograms of corn), using only two inputs: days of labor (L) and hectares of land (K). That is, the production function illustrated in the figure below looks like this: $Q = F(L,K)$. The function itself ($F(\cdot)$) represents the technology that turns inputs into output. To make things even simpler, let's assume land is fixed; the farmer cannot change how much land she plants in corn, at least not in the short run. The assumption of fixed land (or other capital) is often reasonable; for example, most crops have to be planted at a certain time of year, and once you plant the crop, you're stuck with it until after the harvest. We can show land is fixed by putting a bar over the K:

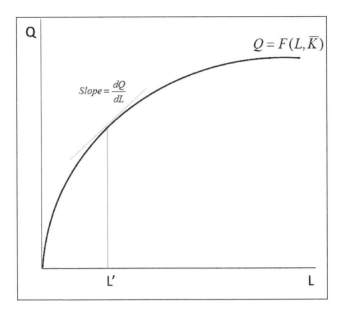

Figure 6.1: The firm's output (Q) increases with labor inputs (L) but at a decreasing rate.

This picture illustrates two important things about production functions. First, the production function slopes upward, indicating that it is increasing in the inputs. Land is fixed, but you can see that as labor increases, so does output. The slope at any point (say, at L' days of labor) gives the change in output from a small change in the input, or the marginal product of the input (here, the marginal product of labor, or MP_L). If you're math-minded, you'll recognize this as the derivative of output with respect to the input, and it's positive.

The other important thing to notice is that the marginal product of labor is not the same for all input levels; it decreases as the amount of labor increases. Think of a fixed plot of land, say, one hectare large. Without any labor, you cannot produce anything on it. Add a little labor, and you start getting output; you can till the land, plant seeds, add fertilizer, weed, and harvest. After a point, though, each hour of labor you add to this single hectare of land will get you less of an increase in output than the previous hour of labor you added. Geometrically, the slope gets flatter as we move out to the right in our diagram. We call this *decreasing marginal returns* to inputs. (Mathematically speaking, the second derivative is negative). Off to the right of our picture the curve flattens out completely. At that point, the MP_L is zero. Beyond it, the MP_L could even become negative: more labor, less output (like when too many workers get into each other's way or trample the crops).

An Aggregate Production Function

Imagine adding up the value of everything produced in the whole economy (that is, the GDP), as well as all the labor and capital used to produce it. This gives you an *aggregate production function*. Just as farms, industries, and service firms take labor, capital, and other inputs to produce a quantity of output (tons of corn, millions of motherboards, or billions of Facebook messages), entire economies combine their labor and capital to produce a GDP. Aggregate production functions are used to describe the relationship between inputs and income in national economies. Neoclassical growth theory is all about how aggregate production grows over time, and where it will end up if a policy or other event (say, war or earthquake) shocks it in one direction or another.

We will use the simplest aggregate production function, which is the staple of the neoclassical growth model. It relates aggregate income (Y) to labor (L) and capital (K): $Y = F(L,K)$.

Under certain conditions, you could increase all inputs by the same factor and output will increase by that factor. Double all inputs, and output will double. This is called *constant returns to scale* (CRS). (There are also *decreasing returns to scale* (DRS) and *increasing returns to scale* (IRS), but like neoclassical growth theory, we'll assume CRS here).

If there are CRS, we could multiply all the inputs by any number, for example *1/L*. Output would increase by a factor of *1/L*, so our aggregate production function would become: $Y/L = F(L/L, K/L)$, or just $y = f(k)$, where *y* is the output-to-labor ratio (*Y/L*) and k is the capital-to-labor ratio (*K/L*). In an economy with constant returns to scale, output per worker depends on capital per worker. We could do the same thing to the production function of our individual farm, above, as long as it also exhibits CRS. (We'll revisit farm production functions in Chapter 7, "Agriculture.")

It's important to keep the distinction between returns to scale and returns to one of the factors of production clear. When we talk about returns to scale, we're talking about increasing *all* of the inputs by the same factor, for example, doubling both labor and capital in our simple two-input case. Even if we have constant (or increasing) returns to scale, we typically have decreasing returns to any single input. Suppose doubling your labor and your capital allows you to double your output. Then imagine doubling only your labor: without also increasing your capital, you won't be able to double your output. It's like increasing the number of cooks in a crowded kitchen; eventually they won't have enough pots and pans to go around and they'll start getting into each other's way.

We can draw a picture of an aggregate production function (Figure 6.2). Given the two properties of production functions we discussed earlier (output is increasing in inputs, but at a decreasing rate), this aggregate production function will look a lot like the individual firm's production function we drew earlier:

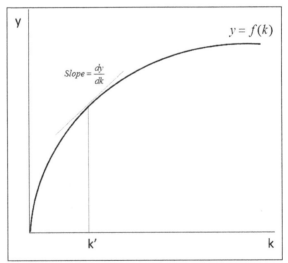

Figure 6.2. Aggregate production per worker (y) increases with capital per worker (k) but at a decreasing rate.

This figure shows output per worker increasing with capital per worker. At any point along the curve, the slope is the change in output per worker that results from a small increase in the amount of capital available per worker in the economy. More capital/worker means more output/worker. But as was the case for an individual farm, for the whole economy, there are diminishing marginal returns to k, that is, to capital/worker.

You can see how important capital is in this model. With no capital per worker, there's no GDP! The factors explaining the amount of capital per worker, then, are the main focus of neoclassical growth models. They are:

- The amount of investment per worker, which is what creates the capital

- Population growth; more workers mean less capital/worker

- Depreciation: capital gets used up in the production process, so like a treadmill, economies have to keep investing in new capital just to stay in the same place

We need a way to represent these factors in our model. Investment comes from savings; in national accounting, total investment always equals total savings (which could include some foreign savings or investment, but let's set that aside for now). Let's use s to represent the savings rate in the economy. Thus, for every dollar/worker that gets created in the economy, $\$s$ gets saved and turns into investment, or capital. Savings per worker, then, is just $s*y$. We can show savings per worker on our graph, as in Figure 6.3:

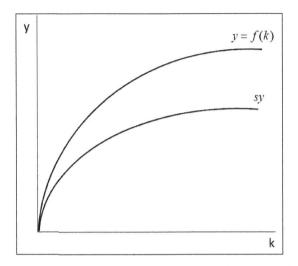

Figure 6.3: Savings per worker is output per worker times the savings rate, s. Since the savings rate is less than 1, the sy curve lies below the y curve.

Next we have to put in the population growth rate and the rate of depreciation. Let's call the population growth rate n, and the rate of depreciation d. Suppose we start the year with 2000 units of capital and 20 workers, so $k=2000/20=100$ units of capital per worker. By the end of the year, 200 units get used up $(d=.10)$. That leaves a total of 1800 units of capital, or 90 per worker. Meanwhile, the labor force grows by one worker $(n=.05)$, so now there are 21 workers sharing 90 units of capital. Depreciation of capital and growth of the workforce thus results in the capital/worker ratio falling to 85.7 (1800/21) units.

The economy will need a minimum of $(n+d)*k$ in savings per worker just to stay in the same place. We can put this in our graph, too. It's a straight line with a slope equal to $(n+d)$ as shown in Figure 6.4.

Nothing catches an economist's eye like two lines crossing in a graph. You can see a crossover at point A, where the savings per worker (sy) just equals what's needed to keep the capital/worker ratio stable $((n+d)k)$. This point, at the capital/labor ratio of k^*, is the economy's steady state. When the economy is at this point, output per worker is constant over time.

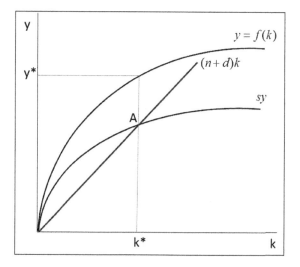

Figure 6.4: To the left of point A, savings per worker exceeds what is needed to keep up with labor force growth (n) and depreciation (d), so capital per worker increases. The opposite is true to the right of A. Thus, A is the steady-state income and capital per worker in the economy.

To the left of the steady state point, savings *exceeds* what is needed to keep up with depreciation and labor-force growth (the savings line *sy* is above $(n+d)k$), so the capital per worker will increase until we get to k^*. To the right of the steady state, there is not enough savings to keep up with depreciation and labor-force growth, so the capital per worker will fall back to k^*.

In short, once the economy is at k^*, there is no reason for it to go anywhere else, and if something throws the economy off of k^*, the economic forces at work in our diagram will always bring it back to the steady state. This is the famous Solow growth model, named after its co-founder, the Nobel laureate Robert Solow. (It is also called the Solow-Swan model after T.W. Swan, who independently came up with a similar model at the same time.)

The big question we want to ask is how to make growth happen. What does the Solow model have to say about this?

At the steady state in our picture the economy is growing just enough to keep up with depreciation and labor force growth. Income per worker is y^*. How can we make it increase?

One thing we can try is raising the savings rate, say, from s to s'. This pivots the savings-per-worker curve upward, from sy to $s'y$, like in Figure 6.5:

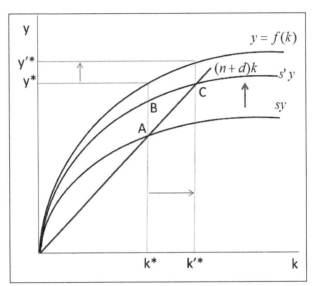

Figure 6.5: An increase in the savings rate leads the economy to a higher steady-state capital-labor ratio and income per worker.

At the existing capital-worker ratio k^*, the amount of savings in the economy jumps from point A to point B. Point B is not a steady state, though, because savings is higher than what is needed to keep up with depreciation and labor-force growth. Capital per worker thus goes up, and with it, so does income per worker. The economy moves up the $s'y$ curve to point C. The new capital-labor ratio is k'^*, and output per worker is now y'^*.

Notice that increases in the labor-force growth rate or depreciation rate have the opposite effect. If n or d goes up, say, to n'' or d'' (see Figure 6.6), the $(n+d)k$ line gets steeper. This shifts the steady state from point A to D in the diagram below, driving down both output and capital per

worker. This does not mean that labor doesn't make the economy grow—
it does. The aggregate production function is increasing in labor. But if
the workforce is growing faster than total income, income *per worker*
will decrease. It should come as no surprise that income per worker is
lower in countries where the workforce is growing rapidly.

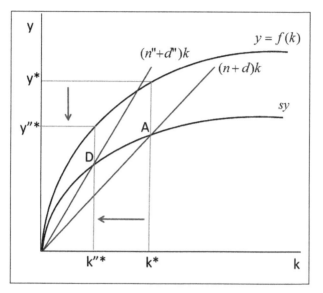

Figure 6.6: An increase in the labor-force growth or depreciation rate
takes the economy to a lower steady-state income and capital per worker.

Technological Change in the Solow Model

What does technology change do to our Solow diagram? Assume as
before that, at any point in time, there are diminishing marginal returns
to capital per worker, so the basic shape of the y and sy curves does not
change. However, technological change and the accumulation of human
capital increase productivity, shifting the income per worker (y) curve
upward over time. Assuming a constant savings rate, the sy curve follows
the y curve upward, as illustrated in Figure 6.7. The figure shows how
the economy's steady state shifts up towards the northeast, raising both
k and y as the productivity of labor and capital in the economy increases.

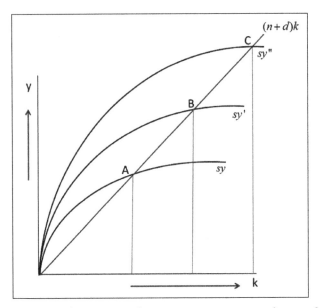

Figure 6.7: As productivity in the economy increases, the steady-state capital and output per worker rises from point A to B to C.

Testing the Neoclassical Growth Model: From Theory to Empirics

Is this a good model?

A good model gives us useful insights and holds up to real-world tests. The Solow model does offer some important insights. In order to grow, countries need both capital and labor. A poor, labor-abundant country is unlikely to increase its income per capita without increasing its capital per worker. "Capital" includes physical capital (e.g., machines) as well as human capital (education and skills). And don't forget public capital like roads, irrigation, and the internet. These are known as *public goods*, because they typically benefit everyone. Governments usually have to make investments in public goods, because private firms cannot capture and profit from many of their benefits; thus, left to the private sector, there will not be enough investment in them.

If you look around the world, you'll find that the major success stories, like the Asian tigers and now China, involved substantial investments providing vast numbers of workers with capital that they did not have before. Employers will not pay a worker a wage that exceeds the value she produces. With more capital, workers produce more value. It's telling that real wages are rising so fast in China (about 10% a year) that they are nearly as high as Mexico's now, as you can see in Figure 6.8:

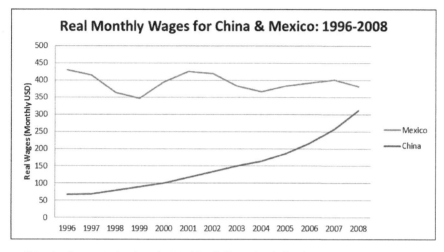

CPI and exchange rate data from the IMF http://elibrary-data.imf.org/;
Nominal wages from the ILO http://laborsta.ilo.org/

Figure 6.8: Real monthly wages in China and Mexico are converging.

Where population is growing rapidly, more investment is needed just to keep pace; otherwise, income per worker may stagnate or even decline. You can't deny that labor is a key input into the production of GDP, but without capital, there are diminishing returns to labor in the production process. It's no surprise that high population-growth countries tend to have low per-capita incomes.

Now it's time to seriously test the neoclassical growth model. We test models by taking their predictions and seeing whether they hold up in the real world. A number of key predictions come out of the Solow model.

One prediction is that when major shocks like war or natural disasters strike, economies will return to their steady-state. Rich country economies tend to bounce back quickly from natural disasters. Post World War

II Europe is a good example (with a little help from the Marshall Plan). There is some evidence that this is true even in poor developing countries (see box: "The Growth Legacy of the Vietnam War"). However, the long-term impact of disaster is challenging to identify, the data to do this are hard to come by, and largely because of this it is a little-researched area in development economics. Recovering from disaster in other ways (e.g., psychologically) is an entirely different matter.

The Growth Legacy of the Vietnam War

The Vietnam War involved the heaviest aerial bombardment of any war in human history. War destroys capital. Neoclassical growth theory predicts that when exogenous events destroy physical and human capital, countries will recover, with no long-term impact on their steady-state equilibrium. Of course, the horrors of war include more than the destruction of capital. War impacts psychology, technology, social institutions, and other outcomes in complex and possibly long-term ways.

A very unique study by Edward Miguel and Gerard Roland tested the long-term impact of U.S. bombing in Vietnam. They authors used actual U.S. military data on bombing intensities in different districts in Vietnam. (The data were provided by the Vietnam Veterans of America Foundation and the Vietnam Ministry of Defense Technology Center for Bomb and Mine Disposal.) The study tested whether districts that were more heavily bombed during the war had higher poverty rates, lower consumption, poorer infrastructure, more illiteracy, or lower population densities three decades later.

The econometric results showed no significant difference in growth outcomes between heavily bombed districts and the country's other districts. The legacy of war did not prevent Vietnam from recovering and experiencing rapid economic growth. Such findings are consistent with a return to the steady state following a major economic shock, as predicted by the neoclassical growth model. The authors warn, however, that Vietnam may have unique features that help explain its post-war economic success, and they advise caution in generalizing their results to other countries.

Edward Miguel and Gérard Roland, "The Long-Run Impact of Bombing Vietnam," Journal of Development Economics Volume 96, Issue 1, September 2011, Pages 1–15

Other predictions of the Solow growth model do not hold up so well. For example, look at the aggregate production function again. It implies that growth in aggregate income can be explained by growth in labor and growth in capital. In the real world, do changes in labor and capital explain all or most of the differences in economic growth we see among countries and in the same countries over time?

The empirical growth economist Xavier Sala-i-Martin says no. By running nearly 2 million econometric regressions, he found twenty-two different variables that appear to be significant in explaining differences in income growth among countries! These variables include capital investment, but they also include a diverse list of other variables, from openness to trade to political rights, black markets, colonial legacy, war, and religion (see box: "The Man Who Ran Two Million Regressions").

The Man Who Ran Two Million Regressions

Econometricians use real-world data to model relationships among variables and test key hypotheses that come out of their theories. For example, if some variable such as capital investment (X) increases income growth (Y), we should be able to take data on these two variables, make a scatter plot, and fit a line (or curve) to the data, like in the picture below:

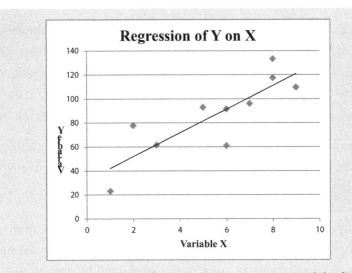

Econometrics is about finding the best way to model relationships, which usually involve not just two but many variables. (You can learn about econometrics in *RebelText: Essentials of Econometrics* or any number of expensive econometrics textbooks.)

Empirical growth economists have found many variables that seem to correlate with countries' economic growth, but often correlations lose their statistical significance when new variables are included in the growth model.

Xavier Sala-i-Martin's big contribution was to come up with a way to estimate many different models, with every conceivable combination of variables, and find the variables that come out significant most often in explaining economic growth. Here's the list he came up with and the sign of the correlation between each variable and economic growth (you can learn more about these variables and how he measured them by reading his article, below):

Equipment investment (+)

Number of years open economy (+)

Fraction Confucian (+)

SD black-market premium (-)

Primary exports in 1970 (-)

Degree of capitalism (+)

Rule of law (+)	War (-)
Fraction Muslim (+)	Non-equipment investment (+)
Political rights (-)	Absolute latitude (+)
Latin America (-)	Exchange-rate distortions (-)
Sub-Saharan Africa (-)	Fraction Protestant (-)
Civil liberties (-)	Fraction Buddhist (+)
Revolutions and coups (-)	Fraction Catholic (-)
Fraction of GDP in mining (+)	Spanish colony (-)

Xavier Sala-i-Martin, "I Just Ran Two Million Regressions," *The American Economic Review*, Vol. 87, No. 2, May 1997.

Another key prediction of neoclassical growth models is that the income levels of poor countries will tend to catch up, or *converge*, with the income levels of rich countries over time. For this to happen, poor countries would have to be growing faster than rich ones. Are they?

In Figure 6.9, we plot countries' annual change in per-capita GNI between 1990 and 2010 (vertical axis) against their initial (1990) per-capita income (horizontal axis). If the convergence hypothesis is correct, the points in this graph should form a clear downward-sloping line.

But that is not what the figure shows. Growth rates are all over the place, especially for poor countries. An econometric regression of 1990-2010 growth against 1990 income shows no significant relationship between the two.

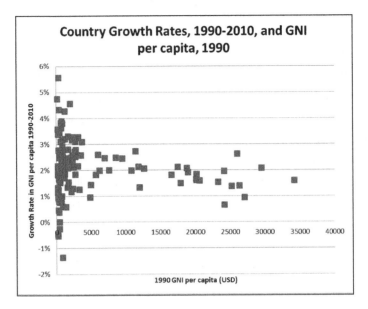

Figure 6.9: There is no significant relationship between initial (1900) per-capita income and country growth rates between 1990 and 2010. Source: Constructed from World Bank data; http://data.worldbank.org/indicator/NY.GNP.PCAP.CD

Although empirical growth studies focus on differences in economic performance across countries, there are tremendous disparities in income growth within countries, too. Almost every country in the world has its "left-behind" regions, from western China to southern Mexico to, as remarkable as it sounds, California's Central Valley, the richest agricultural land in the world, where many towns have per-capita incomes lower than Mexico's! Economists have not done much work on why we do not see economic convergence within countries. Like in the case of inter-country comparisons, it seems that the facts are inconsistent with the predictions of neoclassical growth models.

Revisiting the Assumptions

Why doesn't the neoclassical growth model describe what actually happened in terms of economic growth? The model is internally consistent:

the math behind it all works. If its predictions do not hold up, we have to look at the model's assumptions. Perhaps our model left out something that stimulates income growth in relatively high-income countries and/ or impedes it in poor countries, thereby preventing convergence from happening.

To check on the model's assumptions, let's go back to where we started. We had an aggregate production function describing a CRS technology in which output depends on labor and capital (the $F(L,K)$ function). One assumption behind the convergence theory is that countries share the same or similar technologies. Another is that the production function does not change. If rich and poor countries have different production functions, or if technologies are changing in ways that favor rich countries, convergence may not occur. Still another assumption is CRS. What if the returns to scale are increasing instead of constant? Could it be that the more an economy grows, the faster it is able to grow in the future? Economies of scale describe a situation in which the larger the economy becomes, the more efficiently it is able to turn inputs into outputs.

Rich countries give us plenty of examples where "game-changing" technologies transformed the relationship between inputs and outputs and created enormous production and income gains. Between 1908 and 1915, the Ford Motor Company introduced the assembly line, which transformed the production function for making cars. Suddenly, the same labor and capital investment could turn out vastly more cars, and mass production made automobiles available to middle-class consumers. In the 1980s and 1990s the internet transformed all facets of production and consumption, laying the foundation for new production activities never even imagined before. New startups sprouted up where information and technology production already was concentrated, like California's Silicon Valley.

In 2012, social networking is transforming the production landscape of the city of San Francisco. Where else in the world could a company like Facebook become a hundred-billion-dollar-plus company within eight years? Facebook produces social networking. Down the road sits Google, which produces searches. How much labor and capital are required to create an additional 100 messages or searches? An additional million? With a gross income of $38 billion in 2011, Google would rank 83rd among countries, above Ghana and about the same as Costa Rica. (Apple would rank 55th, just ahead of Vietnam.) What country in the world has an income production function that looks anything at all like Google's?

It is indeed hard to argue that the technologies that combine inputs to create outputs are similar in rich and poor countries, or that they stay the same over time. The far-reaching technological transformations concentrated in high-income countries do not seem to have a place in the neoclassical growth model. Economies of scale might go a long way toward explaining why we do not see convergence.

Endogenous Growth Theory

A new generation of growth theory, called endogenous growth theory, emphasizes technological change and "knowledge spillovers" while explaining differences in income growth over time and among different countries. The economist Paul Romer, who along with Robert Lucas helped found the new growth theory, describes what he did this way:

> "Robert Lucas…and I…cited the failure of cross-country convergence to motivate models of growth that drop the two central assumptions of the neoclassical model: that technological change is exogenous and that the same technological opportunities are available in all countries of the world:

> He goes on to argue:

> … each unit of capital investment not only increases the stock of physical capital but also increases the level of the technology for all firms in the economy through knowledge spillovers."[4]

This is a good example of how new theories build upon old ones that do not stand up to tests against real-world data and events. In the Solow model, investment raises the stock of capital. In endogenous growth theory, it also raises the level of technology for all firms by creating knowledge spillovers. Just think of the knowledge spillovers the internet created! When there are significant knowledge spillovers, the whole production function changes when capital investment goes up. There are incentives for new activities to set up around existing ones, like in California's Silicon Valley where internet start-ups are drawn together like iron to magnets. The benefits of setting up where other successful firms already operate are called *economies of agglomeration.*

Neoclassical and endogenous growth theory stress different determinants of economic development. In neoclassical theory, as Romer writes, "Nations are poor because they lack valuable objects like factories, roads, and raw materials." In endogenous growth theory, "Nations are poor because their citizens do not have access to the ideas that are used in industrial nations to generate economic value." Romer calls the first explanation an "object gap" and the second an "idea gap." Closing the object gap requires savings and investment, as emphasized by the Solow model. Closing the idea gap requires focusing attention on "the patterns of interaction and communication between a developing country and the rest of the world." Some measures, including good macroeconomic policies, educational investments, and the development of well-functioning legal institutions, can help close both gaps.

In Romer's view, closing both the idea and object gaps is the key to achieving the upward shifts in productivity illustrated in Figure 6.7.

Figure 6.10 illustrates how endogenous growth theory builds upon neoclassical growth theory by incorporating new elements of economies of scale, technology change, and agglomeration. The part of the figure in bold depicts the circular relationship between income change and investment that we learned about in the neoclassical growth model: an increase in capital per worker raises output per worker, which in turn generates savings that are used to invest in new capital. Endogenous growth theory adds a new "technology loop" at the bottom of the diagram. New investments in capital, including human capital, lead to technological change and create spillover and agglomeration effects, which in turn stimulate new increases in incomes. This is the way most economists think about economic growth today.

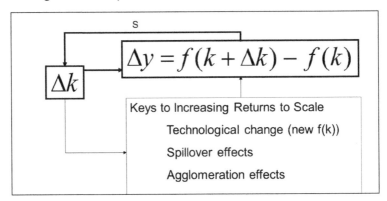

Figure 6.10: Endogenous growth theory adds a new "technology loop" to the growth model.

We've noted that countries with rapid population growth have lower growth in per-capita incomes. Endogenous growth theory explains why this is true. Rapid labor-force growth retards income growth because it creates *negative* spillover effects. When there is plenty of labor, producers don't have an incentive to invest in labor-saving innovations that can generate positive spillover effects in the economy. Without a good reason to invest in labor-saving capital and technologies, productivity per worker stagnates.

Economic development is all about transformation, including technological change. Here's a particularly thought-provoking passage that raises fundamental questions about the meaning of "economic development:"

Sustained economic growth is everywhere and always a process of continual transformation. The sort of economic progress that has been enjoyed by the richest nations since the Industrial Revolution would not have been possible if people had not undergone wrenching changes. Economies that cease to transform themselves are destined to fall off the path of economic growth. The countries that most deserve the title of "developing" are not the poorest countries of the world, but the richest. [They] need to engage in the never-ending process of economic development if they are to enjoy continued prosperity.[5]

Incentives and Poverty Traps

When most development economists think about growth these days, it's endogenous growth. Technological change, in addition to increasing capital per worker, is needed to raise incomes. But what makes technological change happen?

William Easterly, an economics professor at New York University, has a straightforward answer: it's incentives, stupid! In his book *The Elusive Quest for Growth*[6] he wrote:

> Many times over the past fifty years, we economists thought we had found the right answer to economic growth. It started with foreign aid to fill the gap between "necessary" investment and saving…[we] thought investment in machines was the key to growth…education was a form of "human machinery" that would bring growth…population control…loans to induce countries to do policy reforms. Finally…debt forgiveness.
>
> None of these elixirs has worked as promised, because not all the participants in the creation of economic growth had the right incentives.

William Easterly explains the failure of aid to Africa.

Easterly argues that without the right incentives for people to work hard, be creative, and invent and adopt new technologies, development won't happen. He is a harsh critic of foreign aid, arguing that the billions of dollars spent on it have little to show for themselves and certainly have failed to foster sustainable growth. Aid, he argues, often operates from a "do-good" mentality instead of trying to create an environment in which markets provide people with the incentives needed to make growth happen.

Jeffrey Sachs, who heads the Earth Institute at Columbia University, takes a different view, one consistent with people being caught in poverty traps (Chapter 3). Sach's 2005 book *The End of Poverty* argues that, with the right policies and carefully targeted aid interventions, it is possible to eliminate extreme poverty within a couple of decades. He points to China, where the number of people living on less than $1.25 per day plummeted from 85% of the population in 1981 to 16% in 2005. To Sachs, a key to eradicating extreme poverty is to dramatically increase foreign aid, with a focus on providing subsistence farmers with improved seeds, irrigation, and fertilizer, as well as supporting micro-credit and health programs.

To make the point, Sachs founded the United Nations Millennium Villages Project. The project started by setting up 12 "research villages" in ten African countries. Each village gets practical aid equivalent to US$250 per villager per year. Here's how the Millennium Project's website describes the project's goals:

> The Millennium Villages are based on a single powerful idea: impoverished villages can transform themselves and meet the Millennium Development Goals if they are empowered with proven, powerful, practical technologies. By investing in health, food production, education, access to clean water, and essential infrastructure, these community-led interventions will enable impoverished villages to escape extreme poverty, something that currently confines over one billion people worldwide.[7]

The first of the Millennium Villages was Sauri, Kenya. In 2010, a *New York Times* article reported:[8]

> Agricultural yields have doubled; child mortality has dropped by 30 percent; school attendance has shot up and so have test scores, putting one local school second in the area, when it used to be ranked 17th; and cellphone ownership (a telltale sign of prosperity in rural Africa) has increased fourfold... There is a palpable can-do spirit."

Dr. Jeffrey Sachs travels with Angelina Jolie to visit Sauri, Kenya, a Millennium Village.

The success of Sachs' Millennium Villages seems to speak for itself. Or does it? Does the success of Millennium Villages hold out the hope for eradicating extreme poverty on a larger scale? Can it be sustainable and self-propagating, or is dependence on foreign aid the only hope for poor villagers? These are important questions, because given the huge number of poor villages in the world today, there clearly is not enough of Jeffrey Sachs nor of aid money to go around.

What does Dr. Easterly have to say about the Millennium Villages? The same *New York Times* article quoted Easterly as saying:

> Sachs is essentially trying to create an island of success in a sea of failure, and maybe he's done that, but it doesn't address the sea of failure.

He goes on to say that, if one attempts to scale up the Millennium Project to thousands of villages, "it immediately runs into the problems we've all been talking about: corruption, bad leadership, ethnic politics."

Who's right, Sachs or Easterly? Is getting the incentives right the key to making development happen, as Easterly argues? China's remarkable progress in combating poverty would be unimaginable without the far-reaching economic reforms that unleashed markets throughout the country and gave people powerful economic incentives that they did not have before. On the other hand, China also made major investments in its rural areas, with new roads, communications, schools, marketing infrastructure, and productivity-increasing agricultural research, and hundreds of billions of dollars of foreign investment didn't hurt. It even had its own "model villages" along the way.

Does the Millennium Villages' success tell us what works and what doesn't? What lessons can we learn from this remarkable experiment to help unlock the secrets to making development happen on a large scale? Asked about scaling up Sachs' Millennium Village project, another economist, Michael Clemens at the Washington D.C. Center for Global Development (http://www.cgdev.org/), answered:

> No one would dream of 'scaling up' the use of a new pharmaceutical in the U.S. without rigorous evidence comparing people who got the medicine to people who did not."

Can development projects be evaluated like drugs? We'll see in chapter 11, which focuses on the evaluation of development policies and projects. But before we learn about what works and what doesn't, we need to look inside aggregate growth to see what happens when countries grow and how markets can create the incentives Easterly alludes to—or not.

Chapter Six Notes

1. Marcelo Mello, "Decomposing the International Variation in Capital Per Worker," *Economics Letters* 113(2011), pp. 189-191.

2. These numbers were compiled from The World Bank's on-line database; http://databank.worldbank.org. All are in constant 2000 US dollars.

3. *Sources:* Life Expectancy: Department of Health and Human Services, National Center for Health Statistics; *National Vital Statistics Reports,* vol 54., no. 19, June 28, 2006. Web: www.dhhs.gov . http://americandigest.org/mt-archives/american_studies/america_in_1900.php; Richard H. Steckel, Ohio State University, A History of the Standard of Living in the United States. http://eh.net/encyclopedia/article/steckel.standard.living.us. US GDP in 1900 (2002 dollars): Angus Maddison, *The World Economy: Historical Statistics.*

4. Paul M. Romer, "The Origins of Endogenous Growth." The Journal of Economic Perspectives, Vol. 8, No. 1 (Winter 1994), 3-22.

5. Peter Howitt, "Innovation, Competition and Growth: A Schumpeterian Perspective on Canada's Economy." C.D. Howe Institute Commentary No. 246 (April 2007), Conclusion. http://www.cdhowe.org/pdf/commentary_246.pdf.

6. William Easterly, The Elusive Quest for Growth, Cambridge, MA: The MIT Press, 2002.

7. http://www.unmillenniumproject.org/

8. Jeffrey Gettleman, "Shower of Aid Brings Flood of Progress," *New York Times,* March 8, 2010 http://www.nytimes.com/2010/03/09/world/africa/09kenya.html#h[TiaPwh]

7.

Agriculture

Seventy percent of the world's poor live in rural areas, and in the poorest countries most rural households are involved in agriculture. Agriculture is a fascinating and crucial sector of the economy. Virtually all countries start out with economies based primarily on agriculture, but agriculture's shares of GNI and national employment fall as economies grow. It would seem, then, that agriculture starts out being important but becomes less so over time.

There is a connection between agriculture and economic growth, though. You can see it in Figure 7.1, which relates countries' growth in agricultural GDP with growth in non-agricultural GNI over time. There is wide variation in both agricultural and non-agricultural growth rates across countries, but the figure shows a significant positive relationship between the two. Agricultural and non-agricultural growth seem to go hand in hand; the countries that had the highest agricultural GDP growth also tended to have the highest non-agricultural GNI growth. If we do an econometric regression using the data in this picture, we find that a one percentage point increase in agricultural growth is associated with nearly a half (0.45) percentage point increase in non-agricultural growth.[1]

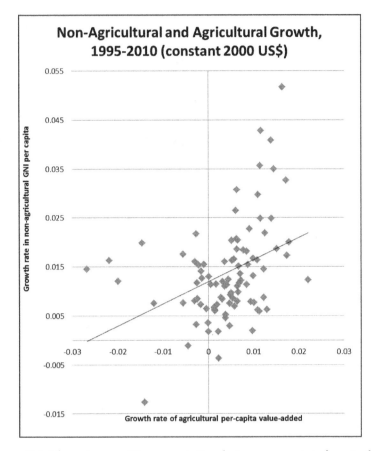

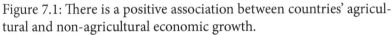

Figure 7.1: There is a positive association between countries' agricultural and non-agricultural economic growth.

This does not necessarily mean that agricultural growth *causes* total income growth. In fact, it could be the reverse: countries that do well overall might be better at growing their agricultural sector. More likely, it is some combination of the two. Increases in agricultural production facilitate growth in other sectors of the economy, and this, in turn, has a positive feedback effect on agricultural growth. In addition, there may be other factors, like technological change, that make both sectors grow.

There are many reasons to believe that countries need to grow their agriculture if they want to grow their whole economy. Agriculture continues to be the main source of income and employment for many people in the world today, making agricultural households an important market for manufactured goods. Agriculture is the principal source of food and labor to fuel expanding urban economies. It provides many intermediate inputs, for example, fruits, vegetables, and grain to food processors. When a large part of the economy is agricultural, where else are the savings to invest in industry going to come from? Countries around the globe have devised a variety of ways to "tax" agricultural income as a way to support investments outside of agriculture. Japan, in the Meiji period (1868-1912), taxed its farmers directly. The former USSR taxed farmers indirectly, by paying them prices below the world price for their crops. Its example has been followed by many agro-exporter countries.

This chapter is an introduction to how economists study agricultural economies in developing countries. The first thing we'll learn is that agriculture is different from other parts of the economy, and agricultural producers in poor countries are also households. They are neither pure firms nor pure consumers, but rather a combination of the two. The microeconomic theory of the firm does not describe their behavior, but neither does the theory of the consumer. We will learn how to model the dual nature of agricultural households as producers and consumers, and what this means for designing policies to address rural poverty and food security.

Next we'll look inside the household. We'll see how unequal access to resources can affect not only how the household's economic pie gets divvied up among household members (equity), but even how big the pie is (efficiency). We'll see that gender divisions within households can result in significant losses in economic efficiency and income, and they can create unintended consequences of development projects.

Finally, we'll look beyond the household and see how diverse households interact within rural economies. We'll see how economic linkages transmit impacts of policy and market shocks among households, often with surprising outcomes.

How Agriculture is Different

Agriculture is different from other sectors of the economy in ways that have far-reaching ramifications for both development policy and economic analysis.

To start with, let's think about the production function. In most sectors of the economy, the production function represents a knowable engineering relationship between inputs and outputs, like how many copies of RebelText can be produced from a given amount of paper, ink, capital (printing machines), labor, and so on. The agricultural production process is biological, and it's full of uncertainty. Farmers rely heavily on inputs from nature, including weather. The good news is that nature provides inputs like sunshine and rainfall for free. The bad news is that you never know when the rains won't come, the sun won't shine, or a swarm of locusts will devastate your crop. Adverse shocks break the engineering relationship between inputs and outputs. Agricultural economists pay a great deal of attention to incorporating risk into the production function. In agriculture, the production function is random or stochastic (from the Greek word στόχος (stóchos), meaning 'guess' or 'target'). Stochastic production analysis is beyond the scope of this book, but as you read on it is important to bear in mind this critical difference between agriculture and other sectors. We will return to the topic of risk and uncertainty in Chapter 10.

Agricultural production involves long time lags—often many months—between purchasing and applying inputs and harvesting outputs. Neither the size of the harvest nor the output price is known at planting time. Farming requires land, so agriculture is spread out over wide geographic areas. Because agricultural production is spread out, seasonal, risky, and involves long time lags, timely access to diverse markets is critical. This includes markets for inputs, output, credit (to finance input costs ahead of harvests), and insurance. Imagine, then, the challenges farmers face in poor countries, where markets don't work well (Chapter 9), banks won't lend money to small farmers, and formal insurance is nonexistent (Chapter 10).

Some sectors, like energy, steel, or automobiles, are dominated by a few large producers. The Minister of Industry might be able to get key industry players to sit down around a table and discuss industrial development policies. Agricultural production is carried out by large numbers of farmers with unequal access to resources, from large agri-businesses (sometimes referred to as "factories in the fields") to hundreds of millions of small farmers. To get agricultural policies right, we have to understand the behavior of thousands, millions, or (in China and India) hundreds of millions of heterogeneous actors whom the Minister of Agriculture couldn't possibly get around a table! Influencing agricultural outcomes thus requires having good economic models of diverse agricultural producers and how they are likely to respond to different kinds of policies. To complicate matters, as we shall see, what's good for big farmers might very well be bad for small ones.

Perhaps the biggest difference between agriculture and other sectors in poor countries is that agricultural production decisions are almost always made within economic units that are also households. This changes the game when it comes to economic analysis.

The Agricultural Household Model

In rich countries, most agricultural producers are firms that produce for the market. Agricultural households in poor countries are different from rich-country farmers as well as from their non-agricultural counterparts, because they consume part or all of what they produce. They also supply many of their own inputs, particularly land and labor. You can think of them as a hybrid of firm and household. Our models therefore have to reflect agricultural households' dual nature as both producer and consumer to provide a reliable basis for understanding the agricultural economy and offer guidance for designing policies.

The analysis of agriculture and development in this way leads to surprises, because what is good for agricultural households as producers often is not good for them as consumers. When the price of food goes up, most crop producers in poor countries are *not* better off, because they also face higher prices as food consumers. Failure to understand the workings of agricultural households has been a source of many ill-fated development policies.

The agricultural household model (also called the household-farm model) is the staple for any kind of micro-economic analysis of agriculture in poor countries, so it is where we begin our journey in this chapter.

Let's start with consumer theory. Figure 7.2 shows the famous indifference curve and budget constraint in the consumer model, which you'll remember from your microeconomics classes. The axes measure the quantities of food (horizontal axis) and other stuff (vertical axis) the household demands. We could have more categories of goods, but each new good adds a dimension to our figure, which makes it hard—or impossible—to draw, so let's keep it at two. Our findings will generalize to more than two goods.

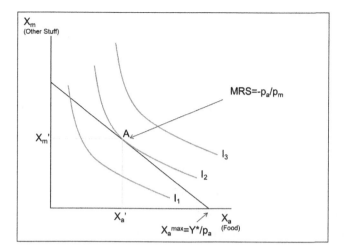

Figure 7.2: The household as consumer optimizes at the point of tangency between the indifference curve and budget constraint. At point A, its marginal rate of substitution between goods equals the ratio of market prices.

The straight line represents the household's budget constraint. In a standard consumer model, we almost always assume the household's income is fixed. In an agricultural household model, though, it includes profits from producing food. Remember this—it's an essential part of the household-farm model.

The point where the budget constraint hits an axis (the intercept) is the maximum amount of the good on the axis that our household could consume if it spent all its available income, Y^*, on that good. To see where the budget constraint hits the two axes, just divide income by the price per unit of each good. The maximum amount of food this household could consume, which we'll call X_a^{max}, is the household's income divided by the price of food. For example, if your income is $100 and food costs $2 per kilo, the most you can consume if you don't buy anything else is 50 kilos. The line between those two points shows all the combinations of food and other stuff the household can afford if it spends all of its money.

The budget constraint has a slope equal to the (negative of the) price of food (or whatever's on the horizontal axis) divided by the price of other stuff (or whatever's on the vertical axis). You can see that this line tells us the rate at which the market trades off food for other stuff. Its slope tells us how much other stuff we could buy if we gave up one unit of food (and vice-versa).

The basic precept of consumer economics is that at the optimum, every household consumes at the point where its own personal (subjective) tradeoff between food and other stuff equals the rate at which the *market* trades off the two goods. The market's rate of trading off food for other stuff is just the slope of the budget line, or the (negative of) the ratio of market prices.

How should we depict the household's preferences, or rate of trade-off in terms of satisfaction (what economists call utility)? Should it be a line, like the budget constraint? Probably not. Your tradeoff in preferences will not be constant: the law of diminishing marginal utility sets in. The more you have of something, the less utility you get from having one more unit; thus, the more you'd be willing to trade to get an additional unit of something else. That's why you'll almost never end up consuming at either end of your budget constraint. You won't spend your whole budget on food (unless you face a very severe nutritional constraint that forces you to do so in order to survive). And you'll never end up at the other end of the budget line, either, because you obviously need to spend some of your budget on food.

Given diminishing marginal utility, we need a curve, not a line, to depict consumer preferences. An indifference curve (I_1, I_2, or I_3 in the figure) depicts all the combinations of food and other stuff that leave the household equally well-off; that is, along each indifference curve, the household's utility is constant. There are many (really, an infinite number of) indifference curves. As we move from the origin up to the northeast in the diagram, we hop onto indifference curves providing higher levels of utility. Most, like curve I_3, describe bundles of food and other stuff that the household cannot afford given its budget constraint. Others, like I_1, describe bundles of goods the household can afford, with money left over.

Point A in the figure is the bundle that gives the highest utility the household can attain given its budget constraint. That's the point where the household's marginal rate of substitution (MRS) between food and other stuff just equals the (negative of) the price ratio. It is where the household's tradeoff in preferences equals the market tradeoff. Every household will set its tradeoff in preferences equal to the ratio of prices. In an economy where every household faces the same market prices, everyone will consume at the same MRS between food and other stuff. When that happens, consumption is said to be *Pareto efficient*: no household can be made better off without making another one worse off.

What happens if the price of food increases? Modeling how an outcome changes when some exogenous variable (here, the price of food) changes is called *comparative statics*. If the household allocated its whole budget to food, it would be able to buy less than before. However, if it spent all its income on other stuff, it could still buy the same amount as before, so the vertical intercept does not change. As a result, the budget line pivots inward, like in Figure 7.3.

You may remember the comparative statics of a price change from microeconomics. Faced with a higher food price, the household substitutes other stuff for food. If it could stay on the same indifference curve as before, the new ratio of prices would drive it from A to B in the diagram. This is called the substitution effect, because consumers substitute away from the good that has gotten more expensive in favor of other goods, which have become less expensive relative to food. In our figure, the substitution effect decreases food demand.

The household cannot afford to consume at point B, though. With the higher food price, its real income falls, forcing it down to a lower indifference curve (point C). A negative real-income effect reinforces the negative substitution effect. That's why demand curves slope downward:

as the price of food (or pretty much any good) increases, consumers demand less of it.

That's the end of the comparative statics of an own-price change in the consumer model, but not in the household-farm model. Remember, agricultural households also produce food. An increase in the price of food hurts consumers, but it makes producers better off, because farm profit goes up.

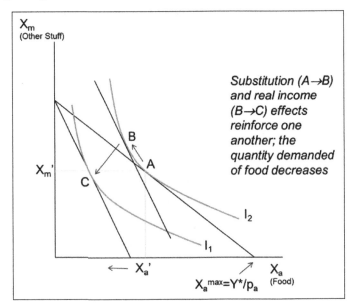

Figure 7.3: In the consumer model, a rise in the price of food triggers substitution (A→B) and real-income (B→C) effects that reinforce one another, resulting in a decrease in good demand.

To show the production-side effect of the price change, we need to borrow a curve from producer theory. You'll recognize the one in Figure 7.4. The marginal cost (*MC*) gives the cost of producing an additional unit of food. A profit-maximizing firm produces where the marginal cost (*MC*) equals the market price. At different prices (vertical axis) we can determine the supply response (horizontal axis) from the *MC* curve. Thus, the *MC* curve is also the firm's supply curve.

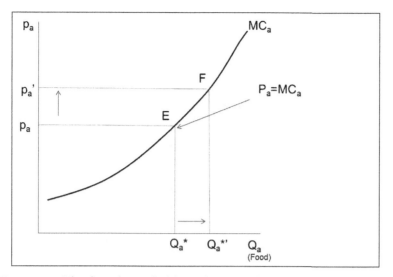

Figure 7.4: The farm household produces at the point where the food price equals the marginal cost of producing food. When the food price rises, so does food production.

The $p = MC$ rule makes good sense. The price is the reward the firm gets for producing one more unit. If the price is higher than the MC, the firm will want to produce more. If the MC is higher than the price, it will cut back on production until it brings MC down to the market price. As a producer, our agricultural household will have the same incentive to do this as a firm would.

At the food price p_a, our household-farm maximizes its profit from food production at point E, producing a level of output equal to Q_a^*. Its profit, $\Pi = p_a Q_a^* - C(Q_a^*)$, is the more-or-less triangular area above the marginal cost curve but below the price in our figure.

What happens when the price of food goes up? At the higher price, p_a', price equals MC at point F. Output jumps to $Q_a^{*'}$ and profit increases (you can see that the triangle below the new price line is bigger).

This is not the end of the story either, because remember: profit is part of the household's income. When the price of food goes up, the household's income goes up because of the profit effect. To see what that does to our comparative statics, we have to go back to our indifference curves.

Before we considered the profit effect, the household was at point C in Figure 7.5. We show an increase in income as a parallel outward shift in the budget constraint (an increase in income changes the point where the budget constraint intersects the axes because the household can afford more of either good). This increases the demand for both food and other stuff, as long as both are normal goods.

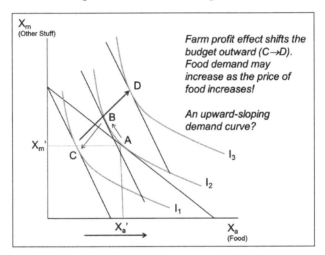

Figure 7.5: The farm profit effect shifts out the budget constraint, possibly resulting in a positive effect of food prices on the household's food demand.

To determine the overall effect of a price change on demand we need to know how much the budget constraint shifts from the profit effect. If the increase in profits only shifted the budget constraint a little, food demand would remain lower than before the price increase. But it could shift the budget constraint out farther, maybe all the way to where it's tangent to indifference curve I_3. At point D, the household consumes a bundle that is actually to the right of where it started, at point A. That means its food demand increased when the price of food went up. An agricultural household's food demand curve can slope upward if the profit effect is big enough! In fact, often when economists estimate household-farm models with real-world data, they find that it does slope upward (see box).

Upward-sloping Demand Curves?

Economists Inderjit Singh, Lyn Squire and John Strauss compared findings from seven agricultural household models, for Taiwan, Malaysia, Korea, Japan, Thailand, Sierra Leone, and Northern Nigeria. Four of the seven studies found a positive own-price elasticity of demand for agricultural goods. In those cases, the positive profit effect was stronger than the negative real income and substitution effects. In all seven cases, the profit effect substantially lowered the effect of a food-price increase on the marketed surplus of food.

Inderjit Singh, Lyn Squire and John Strauss (eds.), *Agricultural Household Models, Extensions, Applications and Policy*. World Bank and The Johns Hopkins University Press, 1986.

The agricultural household model changes the way we think about most of the agricultural producers in the world. It also has some important lessons for agricultural development policy.

First, if a government wants to increase the supply of food for its urban consumers, raising the price of food will not necessarily help. The amount of food available from domestic producers to the market, or marketed surplus (MS_a), is the difference between what the farm household produces and what it consumes; that is: $MS_a = Q_a - X_a$. Assuming the household does not face serious production constraints, production increases when the price goes up. This would increase the marketed surplus if the farm-household's demand stayed the same—but it doesn't. The greater the household-farm's consumption increases because of the profit effect, the smaller the marketed surplus effect. Governments often are disappointed when they offer farmers expensive price supports but the market supply doesn't change much.

Second, most people—including economists—assume that if the price of food goes up, that's bad news for urban consumers but good for farmers. The household-farm models shows that this might not be the case. If a household is to benefit from higher food prices, the positive profit effect has to outweigh the negative consumption effect. In order for that to happen, the household has to be a net seller of food—that is, its marketed surplus must be positive.

It might surprise you to discover that most of the world's farmers produce less food than they consume. The development economist Chris Barrett compared findings from 23 agricultural household surveys in eastern and southern Africa. He found no case in which most farmers were net sellers. The percentage of agricultural households that sold their crops ranged from a high of 45% (maize in Zimbabwe) to lows of 10-12% (barley, sorghum, and wheat in Ethiopia). This means that most farmers – those who produce less than they consume – lose if the price of the crops they grow goes up.[2]

Another development economist, Angus Deaton, came up with a handy way to determine how much welfare increases if the price of food crops goes up: the ratio of net agricultural sales, or marketed surplus (MS), to the household's total expenditures on all goods (E). He called this the net benefit ratio (NBR):

$$NBR = \frac{MS}{E}$$

The NBR can be interpreted as the percentage change in welfare resulting from a 1% change in the crop's price. Table 7.1 gives NBRs for different rural household groups in El Salvador, Guatemala, Honduras, and Nicaragua.[3]

Table 7.1: Net Benefit Ratios by Rural Household Group
in Four Central American Countries

Household Group	Country			
	El Salvador	Guatemala	Honduras	Nicaragua
Landless	-0.16	-0.36	-0.63	-0.49
Subsistence	-0.01	-0.32	-0.78	0.00
Small Commercial	0.31	-0.12	-0.13	0.39
Medium Commercial	1.20	0.07	1.01	0.62
Large Commercial	3.88	0.64	1.71	1.79

Source: J. Edward Taylor, Antonio Yúnez-Naude, and Nancy Jesurun-Clements, "Does Agricultural Trade Liberalization Reduce Rural Welfare in Developing Countries? The Case of CAFTA," *Applied Economic Perspectives and Policy* 32(1):95-116, 2010.

The NBR is almost always negative for small-farm households. For subsistence producers in Honduras, a one-percent increase in food prices *reduces* welfare by 0.78 percent. An important implication of these findings is that trade agreements that lower import tariffs on food actually benefit most food producers in these Central American countries.

A third lesson from agricultural household models is the importance of the production response. When we talk about agricultural households we mean small farmers. Big corn farms in the United States are family operated, but for all practical purposes they are pure firms, because they consume a negligible part of their harvest. Farm households, in order to survive and help feed the burgeoning urban population in their countries, have to be able to increase their production in response to price changes.

The Elasticity of Agricultural Supply

The MC curve is the household's supply curve. The flatter (more *elastic*) it is, the more it will respond to an increase in price by producing more.

In the extreme case where the supply curve is vertical (perfectly *inelastic*), no change in price will lead to an increase in output.

Why would an agricultural household ever have a vertical, or nearly vertical, supply curve? In the real world, small farmers face many different kinds of production constraints that large farmers in rich countries typically do not face. A few of the most common ones are:

- Limited access to land, and especially irrigated land
- Poor land quality
- Technological limitations, including lack of access to high-productivity seeds
- Limited access to modern inputs, like fertilizer
- A lack of cash to purchase inputs, and limited or no access to credit
- Limited or no access to insurance to protect against crop failure
- Labor constraints

Typically, a constellation of constraints restrict small farmers' capacity and willingness to increase production and shift into higher-value crop activities. Small landholdings mean limited collateral to offer banks as security against loans to pay for inputs, as we'll see in Chapter 10. High production risks and a lack of crop insurance make banks even more unwilling to lend to small farmers. All of these constraints can also make small farmers unwilling to "risk the farm" and take out loans, even if banks are willing. Households that lack the cash to hire workers from their village, or who face a limited supply of potential workers, have to farm their land themselves; families with few, old, or unhealthy members often then have little choice but to leave land fallow. The result can be a vicious circle between poverty and production, a poverty trap (see box).

Vicious Circles

For millions of poor agricultural households, increasing food production is a key to escaping from poverty, but being in poverty makes this difficult. In Nicaragua, only 19% of poor agricultural households purchase fertilizers. In Panama the share is 11%; in Bulgaria, 17%; and in Pakistan, 55%. In Malawi, Ghana and Madagascar, half or fewer of rural households in the lowest land quintile purchase fertilizer, and 12.9% or fewer purchase pesticides. The differences in input use between poor and non-poor agricultural households are magnified when one looks at the amounts of inputs purchased per hectare, which tend to be much lower for the poor.

J. Edward Taylor, Alberto Zezza and AliArslan Gurkan, "Rural Poverty and Markets," Background paper for the IFAD Rural Poverty Report 2011, March 31, 2008, http://www.ifad.org/rpr2011/background/8.pdf

Our agricultural household models need to include these constraints if we want them to reflect the way agricultural economies work. This is necessary for our models to be a useful basis for designing policies to increase food production and combat poverty in agricultural areas. In fact, there have been many extensions of the agricultural household model to incorporate these constraints.

Agricultural Technology

Let's begin with the most fundamental constraint on agricultural production: technology. Technology is reflected in the production function, which specifies the maximum output obtainable from a given set of inputs. Graphically, it is reflected in the shape and position of the supply curve. When new technologies come along enabling farmers to get more output from the same set of inputs (or use fewer inputs to get the same output), the supply curve shifts outward, as illustrated in Figure 7.6.

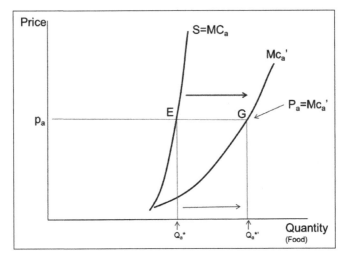

Figure 7.6: Productivity-enhancing technological change shifts the agricultural supply (marginal cost) curve outward to the right, increasing the quantity supplied at a given price.

Agricultural production technologies took great leap forward with the advent of the Green Revolution. The Green Revolution was a series of agricultural research initiatives begun in 1943 by Norman Borlaug, an agronomist and eventual winner of the Nobel Peace Prize who has been credited with saving more than a billion lives."[5] Borlaug's idea was biological: to breed new varieties of plants that would produce more food. His initiatives began in Mexico, but his ideas were put to the test in India, which in 1961 was on the brink of mass famine. Its rice yields at the time were only around two tons per hectare. By the mid-1990s, Indian rice yields had tripled, rice prices had fallen (despite continuing population growth), and India had become a rice exporter.

How did this huge technological change happen? New rice varieties developed at IRRI (the International Rice Research Institute in Los Baños, Philippines) were bred to more efficiently exploit the nutrients in the soil. This, together with an expanded use of fertilizer and irrigation, vastly increased the world's ability to feed itself—and then some. Rice isn't the only crop that experienced a Green Revolution. Between 1950 and 2005, wheat yields in the world rose from around 750 kilograms per hectare to more than 2,500.[6] Today, a network of international crop research institutes, called the CGIAR (cgiar.com), continues to seek new solutions to feeding the world's (still growing) population. The CGIAR's main job is to continue shifting out the agricultural supply curve. Today, this means taking on environmental as well as biological challenges:

Feeding the world's millions.

Other Constraints

Let's consider a liquidity constraint in our comparative statics example above. Suppose that at the initial food price, the household is spending all the cash it has to buy inputs. It faces a liquidity constraint. A basic problem in agricultural production is that inputs have to be purchased a long time before the harvest comes in. Unless the household can borrow against the harvest, which poor small households cannot, its input demand is constrained by its available cash. In In Figure 7.7, the food price goes up, but the liquidity constraint prevents the household from increasing production. The liquidity constraint is represented by the vertical line in the diagram. The MC curve is the same as before, but because the household cannot expand production beyond the constrained level, its supply curve effectively is "kinked," so it is given by GEH. The shaded triangle is the welfare loss to the household from not being able to adjust its production to the higher level. The only way to increase production and raise the household's welfare in this case is to loosen the liquidity constraint.

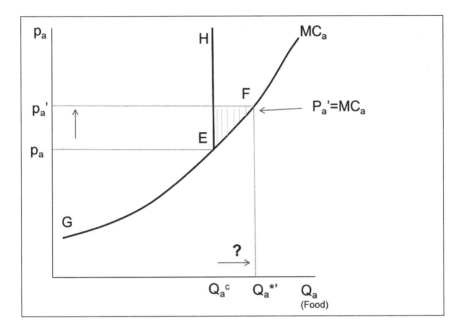

Figure 7.7: A liquidity constraint (segment EH) can result in suboptimal production and a welfare loss.

A lack of access to credit, insurance, or hired labor may reflect market failures due to information and other problems, which we will look at in Chapters 9 and 10. The household also may face high transaction costs in selling its output or purchasing inputs, for example if transportation to markets is very expensive. If transaction costs are high enough, the household's best bet may be to withdraw from the market completely and become a subsistence producer.

If households lack information about new technologies, the spread of knowledge needs to be part of agricultural development programs (see box: "Learning from Others"). But without access to credit, insurance, and markets, simply knowing about new technologies is not likely to be sufficient to raise productivity on small farms.

Learning from Others

The Green Revolution brought new high-yielding seeds to India's farmers, whose production technology had changed little for decades. Many did not adopt the new seeds, even though agronomic field tests had shown them to be significantly more productive than traditional seed varieties. Andrew Foster and Mark Rosenzweig, using data that tracked farmers over time, found that a lack of knowledge about how to manage new seeds was a significant deterrent to adoption. The profitability of the new seeds for farmers increased as their neighbors gained experience growing them. Because of this, farmers whose neighbors had experience growing the new seeds planted more of their own land in high-yielding varieties. Thus, the authors concluded, farmers who adopted the new technology created benefits not only for themselves but also for others, by providing important "knowledge spillovers." This study was influential in documenting how the spread of information about new technologies can be critical in making farmers in poor countries more productive.

Andrew D. Foster and Mark R. Rosenzweig, "Learning by Doing and Learning from Others: Human Capital and Technical Change in Agriculture. *Journal of Political Economy*, Vol. 103, No. 6, pp. 1176-1209.

Food Security and Self Sufficiency

Food security is the most fundamental of all human rights and the most basic objective of economic development. Food self-sufficiency is not. The two have nothing to do with each other, as long as markets exist. I have a measly garden that yields a few organic greens and herbs, along with an orange or lemon from time to time. I am certainly not self-sufficient in food, but I am not food insecure. If something happens that keeps markets from working, however, food security and food self-sufficiency have everything to do with each other.

The point that food security and self-sufficiency are different concepts might seem obvious, but over the years many countries have confused one with the other and launched expensive programs in an effort to achieve self-sufficiency in food production. Japan has striven to achieve self-sufficiency in rice by offering farmers up to ten times the price in other countries. In 1980, Mexico launched an expensive program, called SAM (*Sistema Alimentario Mexicano*), to reduce its dependence on corn imports. It became so expensive that it was aborted in 2002.

We can use our agricultural household model to learn why self-sufficiency is not a good idea. The Oxford Dictionary defines self-sufficiency as "needing no outside help in satisfying one's basic needs, especially with regard to the production of food." What happens when our agricultural household has to be self-sufficient?

To explore this question, suppose the household can allocate its fixed resources (for example, land) between two production activities. When I conducted surveys in China's Jiangsu Province, I saw many family farms converting some of their rice fields into fish ponds, so let's consider rice cultivation and fish ponds as an example. Land is not perfectly transformable between these two activities; there are likely to be decreasing returns to scale in each one. (If you're smart, you'll dig out your least productive rice land for fish ponds.) The various combinations of rice and fish production the households in a region can produce are given not by a straight line, but instead by a concave production possibilities frontier (PPF) like in Figure 7.8. Where the PPF touches the axes, it tells us how much of each good the region could produce if it produced only that good. If we start where it crosses the x-axis (the economy is producing only rice) and move along the PPF, we see how much fish could be produced as less rice is produced. The PPF is curved due to diminishing marginal returns: each subsequent unit of fish requires the economy to give up more rice as land more suited to rice cultivation is converted to fish ponds.

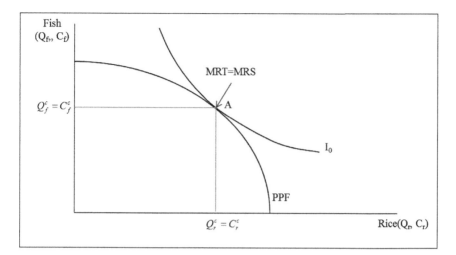

Figure 7.8: A self-sufficient household will produce at point A, where the marginal rate of transformation in production equals the marginal rate of substitution in consumption.

Where along the PPF will our households produce? If they are self-sufficient, they will produce exactly as much as they consume. We'll need to bring in an indifference curve to figure out where the optimal production (which equals consumption) choice will be.

The slope of the indifference curve I_0 in this figure describes the households' tradeoff in preferences between rice and fish: how much of one it would *be willing to give up* to get one more unit of the other. The slope of the PPF is its technological tradeoff: how much of one good it would *have to give up* in order to *produce* an additional unit of the other. The point of tangency between the two is the optimal solution to the households' problem given self-sufficiency. It is where the slope of the PPF, the marginal rate of transformation (MRT) of rice into fish, equals the MRS of rice for fish.

Suppose now that the households can trade rice and fish at the going market prices of p_a and p_f respectively. The market tradeoff between rice and fish is the ratio of these two prices, represented by the price line in Figure 7.9.

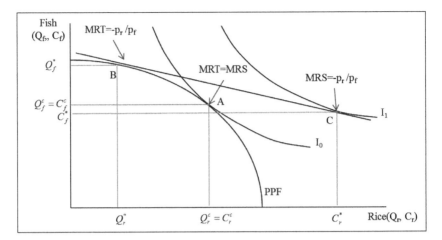

Figure 7.9: Markets enable the household to increase its welfare by separating its production and consumption decisions.

With a market to trade in, the households no longer have to be self-sufficient in rice or fish. They can sell one and buy the other. The market makes it possible to decouple production from demand, just like you and I do. I can be a professor, and someone else can be the farmer.

On the production side, the households will now equate their MRT with the ratio of market prices. They'll produce at point B. Notice that at point B they produce more fish and less rice than when they have to be self-sufficient. Then they can trade along the price line and climb onto the highest indifference curve they can reach. On the consumption side, they'll end up at point C. They've produced more fish than they demand and traded fish for rice. As a result, they consume more rice than they could possibly produce: C_r^* is to the right of where the PPF hits the Rice axis.

The moral of this story is clear: Markets let our household-farms trade up to a higher indifference curve (I_1) than they could reach if they were constrained to be self-sufficient. In other words, markets improve welfare. This, in a nutshell, is the argument for free trade. We'll come back to this argument (as well as its limitations) in Chapter 9. For now, remember how important markets are to us, and what it meant to lose them if you lived in Tigray in northern Ethiopia in the 1980s (see Chapter 9).

Protective trade policies, like import tariffs and quotas, prevent countries from trading. For agricultural households, prohibitive costs of buying and selling prevent trade. In Tigray in the 1980s, the cost of trading was that you'd likely be shot on sight if you walked the highway. For most agricultural households, it's far less dramatic than that. Poor roads, communications, and information make it too expensive to get produce to or from the market, which might be tens of kilometers away over roads that are impassible part of the year.

When it comes to food, it turns out that very few households are truly self-sufficient; everyone seems to buy and sell little bits here and there in their village, in periodic markets or through "door-step trade." However, many villages and regions are largely cut off from outside markets. When droughts strike, instead of markets drawing in food from other places, local prices skyrocket, food stocks dwindle, and families' nutrient intake falls. The consequences can be dire and long-term, especially for children (see box: "The Long-term Effects of Famine").

The Long-term Effects of Famine

China's Great Leap Forward policies (1958-61), including the abolition of land ownership and diversion of peasant labor to industry, created the worst famine in history: between 16.5 and 30 million people perished. What human capital legacy did the famine—and the ill-designed policies that caused it—leave behind?

Four development and health economists studied the effect of being exposed to the famine *in utero* on people's economic and health outcomes. They followed cohorts of children born during the famine (1956-64) into their adulthood, using data from the 2000 Chinese Population Census.

The results show that there are long-term economic and health consequences when mothers are exposed to famine. Males exposed to famine *in utero* were significantly more likely to be illiterate, less likely to work, and less likely to be married four decades later. Females were also more likely to be illiterate and less likely to work, and they tended to marry men with less education. Fetal exposure to famine also substantially reduced the sex ratio; males are more vulnerable to maternal malnutrition, so fewer males survived.

The adverse impacts of famine did not end with the generation exposed in utero. The authors uncovered what they call an "echo effect" of the famine on the *next* generation. Women who had been exposed to famine in utero, once they became mothers, were more likely to give birth to daughters.

Maternal malnutrition is a major problem throughout the developing world. This study gives us insights into some of the long-term consequences not only of famine but maternal malnutrition in general.

Douglas Almond, Lena Edlund, Hongbin Li, and Junsen Zhang, "Long-Term Effects Of The 1959-1961 China Famine: Mainland China and Hong Kong," National Bureau of Economic Research Working Paper No. 13384, September 2007.

Food aid may rush in to try to fill the vacuum. But emergency food relief, while of course necessary to keep famines in check, sets back local farming by driving prices to zero. Development practitioners can labor for years helping to develop more vibrant local farm production systems, only to see their efforts set back when drought hits and food aid rushes in.

Imagine an alternative world, in which farmers have access to crop insurance and agricultural households are integrated with outside markets. A drought hits, insurance pays off, and the payoff is used to buy food that the market brings in the minute prices begin to rise. At most, the local price of, say, rice, would rise to whatever the world price is at the nearest port, plus the cost of getting the rice out to the village.

In short, food insecurity and their extreme form, famine, are not just a production problem. They are a problem with markets, and ultimately, governments. Oxfam, one of the world's major aid and development organizations, explains it this way:

> Famine is the "triple failure" of (1) food production, (2) people's ability to access food and, finally and most crucially (3) in the political response by governments and international donors. Crop failure and poverty leave people vulnerable to starvation – but famine only occurs with political failure. In Somalia years of internal violence and conflict have been highly significant in creating the conditions for famine.[4]

Inside the Household

So far we've been considering households as if they were single, homogeneous units. But in real life, they are a composite of individuals, each with different access to resources and their own preferences and needs. Human development depends on the distribution of food and other resources within as well as among households. Households bring together groups of individuals, usually family members, who can share in production and consumption. But power asymmetries within households can profoundly influence how resources get allocated. They not only determine who gets to consume what; they also can determine whether households act in ways that can make the pie as big as it can be. In other words, household dynamics can affect efficiency as well as equity.

Nutritionists focus on individuals, not households. A new generation of agricultural household models has emerged that takes into account conflict within households and is ramifications for efficiency as well as equity.

Nash Bargained Household Models

In the agricultural household model, income was pooled, and consumption decisions were made as though the household acted as a single unit. That model works if the household members share the same preferences. Alternatively, in the "dictator model," one person has all the power, and his or her preferences determine expenditures. We call these unitary households.

In the Nash-Bargained household model, in contrast, different members have different preferences and access to income. (This model is named after Nobel laureate mathematician John Nash, subject of the Hollywood film *The Beautiful Mind*, who invented the game theoretic model on which it is based.) Household members naturally influence expenditures in ways that reflect their preferences.

How do we model such a household? Two people, person m and person f, decide whether to stay single or form a household. Let v_m be m's utility or welfare if they do not form a household, and let v_f be person f's. If they form a household, they'll combine their income and spend it on things either or both care about. Person m's welfare will be U_m and f's will be U_f. Neither one will want to form a household unless there's a positive welfare gain in it, so both $U_m - v_m$ and $U_f - v_f$ must be positive (that is, unless it's a forced marriage).

Once the household gets formed v_m and v_f are "threat points", the utilities that each person would have if they were single. The higher a person's threat point, the more bargaining power s/he has in the Nash-bargained household. Thus, anything that affects a person's threat point can help explain what the household spends its income on. If my threat point is high, I should be able to influence my household's spending in a big way.

What's in a threat point? Lots of things, potentially, but one of them certainly is unearned income. Earned income, like wages, might be affected by what one's spouse earns, but unearned income (from assets, for example) is the same regardless of whether or not a person is part of the household. If I'm independently wealthy, my threat point will be high. If I'm penniless, it will be low.

In a unitary household model it wouldn't matter who had the unearned income because all the income would get pooled. In a Nash-bargained household, it would matter. Who controls the unearned income determines who has the most bargaining power within the household, and therefore, how much money gets spent on what. Tests for whether we've got a unitary or Nash-bargained household boil down to this question: Does who controls the non-earned income explain household expenditures? Or is total household income the only thing that matters—that is, a rupee is a rupee, no matter who controls it?

A number of studies find that it does matter who controls the income (see box: "Who Controls the Cash?"). Their findings demonstrate that power asymmetries within households can profoundly affect spending and equity.

Who Controls the Cash?

A number of studies find that it matters who in the household controls income. Using data from a household survey in Brazil, Duncan Thomas tested whether unearned income controlled by fathers and mothers had the same effect on how households spent their money. He found significant differences between the two. Income controlled by mothers had a much bigger positive effect on children's health than income controlled by fathers. The effect of mother's income on child survival probabilities was almost twenty times larger. This is one reason why cash transfer programs in developing countries often give the money to poor women instead of men. (We'll learn about cash transfer programs in Chapter 11). The study also found that mothers are more likely to spend their income on daughters and fathers on sons.

A study from Thailand found that the more property income males had, the more likely they were to marry. But for women, unearned income had the opposite effect. It seems marriage is an "inferior good" for Thai women!

Both of these studies were influential in showing that, at least for some types of research, the assumption of unitary households may not be appropriate.

Duncan Thomas, "Intra-Household Resource Allocation: An Inferential Approach," *Journal of Human Resources* 25(4): 635-664, 1990.

T. Paul Schultz, "Testing the Neoclassical Model of Family Labor Supply and Fertility," *The Journal of Human Resources* Vol. 25, No. 4, pp. 599-634, 1990.

Are Households Efficient?

Does who has control within the household also affect efficiency? When economic power within households is unequal, does this affect the size of the economic pie as well as its distribution?

The Nash-bargained model described above assumes there is no reason why households would not maximize their incomes, even if power relations within households affect expenditures. If I exert a large influence on how my household's income gets spent, shouldn't I try to make that income as large as possible? And if I do not, wouldn't I still want my household's income to be large? Having a little influence over a larger pie is better than having a little influence over a little pie.

This is an important question. If someone in the household could be made better off without making others worse off, the household economy is said to be *not Pareto efficient*.

Testing whether who controls income and wealth within households affects expenditures is easier than testing whether it affects efficiency. A pioneering study in the African country of Burkina Faso found a way, though. It concluded that power asymmetries within households reduce efficiency. The economic pie in society would be larger if women controlled more of the assets (see box: "Bad to Be a Female Plot").

Bad to Be a Female Plot

In many African countries, crops are produced on plots controlled by different members of the household. Pareto efficiency implies that these plots are managed so as to maximize income—that is, make the pie as big as it can be, however it might end up being divvied up. Are household economies Pareto efficient? Chris Udry explored this question using data on male and female plots in Burkina Faso households. If the household is efficient, it will allocate its fertilizer such that the benefit of the last bit of fertilizer (the marginal product) is the same on all plots. Udry's econometric analysis refuted this. It found that plots controlled by women were farmed much less intensively than the male-controlled plots; yields were 30 percent lower on female plots within the same household. This study was influential, because it demonstrated that heterogeneous preferences and access to resources within households affects not only equity, but also efficiency.

Christopher Udry, "Gender, Agricultural Production, and the Theory of the Household," *The Journal of Political Economy*, Vol. 104, No. 5. (Oct., 1996), pp. 1010-1046.

Beyond Households

Households do not exist in isolation from one another. Diverse, heterogeneous households interact within rural economies, like individual cells that together make up a complex organism. When a policy, market, environmental, or some other shock strikes one household, its effects reverberate through the economy, like ripples in a pond. The models we have looked at so far in this chapter focus on individual households; they ignore linkages among households.

To illustrate the importance of these linkages, suppose a poor household receives a 100 peso transfer from a government welfare program like the ones we will look at in Chapter 11. The immediate effect of the transfer is to raise the poor household's income by the amount of the transfer. But that is not the end of the story, because the poor household spends the money. Suppose it spends 50 pesos to buy meat from a herder in the same village. The herder's income goes up by 50 pesos. So far, the 100 peso transfer has increased village income by 150 pesos. Now suppose that the herder spends half of her new income in the village, hiring a mason to fix her house. The mason now has 25 pesos. As the money circulates through the village, it creates more income. Some of the money leaves the village along the way, contributing to income somewhere else in the country (or world). But the money that stays in the village has a multiplier effect on income in the village. Most people's income gets spent not far from home. If people spend half of their income in the village, it can be shown that every peso of income transferred to a poor household ends up creating two pesos of income in the village.

If you have taken a macroeconomics class, you might recognize this story. It is just like the Keynesian income multiplier, which became an important part of economic policies in rich countries following the Great Depression and, most recently in the United States, "Obamanomics."

A relatively new area of research in development economics takes models of individual households and "nests" them within models of the larger economies of which these households are part: villages, regions, or nations. Economy-wide impacts created by interactions among economic agents, like income multipliers, are called "general equilibrium effects." General equilibrium effects can take many forms, and they can dramatically alter the ways development policies affect incomes, employment and welfare in poor economies (see box "The Mystery of Maize in Mexico"). We'll look at general equilibrium effects again in Chapters 8 and 11.

The Mystery of Maize in Mexico

In 1995, Mexico did away with policies that guaranteed farmers high prices for their maize and other basic crops. The producer price of maize in Mexico immediately fell by around 40 percent, but this was followed by a record-high maize harvest that couldn't be explained by the weather. Why would maize production increase after the price fell?

A study by three UC Davis economists offered an answer. Most maize producers do not sell their crop; they are subsistence farmers. When the price of maize fell farmers who were not in the market were not directly affected.

Typically, villages have many subsistence farmers and a few commercial ones. They interact with each other in local labor markets, as subsistence households hire out labor to commercial farms.

When the price shock hit, commercial maize farmers cut back their production and hired less labor. This transmitted a negative impact to the subsistence households, even though they did not sell maize. Unable to find employment, subsistence farmers had to find another use for their labor. Their solution? Grow more maize for home consumption!

The result seemed paradoxical: the price of maize fell, but maize production on subsistence farms increased. The authors refer to this as a "retreat into subsistence." Across Mexico, maize production went up on rain-fed lands, where subsistence farmers are concentrated. Despite higher maize production, though, Mexico's maize farmers were worse off after the price plunge.

George A. Dyer, Steve Boucher and J. Edward Taylor. "Subsistence Response to Market Shocks." *American Journal of Agricultural Economics* 88(2):279-291, 2006.

An on-line application, the Gapminder agricultural lab, makes it possible to visualize in detail the evolution of agriculture in a large set of countries over time:

 Gapminder Agricultural Lab

Chapter Seven Notes

1. This point was made by Peter Timmer in his paper, "The Agricultural Transformation," Chapter 8 in the *Handbook of Development Economics, Volume 1*, edited by Hollis Chenery and T.N. Srinivasen, back in 1988. The data in this figure are from The World Bank (www.worldbank.org).

2. Christopher B. Barrett, "Smallholder Market Participation: Concepts and Evidence from Eastern and Southern Africa," *Food Policy* 33 (2008) 299–317.

3. The source for this table is: J. Edward Taylor, Antonio Yúnez-Naude and Nancy Jesurun-Clements, "Does Agricultural Trade Liberalization Reduce Rural Welfare in Developing Countries? The Case of CAFTA," *Applied Economic Perspectives and Policy* 32(1):95-116, 2010.

4. http://www.oxfam.org/en/emergencies/east-africa-food-crisis/famine-somalia-what-needs-be-done.

5. Gregg Easterbrook, Forgotten Benefactor of Humanity, *The Atlantic*, January 1997 (http://www.theatlantic.com/magazine/archive/1997/01/forgotten-benefactor-of-humanity/306101/)

6. United Nations Food and Agricultural Organization (FAO).

8.

Transformation

In January 2006 the United Nations Food and Agricultural Organization (FAO) held a workshop called "Beyond Agriculture." This was a striking thing for the FAO to name its conference. Consider the FAO's mandate:

> "To raise levels of nutrition, improve agricultural productivity, better the lives of rural populations and contribute to the growth of the world economy."[1]

For years, with most of the developing world's population living off agriculture, these were compatible objectives. For example, high-yielding seeds could raise agricultural productivity, reduce poverty, and provide people with more secure access to food.

The FAO was telling us that wasn't the case anymore.

On May 23, 2007, the world became more urban than rural. That's the day that, according to the United Nations, more than half of the globe's population was living in towns and cities, for the first time ever.[2,3]

Not only is the world becoming less rural; rural populations are becoming less agricultural. Rural households in Malawi and Ghana still get 55-56% of their income from crop production, but the crop share is 41% in Vietnam, 21% in Nicaragua, and only 15% in Bangladesh.[4] In Mexico, the share of agriculture in rural household income was 14% in 2002 and 11% in 2007; only around 2% came from corn.[5] Even substantial increases in agricultural productivity are unlikely to raise rural incomes very much when most income is non-agricultural.

The FAO found itself grappling with the question of how to achieve multiple objectives that, in the modern world, are less and less related to one another.

How did we get here?

The growth models in Chapter 6 give an aggregate, birds-eye view of income growth and why some countries grow faster than others. The empirical growth model of Sala-i-Martin suggests that growth involves a complex array of variables, and there may be more than one way to make growth happen. As endogenous growth theorists point out, there are important feedbacks that shape growth in different countries. Economic incentives are important in shaping these feedbacks. Poverty trap models suggest that exogenous interventions are required to "kick-start" asset accumulation and income growth, like in Jeffrey Sach's Millennium Village Project.

Unfortunately, aggregate models mask far-reaching transformations that have to occur within economies in order to make growth possible and that are themselves a product of growth. Countries start out being mostly agricultural, in terms of where their income comes from as well as where their people are employed, with most people living in villages. As economies grow, they morph into manufacturing-and-service economies.

The transition from largely agricultural to nonagricultural societies is one of the most fundamental features of economic development. The Nobel Laureate W. Arthur Lewis (whom we will learn about below) called it the heart of the development process. Whatever nostalgia you might have for picturesque villages and the rural way of life, you'd better get over it, because people leaving the farm is an inescapable part of development. (Of course, a society can invest in trying to keep picturesque villages alive, as France has, but it will not be cheap, and not very many people will live in them.)

Figure 8.1 drives home the point. It shows a scatterplot of countries at different levels of per-capita income (PPP adjusted, measured on the horizontal axis) and shares of the workforce employed in agriculture (vertical axis). Each country is represented by a ray whose starting point tells us where the country was in 1990 and whose tip shows where it was in 2010. The very top arrow belongs to Burundi, with a per-capita income of $620 per year and 94% of the workforce in agriculture. The rightmost rays correspond to countries with very high per-capita incomes and almost none of their workforces in agriculture. There you would find the United States and even France and Japan, which have expensive government programs to support farmers and rural villages.

Changes in Per-Capita GOP and Agriculture's Share of Employment, 1990–2005

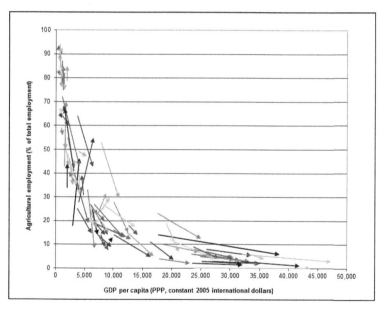

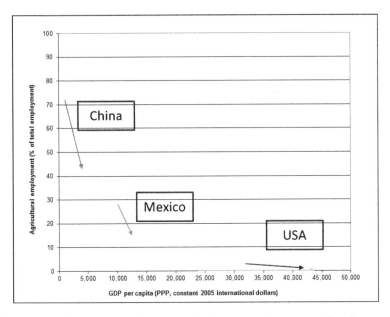

Figure 8.1: As countries' per-capita incomes increase, the share of the labor force doing farm work decreases. Source: GNI per capita, PPP (current international $ x 1000): World Development Indicators (WDI), 2005, The World Bank. Agricultural labor: 99-04: CIA World Factbook. 2005.

As country per-capita incomes rise, the share of the workforce in agriculture doesn't just decrease—it falls off a cliff. First, look at how the arrows line up. With no exceptions, the countries with low per-capita GDPs have high shares of their workforces employed in agriculture. As per-capita incomes rise, the arrows fall sharply, forming a hyperbolic curve. Not only that—almost all the arrows slope toward the southeast. (If you see an exception, there is a unique story behind it, like a resource-extracting country without agriculture, or a former Soviet republic struggling to adjust to a post-socialist existence.)

The sloping arrows tell us that between 1990 and 2005, per-capita incomes increased while farm labor shares fell. At high per-capita incomes, the arrows converge towards the horizontal axis, where agriculture's share of the workforce is zero. No country ever reaches zero—you can't grow crops without *any* workers. However, some rich countries have agricultural labor shares of 2% or less. Some of the smallest farm workforce shares in the world are in countries with expensive government programs to support agriculture, like the US, the EU countries, or Japan, whose domestic price of rice is as high as seven times the world price.

The right-hand diagram removes all but three of the countries on the graph: China, Mexico, and the United States. China is the economic miracle with income growth exceeding 10% in some years. You can see that it starts out in 1990 with over 75% of its workforce in agriculture. In 2010, 49% of Chinese workers had farm jobs—and the farm share was falling fast. Mexico began the period with a higher income and a much smaller workforce share in agriculture than China. Its income continued to grow and its farm-employment share fell, though at a slower rate than China's. The United States began the period with one of the world's highest per-capita incomes and around 2% of its workforce in agriculture. Most US farm workers are immigrant workers from Mexico.[6]

Modeling the Transformation

In order to understand what drives this economic transformation, we need to dig underneath the aggregate growth numbers we looked at in Chapter 6. Multi-sectoral models allow us to study the interactions between agriculture and the non-agricultural sectors in an economy, including the movement of people between them. They offer insights into what has to happen to get growth going and how economic growth transforms poor economies. We'll see what development economists have to say about how the transformation from agricultural to industry-and-service economies unfolds and the ramifications for economic development research and policy.

The simplest multi-sectoral models involve only agriculture (often called the "traditional sector") and the non-agricultural sectors (the "modern sector"). Because they have only two sectors, these are called dual-economy models. They are a good starting point for learning about interactions between sectors. Today, though, almost all multi-sectoral models used in development economics have many different sectors as well as many different actors: households, governments, and others. After learning about two-sector models we'll take a look at multi-sectoral models and how they are being used for development policy and research.

Leaving the Farm

Francisco is a farmer in a village in southern Mexico.[7] He and his wife Alde have a three-hectare (about 7.5 acre) plot of good land, three sons and two daughters. A horse, a team of oxen, and some goats and chickens fill out the family.

A construction job opens up in the city of Oaxaca 50 miles away, and a contractor comes to the village to recruit able-bodied villagers willing to work. Francisco and Alde's 17-year-old son, Alejandro, asks if he can go. His best friend migrated to Oaxaca a few months earlier. Alejandro reminds his parents that his friend sends home $50 a month to help his family. "I could do the same thing," he assures them.

Should they let him go? Alejandro's 15-year-old brother, Ramiro, says he can fill in for Alejandro on the farm. "There isn't enough work for all of us here, anyway," he says.

The next morning Alejandro hops on the bus for Oaxaca.

A month later, Francisco and Alde's daughter Alicia's friend heads off to work in an electronics plant in Tijuana. Alicia says she's already sending back $25 a month to her parents. "I could do that, too," she tells them.

"But if you go, who will watch the animals and help me around the house?" her mom asks.

"I will," her little sister, Silvia, assures her.

The next week, Alicia is gone. Within a month, Francisco and Alde get $75 a month in migrant remittances, the income sent home by their two kids. Not only that, they now have fewer mouths to feed. Ramiro and his dad have no trouble bringing in the harvest, with a little help from the youngest daughter, Norma, and her little brother Tomás. The extra income from Alejandro and Alicia helps pay for Norma and Tomás to go to school.

A year later, Alejandro comes back to visit for the Fiesta of the Virgen de Guadalupe. "The work's good," he tells Ramiro. "Ever think of going to the city?"

"Don't think of it!" Alde tells them. "Who will help your father in the field?"

"I will!" little Tomás and Norma exclaim in unison. "I'm *never* leaving home!" Norma insists.

Their father shakes his head, knowing all too well that kids with schooling don't stick around the village. "I'm not getting any younger, Ramiro. If you go, I fear there will be no harvest," Francisco sighs.

Ramiro stays, gets married, and his new wife moves into Francisco and Alde's house. Little by little Ramiro takes over the farm, with some financial help from his migrant siblings when there's an investment to be made or when the harvest isn't good. Tomás and Norma both migrate to the city the summer after their high school graduation.

This story is a composite of families all over rural Mexico, and indeed, the world. It's so universal that there's an economic model about it.

The Lewis Model

The economist W. Arthur Lewis, a Nobel laureate, wrote a famous paper called "Economic Development with Unlimited Supplies of Labor." Lewis looked at the surplus labor in rural areas and recognized a tremendous potential there for economic development. He argued that the marginal product of labor in the subsistence sector (agriculture) is virtually zero—or at least very low compared to the "subsistence wage," or what it takes to keep a person alive in the rural economy. This means that, at the margin, agricultural workers produce next to nothing, yet naturally everyone has to consume enough food to survive (a "subsistence bundle"). Think of the subsistence wage, w_s, as the cost of this subsistence bundle.

An employer in the city, in theory, only has to offer a wage equal to the cost of subsistence—plus maybe a little extra for the bus fare and the higher urban cost of living—in order to induce a worker to move off the farm and migrate to a modern-sector job.

The power of Lewis' argument is this: workers can move out of the subsistence sector without the economy suffering any loss in agricultural output. In effect, the movement of labor off the farm could provide a seemingly endless supply of labor to the expanding modern (industrial and service) sectors, and farms would still be able to produce the food to feed them (as long as there are good markets to get the food to the city; see Chapter 10). As the urban economy expands, urban employers do not have to offer higher wages to get more workers to come, as long as there is a surplus of labor ready to move off the farm. The supply of labor to urban jobs, therefore, is perfectly elastic: the urban labor supply curve is horizontal. If urban capitalists create jobs, the workers will come—from the farm to the city.

…And jobs they'll create, if the wage stays flat. Low wages mean high profits, which in turn can be re-invested to make the urban economy grow even more.

Figure 8.2 illustrates the Lewis model. The horizontal axis in each represents labor. The economy starts out with an amount of labor equal to $\overline{L}$, all of it in the traditional (or agricultural) sector. Since the economy starts out with virtually all its labor in the traditional sector, any gain in labor to the modern sector implies a loss of labor from the traditional sector.

The top figure represents agriculture. You should start out at its south-east corner and read from right to left. The curve depicts the marginal value product of agricultural labor (MVPL), given the other inputs (land, capital) available to farms. This curve is drawn steeply to reflect sharply decreasing marginal returns to labor under traditional technologies. For the first few workers, the MVPL is high. These workers would include Francisco and Ramiro. As more and more people work the land, the con-tribution of the last worker becomes smaller. Eventually, Lewis argues, it bottoms out at zero; there is surplus labor, and the MVPL curve flattens out along the horizontal axis. Over the flat range of the MVPL curve, workers can leave the farm without having any adverse effect on agri-cultural output.

The bottom figure is about the modern (industrial and service) sector. We have to read it from left to right, because any gain to the modern-sector workforce implies a loss for the traditional-sector workforce. This figure shows three MVPL curves in the modern sector, each correspond-ing to a different level of capital investment. As more capital is invested in new plants and equipment, the MVPL shifts out to the right. Like the MVPL curve in agriculture, each modern-sector MVPL curve is decreasing with labor: an additional worker adds less and less to output at a given level of capital. New investments increase this MVPL, though.

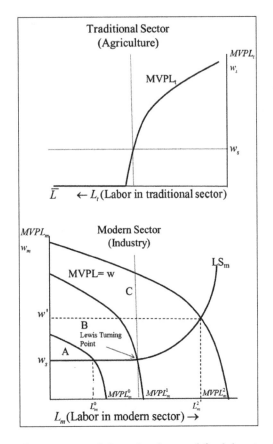

Figure 8.2: In the Lewis model, as the demand for labor in the modern sector increases (bottom figure), surplus labor is drawn from the traditional sector (top figure) without putting upward pressure on wages until the Lewis turning point is reached.

The bottom figure also shows the labor supply (LS) curve for the modern sector. You can also think of it as the wage curve: for each wage (vertical axis), we can read off this curve the amount of labor the traditional sector is willing to supply to the modern sector. It will not supply any labor if the wage is less than subsistence.

Lining the bottom figure up with the top figure, you can see that the modern-sector LS curve is horizontal until the traditional-sector MVPL exceeds the subsistence wage. Over this range, the traditional sector will supply all the labor the modern sector demands—that is, until the labor surplus dries up and the agricultural MVPL rises above the subsistence wage. This is called the "Lewis turning point."

Beyond the Lewis turning point, if more workers leave the farm, the value of agricultural production goes down by more than the subsistence wage. Modern-sector employers will have to pay higher wages to induce more workers to move off the farm. They'll have to convince people like Ramiro. That's why the LS curve turns upward beyond the Lewis turning point.

How much labor will the modern sector hire? The MVPL for the modern sector tells us how much revenue will increase if another worker is hired. The wage line tells us how industries will have to pay for that additional worker. Modern-sector firms will hire additional workers up to the point where their MVPL just equals the wage they have to pay. The modern sector starts out with a low level of capital, at $MVPL_m^0$, paying a wage equal to w_s; thus, it demands L_m^0 workers.

The difference between the MVPL and the wage at leach level of labor use is the marginal worker's contribution to profit. Cheap labor creates high profits.

For any MVPL curve, profits are the area underneath the curve but above the wage (or labor supply) curve, and wages are the area underneath the wage line. At $MVPL_m^0$, the modern sector's profit is given by area A, and wages are the area of the box defined by $w_s * L_m^0$. Part of this profit is invested in new plant and equipment, which shifts the MVPL curve out to $MVPL_m^1$. You can see that the new profit, depicted by areas A+B, is much larger than the original profit (A). Modern-sector growth, then, is self-perpetuating, as long as a large part of the profit is re-invested.

Eventually, the surplus labor in the traditional sector becomes exhausted. Once the MVPL in agriculture exceeds the subsistence wage, the modern sector has to offer higher wages to attract new workers. At that point, the income distribution begins to shift in favor of labor. At

$MVPL_m^2$, total modern-sector wages are the box given by $w' * L_m^2$, and profits are given by the area above the w' line (C).

Why was this model important?

The Lewis model gets us inside the "black box" of the aggregate growth model. It illustrates what has to happen in order for incomes to grow: the economy has to transition from a traditional, agricultural one to a modern, industrial and service one. Growth in the modern sector cannot be understood in isolation of the traditional sector. Lewis pioneered what is known as "dual-economy" or "two-sector" economic models. As income grows, the workforce shifts out of the traditional sector.

The Lewis model is not without its critics or limitations. Theodore Schultz, an economist who shared the Nobel Prize with Lewis, questioned the assumption of a zero marginal product of labor in agriculture. (Leave it to the Nobel committee to give the prize to two economists who contradicted each other!)

Lewis largely ignored the importance of agriculture in his model. An influential study by Gustav Ranis and John C.H. Fei pointed out that agricultural production has to be sufficient to support the whole economy with food and raw materials—otherwise, rising food and raw-materials prices will choke off the expansion of the modern sector.[8] Their work shows the importance of investing in *agriculture* if a country wants its *modern* sector to grow. Agricultural investments can make it possible to produce more with fewer workers, thereby freeing up labor for the growing modern sector.

Although dual-economy models offer new insights into the economic and social transformations accompanying growth in poor economies, they are still aggregate models (though less so than the models in Chapter 6). They do not tell us much about what has to happen on a micro level to enable people to move up economically by moving off the farm, or how to feed them once they are in the city. For food to be available to urban workers, markets have to work. Market failures are a quintessential feature of poor countries, especially in rural areas (Chapters 9 and 10).

Can countries continue feeding themselves as people leave the farm? The answer to this question depends on farmers' ability to raise productivity. Poor access to credit, insurance, and markets for inputs and output severely limit small farmers' capacity to invest in new technologies and production activities. Family members who migrate can provide farmers with capital they need to raise productivity, via remittances. There's no place for this kind of feedback of migration on agricultural investment in Lewis' or Fei and Ranis' models.

Finding the data to test how off-farm labor affects crop production is not easy, because few household surveys provide good information on both migration and crop production. The studies that do, though, almost unanimously reject the Lewis hypothesis of zero marginal product of labor. However, they also find that off-farm work may help farmers overcome the lost-labor effect and raise productivity (see box "Can China Feed Itself as People Leave the Farm?").

Can China Feed Itself as People Leave the Farm?

If agriculture is past the Lewis turning point, farm households cannot sacrifice labor to the non-farm sector without losing production. A study of agricultural households in the northeast of China found that crop yields fell sharply when family members migrated from farm to nonfarm jobs. However, the study also found that those who left the farm sent home remittances, and remittances, in turn, raised crop yields. This finding suggests that the income family members send home loosens financial constraints on investing in fertilizer and other inputs that raise crop production. This study concluded that, on balance, the migration of labor off the farm has only a small effect on the aggregate supply of food in China.

Scott Rozelle, J. Edward Taylor, and Alan deBrauw. "Migration, Remittances, and Agricultural Productivity in China," *The American Economic Review*, Vol. 89, No. 2 (May):287-291, 1999.

From Farmer to Factory Worker

The skill demands of modern-sector jobs are different than sub-sistence production. The Lewis model leaves us with big questions in this regard. There's no human capital in the Lewis model—only hands. Lewis does not offer insights into who leaves the farm and who does not. Do countries have to invest in preparing people to enter nonfarm jobs? Without investments in education, people will not be prepared to work in the modern sector. China had an unusual situation when its market reforms happened: a massive workforce with secondary education, ideal to fill factories with skilled workers and make China the world's workshop. Ireland had a similar situation but at a higher skill level. Its policy of free university education created a very highly trained workforce, and it became the headquarters for many corporations positioning themselves to supply the European Union's markets.

Research shows that the people who migrate off the farm look different than those who stay behind. These differences teach us about the things people—and countries—need in order to make the transition from an agricultural to a manufacturing and service economy.

Who Leaves, Who Stays, and Who Succeeds?

In a happy world, there would be jobs for people wherever they wanted to work, and people would have whatever skills they needed to fill those jobs. Reality is not much like that, even in the best of worlds. A student may love Davis, but the chances of finding a job in a small college town after graduation are small. In poor countries, millions of people leave their villages to work in the city and end up unemployed because they do not have the right skills, the jobs aren't there, or they just aren't in the right place at the right time. The transition from agriculture-based to industrial-and-service economies involves huge dislocations and wrenching adjustments. Hundreds of millions of people move off the farm and have to compete and live in a very different, urban, world. As populations shift from rural- to urban-based activities, pressures on food production as well as public services in urban areas increase. Many people—though a tiny minority of the world's population—migrate to other countries.

Industry and service jobs may not materialize because investors do not believe that workers with the right skills will be available. In the 1989 Hollywood movie *Field of Dreams*, an Iowa corn farmer (Kevin Costner), hearing voices, interprets them as a command to build a baseball diamond in his fields; he does, and the players come. Good players. If you build a factory, will the right workers come?

In the story of Francisco and Alde, Alejandro and Alicia both migrate to nonfarm jobs, one in construction, the other in an electronics factory. In real life, can *any* kid raised for farm work simply shift over to a nonfarm job? Why did Francisco know that his two youngest kids would migrate away as soon as they finished school?

The Lewis model doesn't answer the questions of who migrates and who does not, or whether factories in the city can get the quantity as well as the quality of labor they need. Instead, it treats workers as homogeneous and ignores human capital.

Human capital theory can help us answer these questions. It posits the following: Workers are paid the marginal value product of their labor (MVPL), as depicted in the preceding figures. A firm will not hire a worker unless the additional value he produces (his MVPL) is at least as large as what the firm will have to pay the worker (that is, the wage). Characteristics that raise workers' productivity, particularly schooling and work experience, therefore, should bring higher wages.

Econometric evidence confirms that there are significant and high economic returns to these human capital variables in the modern sector—higher than in farm work. At the very least, basic literacy, and possibly schooling beyond the primary level, may be required in order to become a productive factory worker.

If this is true, then a human capital migration model would predict that people with more schooling are more likely to migrate from the traditional to the modern sector. Empirical studies consistently find this to be the case (for example, see the box: "Who Migrates and Who Doesn't?").

Who Migrates and Who Doesn't?

A study using survey data from rural Mexico found that migration is highly selective: the characteristics of those who migrate off the farm are different than those who stay, in ways consistent with human capital theory. Like in the story of Francisco and Alde, migration seems to be a household strategy. Household heads are significantly less likely to migrate to the city than their children. Each year of additional schooling raises the likelihood that a child migrates by 0.6 percentage points. This is not a small effect, considering that 7% of all rural Mexicans were found to be internal migrants. (Another 6.7% were international migrants, working in the United States.) An additional year of work experience also increases the likelihood of migration. Thus, a child with 10 years of schooling and work experience is more than 11% more likely to migrate to the city than a person without any schooling or experience. The probability of migrating is lower for women than men, and it is lower the more land the family has (why?). If one family member migrates, the likelihood of another family member migrating rises. Each family migrant raises the odds that another family member will migrate by 3.5 percentage points. Thus, migration is a network-driven process.

Human capital theory would predict that schooling would have the largest effect on migration to jobs where it raises workers' productivity the most. The study found that higher schooling *decreased* the likelihood of migrating to farm jobs. Schooling was found to have *no significant effect* on the likelihood of migrating to the United States. Most people who migrate from rural Mexico to the United States do so illegally, and education does not help much if you're working abroad as an undocumented immigrant.

"Determinants of Migration, Destination, and Sector Choice: Disentangling Individual, Household, and Community Effects," by Jorge Mora and J. Edward Taylor. In Ça–glar Özden and Maurice Schiff, Eds., *International Migration, Remittances, and the Brain Drain*. New York: Palgrave Macmillan, 2005, pp. 21-52.

Transformation and migration in China.

The "De-agriculturalization" of Rural Economies

As people move off the farm, rural households diversify their income sources. A poor rural household in Burundi is likely to get most or all of its income from farming. But in Latin America, Asia, and increasingly even sub-Saharan Africa, it is hard to find households that specialize in farming. Most are income diversifiers. Table 8.1 illustrates this for several countries in Africa, Asia, and Latin America:

Table 8.1: Non-farm Income Shares of Selected LDCs

Country	Year of Survey	Non-farm Income Share
Bangladesh	2000	63.1
Botswana	1985/86	77
Burkina Faso	1981/84	37-40
Ethiopia	1989/90	36-44
Gambia	1985/86	23
Ghana	1998	39.1
Guatemala	2000	50
Kenya	1987/89	80
Lesotho	1976	78
Malawi	2004	23
Malik	1988-89	59
Mozambique	1991	15
Nicaragua	2005	43.1
Niger	1989/90	43-52
Nigeria	1974/75	30
Rwanda	1990	30
Senegal	1988/90	24-60
South Africa (former homelands)	1982/86	75
Sudan	1988	38
Tanzania	1980	25
Vietnam	2002	37.7
Zimbabwe	1990/91	31-38

Sources: Thomas Reardon, "Using Evidence of Household Income Diversification to Inform Study of the Rural Nonfarm Labor Market in Africa," *World Development* 25(5):735-747, 1997 and Erik Jonasson, Mateusz Filipski, Jonathan Brooks and J. Edward Taylor, "Modeling the Welfare Implications of Agricultural Policies in Developing Countries," Scandinavian Working Papers of Economics No. 2012:11 (http://swopec.hhs.se/lunewp/abs/lunewp2012_011.htm)

It is clear from these data that when we think "rural" we should not automatically think "agricultural." To end up with average shares as high as these, many households must have nonfarm income shares that are very high indeed.

High shares of non-agricultural income in rural households have important implications for development policies as well as for research. Following are two of the most important ones:

Productivity and Poverty

If poor rural households get a small share of their income from agricultural production, even a large increase in agricultural productivity is not likely to have a big effect on poverty. For example, take a poor household that gets 20% of its income from growing and selling staples. Suppose a new technology (say, a Green Revolution seed) raises staple productivity by 10% for this poor household. How much will income go up? The immediate effect of the new technology will be to raise this household's income by 2% * 20% = 4%. In other words, the income effect is much smaller than the production effect. In time, the household might be able to put more effort into staple production and get a higher return from the new seeds. But the point is clear: in a rural economy where most income does not come from growing staples, raising productivity in staples might not be the best way to move households out of poverty.[9]

In a diversified economy, households' income sources can span different activities as well as different locations. The key to moving up, out of poverty, might well be to move out of agriculture and into higher-paying nonagricultural jobs. Policies that stimulate non-agricultural activities inside rural areas can play an increasingly important role in combatting poverty. So can employment growth in urban areas, which may benefit poor urban households as well as rural households, through migration.

Consumers vs. Producers

Some countries try to support their rural households by offering farmers artificially high prices for their crops. In many cases, this means that crop producers get higher prices, but consumers pay more for food. Agricultural households are both producers and consumers of food. We say in Chapter 8 that when the price of food goes up, these households win as producers but lose as consumers. If only a small share of income comes from food production, the consumption effect will outweigh the production effect, and higher food prices will hurt rural (as well as urban) households. Never assume that higher food prices are necessarily good for rural households, particularly the poor.

Another implication of diversification away from agriculture concerns the benefits of technological change. If everyone is a farmer, the main benefits of new technologies that raise food production will be on the farm. As more and more people move away from farming, the benefits become indirect, through lower food prices. Keeping ties with rural households might be an important form of livelihood insurance for migrants in distant labor markets.

Who Diversifies and Who Doesn't?

Economists often talk about the gains from specializing. The economists David Ricardo advised countries to specialize in producing goods in which they enjoy a "comparative advantage" and trading to get whatever else they wish to buy. As rural economies diversify, it is natural to ask whether the same advice applies to rural households. Mark Twain once said: "Put all your eggs in one basket—and watch the basket." Clearly, most rural households do not follow Twain's advice. Should they?

An economist would look at diversification and conclude that it is welfare-maximizing. Otherwise, why would households diversify? Or maybe households would like to specialize in wherever their comparative advantage lies, but for some reason they cannot. Perhaps there is a market failure or some other barrier to maximizing income. (Market failures will be a topic of Chapters 9 and 10.)

An action can be welfare (or constrained-welfare) maximizing even if it does not maximize income. For example, a household might be willing to sacrifice income in order to reduce income risk. In that case, its welfare depends not only on expected income but also on income uncertainty, which might be measured by the variance of income or the probability that income will fall below some minimum subsistence threshold. Does aversion to risk prevent poor households from making the investments needed to lift themselves out of poverty? This is an important question in development economics.

What is the relationship between diversification and income? The answer to this question depends on why households diversify. Are they "pushed" into diversifying for some reason other than to increase their income? Or are they "pulled" into diversifying because they can get higher income by investing in non-agricultural activities?

The "diversity push" view mostly emphasizes risk. A poor farmer could put all his effort and cash into crop production, but if the crop fails, he will not be able to put food on the table for his family. Poor farmers around the world lack any access to crop insurance. If the crop fails, that's it. Diversification allows a poor household to fall back on its other income sources should the crop fail.

The "diversity pull" view stresses diminishing marginal returns in crop production or intra-household considerations. Beyond a point, the more you invest in crop production, the smaller the marginal returns to that investment—whether it is cash spent on fertilizer or family labor. If a farmer could earn more by working an additional day for a wage or in some non-crop production activity than in his own fields, it makes sense for her to diversify into wage work or non-crop production. The same applies to different family members. A strong son with little schooling might be a productive crop producer but have few prospects as a factory worker, whereas his sibling (sister, perhaps) with secondary schooling would be ill-placed in the fields.

These two theories of why households diversify provide different hypothesis, which might be testable using survey data. If the diversify push view is right, we would expect that households most vulnerable to risk (and with the least access to other forms of income security) would diversify, and this would lead to lower incomes relative to households less vulnerable to risk. If the diversify pull view is correct, we would expect diversification into non-crop activities to be associated with higher incomes. That's what a survey of research findings from African countries found—but not everyone can do it (see box: "Do Non-farm Activities Increase Inequality?").

Do Non-farm Activities Increase Inequality?

A survey of findings from several African countries found that many rural households diversify into non-farm activities, including non-farm rural enterprises like food processing that rely on agriculture for inputs. In most areas, non-farm wage work and non-farm production generate higher income than agricultural work, and they constitute an important part of rural household incomes. However, poor households face severe barriers to entry into these non-farm activities. Taking a chance on a non-farm investment entails risks and requires capital, both financial and human. Getting access to a non-farm wage job requires schooling and skills. These are all things that the poorest households generally cannot afford. As a result, most of the gains from diversifying into non-farm activities bypass the poor, and as a result, off-farm income increases inequalities in rural areas.

Thomas Reardon, "Using Evidence of Household Income Diversification to Inform Study of the Rural Nonfarm Labor Market in Africa," *World Development* 25(5):735-747, 1997.

The Transformation of Agriculture and the National Economy

The economist Peter Timmer identified four stages of the transformation of agriculture and its role in national economies.[10] First, agricultural productivity per agricultural worker begins to rise, creating an economic surplus. Second, this surplus is tapped in ways already discussed in Chapter 8 (taxes, surplus labor migrating to the city, or government price policies). The second stage is the main focus of the dual economy models, like the Lewis model. In stage three, the agricultural sector becomes increasingly integrated with other sectors of the economy. This happens as markets develop, linking agriculture with the urban economy, and also as the rural economy diversifies into non-agricultural activities, as discussed earlier in this chapter. Eventually, in stage four, agriculture is just another sector of the economy. As Timmer writes:

> The role of agriculture in industrialized economies is little different from the role of the steel, housing, or insurance sectors.

Even in poor countries, it is important to view agriculture in the context of an increasingly diversified and integrated national economy. As we shall see next, seeing agriculture as one of many interacting sectors in a complex economic system changes the way we think about, and model, developing economies.

Beyond the Dual Economy: Economy-wide Models in Development

Empirical research using survey data finds that rural households engage in an array of farm and non-farm activities as well as rural-to-urban migration. Urban economies are more complex, with a large number of inter-acting production sectors, factors, labor types, and households. An economy is really a complex organism, a vast marketplace in which millions and millions of decisions by a diversity of actors lead to both aggregate (for example, national) and micro (for example, household-level) economic outcomes. The interplay of demand and supply determines both prices and quantities of goods as well as factors.

Both aggregate growth models and dual-economy models miss these complex interactions that are the essence of modern economies. Over the past quarter century, a new breed of economy-wide models has emerged to enable researchers to simulate the ways in which development policies impact whole economies and the actors within them. These models are called *computable general equilibrium (CGE)* models, and they have become a staple of development policy analysis.

CGE models are complex, and building one is beyond the scope of this course.[11] Like climate models and even computer games, constructing CGE models requires having an understanding of the system being modeled (in this case, the workings of the economy) and the mathematical and programming skills to create the simulation model.

Nevertheless, development economics students, researchers, and practitioners are likely to come across them at some time or another, so having a basic understanding of how they work has become an "essential of development economics." Mary Burfischer, in the preface to her "how-to" book on CGE modeling, writes:

> A CGE model is a powerful analytical tool that can help you to gain a better understanding of real-world economic issues…Economists today are using these models to systematically analyze some of the most important policy challenges and economic "shocks" of the twenty-first century, including global climate change, the spread of human diseases, and international labor migration.

The Anatomy of a CGE Model

So what is a CGE model? Actually, we already saw a miniature one in Chapter 7. An agricultural household model, estimated with real-world data, is a CGE model for a very small economy: that of a household-farm. It includes both supply and demand. If agricultural households are involved in many different kinds of activities, both farm and nonfarm, the household-farm model can be expanded to include these activities. Then it is a multi-sector model. A household-farm model can be used to simulate the impacts of policies and other shocks on the agricultural economy.

Now imagine combining a household-farm model with similar models of *all* producers and consumers in the national economy. There would be models for urban as well as rural households, and urban firms as well as rural household-farms. Most CGE models are national. Some even link models of several nations into an international CGE model. They commonly include several different household groups and scores of different production sectors.

To a non-expert, CGE models are likely to appear complex and black-boxish. In this sense, they are like any simulator, from flight simulators to World of Warcraft (or whatever your favorite computer game is). All involve a set of equations describing the behavior of the system they are simulating. For example, a flight simulator contains equations describing the physics of flight and aerodynamics. Assuming these equations are correct, it can teach pilots how to fly. Similarly, a CGE model with equations describing the behavior of an economy can teach us how economies function, how they evolve over time, and how they change when "shocked" by a policy, market, or environmental change.

A CGE model is an "economy-wide model" because it is created to represent the economic behavior and interactions among *all* of the actors in an economy, producers as well as consumers.

Let's take a brief tour through a typical CGE model to see how it works, using the tools we already know from microeconomics courses and previous chapters of this book.

Producers (Firms or Farms):

The behavior of producers in a CGE model is represented by production functions describing the technologies that combine inputs to produce output (for example, Cobb-Douglas production functions), as well as the classic conditions for profit maximization: that firms demand inputs at the point where their marginal value products just equal their prices. Each sector in the economy has its own set of equations in the model.

To produce output, firms purchase inputs. Payments for intermediate inputs become demands for the output of other firms. The income firms generate, above and beyond these intermediate input costs, is the firms' value-added, which we saw in Chapter 2 add up to a country's GDP. Firms also pay taxes, for example, sales taxes, also called indirect taxes. They also may save (retained earnings). At the end of the day, each firm's total revenue must equal its total expenditures; all of the money has to go somewhere.

Households:

The value-added generated by firms gets channeled into households, in the CGE model like in the real world. It, along with any other income households might receive, determines households' budget constraints. Expenditure functions in a CGE model describe how households spend their income, as a function of their income as well as prices. The equations describing households' expenditures are derived from the maximization of household utility functions, subject to the budget constraint. In addition to demanding goods and services, households save and pay taxes (called direct taxes). At the end of the day, households' total expenditures must equal their total income (plus borrowing). Each household group in the economy has its own set of expenditure equations in a CGE model, and sometimes there are many different groups, depending on the model's focus. Households can be grouped using many different criteria, for example, by their main economic activities, demographic makeup, ethnicity, location, or poverty status.

Governments:

The taxes paid by firms and households determine the government's budget constraint. Governments use their income (often supplemented by borrowing) for many purposes, most of which involve demanding goods and services in the economy or transferring income back to households.

Investors:

Savings by households and firms (perhaps supplemented by other sources, including foreigners) turn into investments. Investments, in turn, create a demand for goods and services in the economy. For example, construction investment involves the purchase of materials as well as labor and capital.

For every economic agent, total income must equal total expenditures. This fundamental identity of economics is critical in building CGE models.

When incomes increase, so do the demands by households, government, and investors, and this stimulates the production of goods and services in the larger economy, which in turn creates new incomes, and so on. Everyone is part of the circular flow of goods, income, and spending in an economy. Like in any ecosystem, an exogenous shock to any part of the economy reverberates through the economic system, carrying impacts from one actor to another.

A CGE model "solves" to find the set of prices and quantities at which the economy is in equilibrium. This is the point at which the quantity supplied equals the quantity demanded for all goods and factors, like at an enormous auction.

Once we have a CGE "base model," we can use it to do experiments. For example, we can ask what will happen if the government implements a particular policy, if there is a change in world food prices, or if climate change reduces crop production. Each of these policies "shocks" the CGE model and throws it out of equilibrium, but the model adjusts, through a series of iterations, to find a new equilibrium set of prices, quantities, and incomes. If the model is detailed enough, it can show us how different shocks are likely to affect different production sectors and household groups, as well as the overall economy (see box: "Climate Change and Poverty").

Climate Change and Poverty

A team of economists and climatologists at Purdue and Stanford Universities used a CGE model to study the effects of climate change on poor households in fifteen different developing countries. Climate change alters crop yields. This can affect poor households directly, if they grow crops, as well as indirectly, by changing food prices. Even poor urban households, which are not involved in crop production, may suffer if food prices increase.

Understanding the impacts of climate change on poverty requires a systems approach that integrates climate science with CGE modeling. Climate simulation models give us predictions of the effects of climate change on key variables affecting crop yields, particularly temperatures and rainfall. These climate predictions are used as inputs into CGE models, which then simulate the impacts of the resulting crop production changes on the incomes of different household groups as well as the prices they must pay for food and related products.

Under one climate-change and food production scenario, prices for major staples rise 10 to 60 percent by 2030. The effects of these higher food prices on poverty are different in different countries. In some non-agricultural household groups, the poverty rate rises by 20 to 50 percent in parts of Africa and Asia. Meanwhile, in other parts of Asia and in Latin America, some households specializing in agriculture actually gain as a result of climate change. Climate change, like most everything else in life, has winners and losers.

This study was unique in bringing together experts in CGE modeling and climate science. Its findings have been influential in alerting policy makers to the adverse effects climate change is likely to have on poverty. The CGE findings also offer insights into where government policies might focus their efforts to protect the most vulnerable households from the negative effects of climate change.

Thomas W. Hertel, Marshall B. Burke, and David B. Lobdell, "The Poverty Implications of Climate-Induced Crop Yield Changes by 2030," Purdue University, GTAP Working Paper No. 69, 2010.

Chapter Eight Notes

1. http://www.fao.org/about/en/

2. "Transition day," as this day has become known, is largely symbolic. The date was estimated from the UN's prediction that the world would be 51.3 percent urban by 2010. Researchers at North Carolina State University and the University of Georgia interpolated the transition date by using the average daily rural and urban population increases from 2005 to 2010.

3. The terms "rural" and "urban" are problematic. At what population does a rural village become a town? (Many governments, including the US Bureau of the Census, use 2,500 as the cut-off.) As expanding roads, communications, and markets integrate town and country, the distinction becomes ever more blurred.

4. Jonathan Brooks, Mateusz Filipski, Erik Jonasson, and J. Edward Taylor, "Modelling the Distributional Impacts of Agricultural Policies in Developing Countries: The Development Policy Evaluation Model (DEVPEM)." Paper presented at the OECD Global Forum on Agriculture, 29-30 November 2010.

5. Aslihan Arslan and J. Edward Taylor. 2012. "Transforming Rural Economies: Migration, Income Generation and Inequality in Rural Mexico," *Journal of Development Studies* (in press).

6. US Department of Labor, National Agricultural Worker Survey (NAWS); http://www.doleta.gov/agworker/naws.cfm

7. Francisco and his family are a composite constructed from field surveys carried out by researchers at UC Davis and the Colegio de Mexico in Mexico City.

8. Gustav Ranis and John C.H. Fei, "A Theory of Economic Development," American Economic Review LI (September): 533-565, 1961

9. In a subsistence household, on the other hand, raising productivity can free up family time for other activities, including wage work.

10. C. Peter Timmer, "The Agricultural Transformation," Chapter 8 in *Handbook of Development Economics*, Volume I, edited by H. Chenery and T.N. Srinivasan, Amsterdam: Elsevier Science Publishers, 1988.

11. For a guide to building and using CGE models, see Mary Burfischer's book, *Introduction to Computable General Equilibrium Models*, Cambridge: Cambridge University Press, 2011.

9.

Markets, Information, and Trade

Imagine you wake up one day and there are no markets. Not for food or other stuff. No credit, either—not that it would matter, without access to goods to spend money on. You'd eat whatever your plot of land gave you—no more, no less. You would be *your own* market; your internal balance of supply and demand would determine how much you consume and produce.

It also would determine how much you value things. If you're running low on food, you'd value it highly. In economics jargon, your "shadow price" of food would be high. If your plot produces too many tomatoes, your shadow price of tomatoes will be low.

I don't know about you, but I'd be in serious trouble without a food market. When people in Tigray province, Ethiopia, lost their access to food markets in 1983, the result was catastrophic (see box: "Famine and Missing Markets in Tigray").

Images of a market in Tigray, Ethiopia.

Things would be better if we could get everyone in town together and form a market. You grow food, I do something else (like teach economics!). Someone else could make us candles, and others could bake us bread (assuming there's wax and wheat around), fire bricks, or carve

185

furniture (assuming there's wood to be had). Having a local market, we could all begin to specialize.

With more far-flung markets, we'd get access to stuff we couldn't possibly produce locally and be able to sell stuff we produce best or have too much of. Tomatoes could be rotting on the vine in your yard, but in a mill town in the next valley over there might be a tomato shortage. They'd pay dearly for your tomatoes and you for their wood, if only the two of you could discover one another, get together, and trade.

Naturally, specializing and trading requires coordination and information. Buyers and sellers need to know about each other. If your "thing" is doing carpentry, you need to know where your buyers are and, in turn, where to get the food you'll need to eat.

One way to coordinate production across space is through centralized planning, as in the former Soviet Union and pre-reform China. Central planners faced an enormous task: coordinating production and demand across millions of producers and consumers and typically very large spaces (those countries were big!). They turned out not to be very good at it, as evidenced by their persistent use of rationing (exemplified by the long bread lines in Moscow in the 1960s), inefficiency, and ultimately the demise of large centrally planned economies altogether.

Interestingly, large corporations in the world today face serious coordination challenges reminiscent in some ways of the ones faced by centrally planned economies. (Imagine the coordination it takes to make a Boeing 747!). Over the years, corporations have tended to oscillate between having highly centralized and decentralized decision models. They have come up with innovations to deal with their information and coordination demands, including structures that mimic markets and, of course, extensive use of computers and the internet to track and coordinate activities.

Famine and Missing Markets in Tigray

Between 1983 and 1985 a widespread famine took more than 400,000 lives in northern Ethiopia. The blame for the famine often is put on drought. However, the drought did not strike until months after the famine was already underway. In fact, as northern Ethiopia suffered famine, record harvests were reported in other parts of the country. Civil conflict against the Derg government and repressive policies shut down rural markets, forcing peasant households into self-sufficiency. When record low rainfall hit, markets could not function to fill the region's food deficit, and the rural population was left without access to food.

In January 2012 Ed visited a village in Tigray, the hardest hit province. The village had only a few hundred inhabitants, but this was market day. Thirty thousand people filed in from smaller villages as far away as twenty miles, all on foot. The line of people coming and going stretched off into the distance as far as I could see. Some hoisted bags of grain over their shoulders, others carried bags of produce or bunches of live chickens bound at their feet, and a few led goats on leashes fashioned from rope.

I asked my guide, an official in the state government, what this market looked like during the famine years. He sighed and said, "You do not understand. The soldiers would not let anyone walk the roads then. There was no market."

de Waal, Alex (1991). *Evil Days: Thirty Years of War and Famine in Ethiopia.* New York & London: Human Rights Watch, and personal interviews in Tigray province.

Since ancient times, markets have been the answer to overcoming local resource constraints and gaining access to new goods. Archeologists have uncovered prolific evidence of ancient trade. For example, ceramic pottery and silver coins from 5th Century Athens are still being unearthed all around the Mediterranean Sea, from Egypt to Sicily. In ancient Athens, the Long Walls connected the city to its port, Pireaus, so that citizens would never be cut off from trade by sea, which provided most of the Athenians' food supplies. When Athens did lose control of the sea in the Peloponnesian war (404 BC), it quickly fell to Sparta and its allies—a vivid illustration of how critical access to markets is.

Today, markets are seen as the key to economic efficiency even in the world's former centrally planned economies. Why is this?

The Nobel laureate economist Friedrich August von Hayek had a simple answer to this question: markets effectively pool information from disparate sources into a convenient measure of market conditions, the price (see box: "All in One Price"). To most people a price is what you pay to buy something or what you get from selling it. To an economist, prices are conveyers of information. A high price tells producers there is excess demand for their good so they should produce more, and it tells consumers to cut back and seek out consumption substitutes. High input prices tell producers to seek out input substitutes while creating incentives for others to develop these substitutes.

Markets are critical to economic welfare because they bring together sellers and buyers, integrate vast amounts of information, and distill this information into prices. In rich countries life would be unimaginable without access to a wide array of reasonably well functioning markets, from food to credit and insurance. It is almost never the case that a rich-country household has to produce something in order to consume it, or that its members cannot sell their labor for a salary or wage. Credit markets function for small businesses and farms to finance investment projects. People pop out credit cards for convenience, to get through a tough time, or to buy things they can't afford at the moment. Insurance markets help protect people from unexpected income and health shocks. More and more people interact in "virtual marketplaces," where buyers and sellers find each other and transact on-line, like on eBay and Amazon.com.

Missing markets create inefficiency. When markets don't work, prices vary from one place to another. Wages are high in my town but low in yours; food prices are low in my town but outrageously high in yours; I lack a forest but you have cheap wood. Almost nothing catches an economist's eye more quickly than price differences across space, because of the obvious efficiency implications. Widely varying prices for the same goods suggest poor market integration and an opportunity to increase the economic pie for everyone.

Access to markets is just as compelling for a poor rural household in Rwanda, India or Peru as for someone in a high-income country. Without good access to markets, a poor household cannot market its produce, obtain inputs, sell labor, obtain credit, learn about or adopt new technologies, insure against risks, or obtain consumption goods at low prices. Equally important, it cannot use its scarce resources like land and labor efficiently. Its decision making is constrained.

All in One Price

As a number of countries were experimenting with centrally planned economies, Friedrich von Hayek was looking inside prices. What he found there can tell us a lot about why centrally planned economies failed and why, without well-functioning markets, the economic prospects for poor societies are dim.

Think of anything that can shift around a supply or demand curve: changing technology, population, ethnicity of consumers, people's expectations, government policies, the weather, the internet, whatever. So many things that it's impossible to keep track of them all. Yet in a market, the intersection of supply and demand determines the price. If any of the multitude of things affecting supply or demand changes, we see it in the price. The Beatles said

"All you need is love." An economist would say "All you need is prices." That's why market economies are better coordinated than centrally planned economies.

The price system, von Hayek argued, is a "communications network" and the most efficient means of making use of economic information. It transmits information from one part of the market to another. For example, a drought might cause a grain-crop failure in one region, pushing up the grain price there. The higher price immediately communicates information to *other* regions where prices are lower. Astute traders see an opportunity to *arbitrage* (buy cheaply in one region and sell dearly in the other). In so doing, they resolve the excess-demand problem in the drought region while driving down prices there. If the market works very efficiently, a local drought will have little effect on local grain prices—all because of the price's role in conveying information. The key to making prices play this valuable economic role is the rough-and-tumble process of market agitation that von Hayek called *market competition.*

Even well-developed market economies sometimes experience system-wide coordination failures that can cause the economy to experience artificial booms and busts and even collapse into economic depression. These failures, von Hayek argued, stem from coordination problems over time. Coordinating activities over time is more difficult than coordinating them at a given point in time. For example, producers have to make decisions today anticipating what other producers and consumers will do in the future. It turns out that prices are better at conveying information at a given point in time than through time. We'll see an example of this when we learn about credit and insurance in Chapter 10.

Von Hayek's work changed the way we think about prices and the critical role of markets in developing as well as developed economies.

Roger W. Garrison and Israel Kirzner, "Friedrich August von Hayek," *The New Palgrave: A Dictionary of Economics*, pp. 609-614, London: Macmillan Press Ltd., 1987; http://www.auburn.edu/~garriro/e4hayek.htm).

Friedrich A. Hayek, "The Use of Knowledge in Society," *American Economic Review* 35 (September): 519–530. Available online at: http://www.econlib.org/library/Essays/hykKnw1.html.

Tradables and Nontradables

When an economy does not have access to outside markets for a good, the good is called a *nontradable*. The price of a nontradable is determined by the interaction of demand and supply within the economy, like in an Econ 1 graph of market equilibrium; that is, it is *endogenous* to the economy. When the economy is integrated with outside markets for a good, the good is said to be *tradable*. The price of a tradable is determined outside the economy; that is, it is *exogenous*. At that price, if there is excess demand for the tradable, the difference is purchased in outside markets (imported). If there is excess supply, the surplus is sold in those markets (exported).

The notion of tradables, nontradables, and where prices come from applies to *any* economy—whether of a country, region, village, or even a household. A subsistence household—one that consumes what it produces and has to produce what it consumes—is a very small closed economy. It even has its own prices, which we call "shadow prices." We cannot see them, but we have ways to estimate them with the right data (see box: "Estimating the Shadow Price of Corn."). Keep this in mind as you read this chapter; it is fundamental to understanding trade and economic development:

For a nation: The minute a country opens up to international trade, world prices replace internal equilibrium prices for tradables. The world price is what people must pay for what they buy, or what they get for what they sell, on the world market.

For a village: When a new road links a remote village up with a regional commercial center, goods that once were nontradable can become tradable. Village prices get replaced by prices determined in the outside market.

For a household: A subsistence household, self-sufficient in food, makes its production and consumption decisions based on its own subjective valuation (shadow price) of subsistence goods. This shadow price gets replaced by an exogenous market price if the subsistence household becomes connected with outside markets.

Estimating the Shadow Price of Corn

You know what a shadow price is—you've surely "felt" one before. Imagine you're backpacking in a remote part of the Sierras and a bear gets your food. (That happened to me once, I'm sad to say.) What you would pay for a freeze-dried pack of lasagna then! That's a shadow price. If you were standing in a backpacking shop, your shadow price would be the same as the price on the shelf. Hungry, isolated, and foodless in the mountains, *where there is no market*, you'd almost certainly be willing to pay more.

We can't see shadow prices, but sometimes we can estimate them. Consider a subsistence corn farmer in a remote village in southern Mexico. Assuming he follows basic economic precepts of optimizing behavior, he will produce at the point where the price just equals the marginal cost, as we saw in Chapter 7. If we can estimate the marginal cost, then, we'll know what price the farmer is using to value his crop, whether it's for the market or his family's own consumption.

A recent study used this approach to estimate the shadow price of maize for Mexican farmers. For commercial farmers, who are integrated with markets, the shadow price was found to be not significantly different than the market price. For subsistence farmers growing traditional maize varieties, though, it was significantly higher. The more remote the farmer was from markets, the higher his shadow price. Indigenous farmers were found to place a particularly high value on their traditional corn varieties.

This study was important because it showed how to estimate the shadow price of a subsistence crop, and it offered an explanation for why small farmers seem to produce corn at a loss: they put a higher value on their corn than the market does. Friedrich von Hayek would not be happy about that!

Aslıhan Arslan and J. Edward Taylor, "Farmers' Subjective Valuation of Subsistence Crops: The Case of Traditional Maize in Mexico." *American Journal of Agricultural Economics* 91(4):895-909, 2009.

Some goods by their very nature tend to be nontradables. Haircuts are an example: it's hard to import them, unless you travel to wherever the hairdresser is. (I "imported" a pretty good haircut from Paris last year, but that's because I happened to be there for a workshop.) Lodging and restaurant food are other examples of nontradables. Sometimes, goods that are nontradable can become tradable. Highly perishable foods, like fish, are nontradables if they have to be carried by hand or on donkey's backs over long distances in the heat. They become tradables if traders appear with trucks and ice boxes, public transport becomes available, or the fisherman gets a motorcycle.

When goods and services that *could* be tradable *are not*, two important questions arise. First, why not? And second, what are the consequences for economic welfare, particularly of the poor?

What Makes Tradables Nontradables?

The explanations for why things that *could* be tradable are *not* fall mostly into two categories: trade policies and transaction costs.

Trade Policies and Nontradables

Figure 9.1 illustrates a country's supply and demand for a tradable good, say, rice. If the country could not trade with the rest of the world, its equilibrium price and quantity of rice would be given by the intersection of its supply and demand curves: the country would consume an amount Q_e of rice at a domestic price equal to p_e. We can call this domestic price without trade the "autarkic" price. (Autarky means economic independence or self-sufficiency—in this case, for a country.)

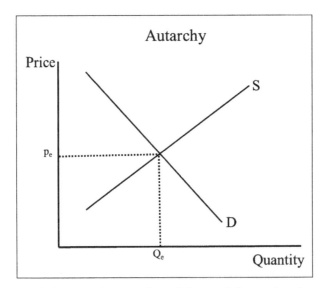

Figure 9.1: Under autarky, supply and demand determine the equilibrium price and quantity.

Rice is a globally traded commodity, so if the country's policies permit it there may be trade. Trade is illustrated in Figure 9.2. There is a world price of rice, which we can call p_w. The world price could be higher or lower than p_e, depending on whether the country is an efficient rice producer (the position of its supply curve) and whether it is a large or small demander of rice (the position of the demand curve). If $p_w > p_e$ the country will supply more rice than it produces and export the difference; if $p_w < p_e$ (like in this diagram) it will do the opposite. Here, we have assumed $p_w < p_e$, so left alone, our country is an importer of rice: it imports an amount M of rice from the rest of the world.

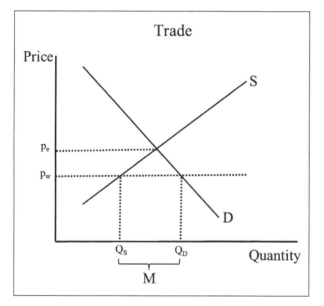

Figure 9.2: With trade the economy is a price-taker, and it imports its excess demand or exports its excess supply.

Trade in this case makes consumers happy: they can pay the lower world price for rice. The country's producers have to sell at this price; if they charge the higher equilibrium price, no one will buy from them.

Many countries impose taxes on the goods they import and/or export. Import tariffs raise the price people in the country have to pay for imported rice by the per-unit amount of the tariff. That is, instead of paying p_w per ton of imported rice, consumers have to pay $p_w(1 + t_{im})$, where t_{im} is the per-ton tariff. Export taxes lower the price the country's producers get for selling their goods abroad; instead of p_w they get paid

$p_w(1 - t_{ex})$, where t_{ex} is the export tariff per ton. The case of an import tariff is illustrated in Figure 9.3.

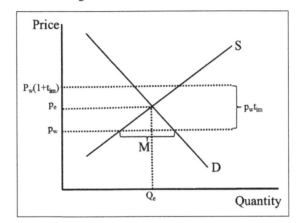

Figure 9.3: A high import tariff can drive an economy into autarky.

Tariffs create a wedge between the import and export price. If the tariffs are large enough, it becomes too expensive for the country to *import or export* rice. In our figure, the import price (including tariff) is above the autarkic (equilibrium) price, and the export price is below it. (Assuming there's no export tariff, the export price is the world price.) If you want to buy rice, you are better off paying the autarkic price p_e than the import price plus tariff. If you are selling, you'll get a better price selling to local consumers, at the autarkic price, than exporting at the world price. (All the more if there is an export tariff, too!) Thus, in our example, consumers will buy from domestic producers, and producers will sell to domestic consumers. There will be no trade. The country will be self-sufficient in rice. (As we shall see below, this self-sufficiency will come at a cost.)

This example illustrates how you can use trade policy to take a tradable and turn it into a nontradable. (A more direct way is simply to restrict imports, by imposing a *trade quota*.)

More generally, trade policies like tariffs may distort trade without eliminating it. In the process, they create winners and losers while reducing overall economic welfare. If the country imposes an import tariff, its consumers will be hurting, but producers of the protected good will thank the government all the way to the bank. That's what rice farmers do in Japan, where the price of rice is often seven times the world price because of trade policies! But if you add up the economic welfare of producers and consumers, it will be lower than without the tariff. That's because import tariffs, like other distortionary trade policies, create what is called a *deadweight loss*.

Welfare Gains from Trade

To understand the importance of trade to economic welfare (and welfare losses from tariffs), we have to start by agreeing on what we mean by "economic welfare." Economic welfare is the sum of producer and consumer surplus, so let's first see what each of these concepts means in the presence of trade.

Figure 9.4 illustrates producers' optimal outcome given the world price, p_w. Following the basic precept for profit maximization, the quantity supplied in the market is given by the point where $p_w = \text{MC}$, that is, where the world price line hits the supply curve. In our figure, optimal output is Q_S^*. Producers make no profit on the last unit supplied (because its MC just equals the price). However, they *do* make a profit on all the other units ($Q < Q_S^*$), because on those units the price exceeds the MC. Total profits are given by the area of triangle A, which is the sum of the difference between price and MC for all of the units supplied, up to Q_S^*. (In calculus terms, in case that's how you like to think, it's the integral from zero to Q_S^* of the function $p\text{-}MC(Q)$.) This is the *producer surplus* (PS in the diagram). For all units from zero to Q_S^*, producers get a price higher than the minimum they would require in order to supply the goods. The producer surplus is our measure of producers' economic welfare.

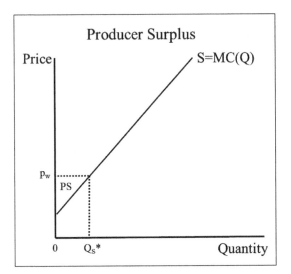

Figure 9.4: The producer surplus (PS) is the area below the price and above the supply curve.

There is an analogue to this for consumers. Not surprisingly, it is called the *consumer surplus*. Have you ever paid less for something than you would have been willing to pay? Maybe picked up what you want on sale, surprised by how cheap it was, then say to yourself "Wow, what will I do with the money I saved?" That difference between what you would have been willing to pay and what you did pay is called your consumer surplus.

Look at the market demand curve in Figure 9.5. It represents consumers' willingness to pay for each quantity of the good. The quantity demanded in the market is given by the point where the world price line hits this demand curve; in this figure it is $Q_D{}^*$. For all the quantities from zero to $Q_D{}^*$, consumers would have been willing to pay more than the world price. The sum of differences between consumers' willingness to pay and the world price, then, is the total consumer surplus in this market. It is shown as the triangle CS in the figure. It will be our measure of consumers' economic welfare.

Total welfare is the sum of producer surplus and consumer surplus.

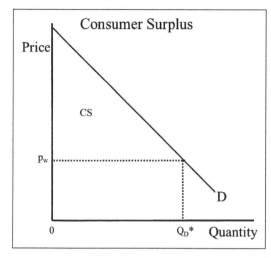

Figure 9.5: The consumer surplus (CS) is the area above the price and below the demand curve.

What does an import tariff do to economic welfare? Suppose the government imposes a tariff of $t per unit of the good, so the relevant price (everyone's *decision price*) is now $p_w(1+t)$ as shown in Figure 9.6. Before the tariff, the country's consumers demanded Q_D^* and producers supplied Q_S^*; the country imported the difference ($M^* = Q_D^* - Q_S^*$). After the tariff is imposed, the country imports a smaller amount, because consumers demand less and producers supply more. The new level of imports is ($M' = Q_D' - Q_S'$).

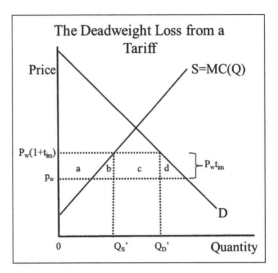

Figure 9.6: With a tariff, consumers lose $a+b+c+d$, government gains c, producers gain a, and there is a deadweight loss of $b+d$.

Let's see what this does to economic welfare.

First, it raises the producer surplus, by an amount equal to the area of the trapezoid a in the figure. Producers now sell at the higher price, so they make more profits than before. Producers' welfare goes up as a result of the tariff.

Second, it generates tax revenue for the government. The government's gain is given by the area of the rectangle c. It is the tariff, t, times the level of imports once the tariff is in place, $Q_D' - Q_S'$. The government, like producers, is better off.

What happens to consumer surplus? Consumers have to pay a higher price than before, so their consumer surplus falls. Remember that the consumer surplus is the difference between the price line and the demand curve. Thus, the fall in consumer surplus is given by the area $(a+b+c+d)$. That's how much the economic welfare of consumers falls when the tariff is imposed.

So, let's take stock of what happened here. Producer surplus went up by a. Government revenue went up by c. But consumer surplus *fell* by *a+b+c+d*. That's *b+d* more than the gains to producers and government. Where did that consumer loss go? Whose gain did it become?

The answer is: nobody's. The tariff distorted the economy and led to an efficiency loss equal to the areas of the two triangles, *b+d*. That's what economists call a *deadweight loss*. Avoiding deadweight losses is pretty much the argument for free trade. Eliminating the tariff makes total economic welfare increase, because the economic pie becomes bigger. If a tariff is eliminated, producers and government lose, but consumers gain more. In short, everyone could be made better off if the government didn't charge the tariff, then taxed consumers and handed some of the proceeds to producers.

Of course, this means the government must have the administrative capacity to efficiently collect taxes from consumers and make transfers to producers. Some taxes are easier to collect than others. Import tariffs are easy to levy at the port. Income taxes are notoriously difficult to levy, because they require having information on incomes of large numbers of people. Sales taxes and value-added taxes are levied on businesses, easier to collect than income taxes but more difficult than import tariffs. In countries lacking the administrative expertise to levy taxes efficiently, there may be large deadweight losses from tax collection. The same is true for making transfers to producers. For example, it is more efficient to hand each farmer a check than to pay farmers an artificially high price for their harvests (why?). However, it is more administratively demanding, as well.

Transaction Costs

Usually government policies do not limit trade within countries. However, *transactions costs* can turn tradables into nontradables within countries in much the same way that import and export tariffs do in international trade.

The market price is what a buyer pays or seller receives as a result of a transaction, like the ones that happen billions of times a day in marketplaces and stores all around the globe. Transacting is not free, though. Buyers and sellers have to know where to find one another. Both have to know the specifics of what is being transacted, including its quality. When I sell something to you, property rights change hands. We both need to be convinced that I had the right to sell it and that you have secure rights to the thing once it is sold. All of these things have to happen every time we buy or sell a potato, a day's work, a piece of property, a loan, or an insurance policy. For many transactions, like buying a lemon, they're trivial: we don't even think about them. But what if the lemon is an old car?

The Power of Information

In 1970, Berkeley economist George Aklerof published a revolutionary paper called "The Market for Lemons."[1] The paper was so novel that it got rejected by three top economics journals before eventually winning Aklerof the Nobel Prize. It was about the power of information to make—or break—markets. Its argument goes something like this:

You want to sell your used car. After taking good care of it all these years, you know it's in top shape, and you want to get a good price for it. But what do the potential buyers know? Only what they can see. There is *asymmetric information*: You know more about your car's quality than they do. Unless you can persuade them otherwise, the most they'll be willing to pay will be the price of the average-quality car out there.

So what do you do? Unless you can figure out a way to resolve this information asymmetry, you either sell below what you know your car is worth, or else you pull it from the market. If you decide not to offer your car for sale, the average quality of cars on the market falls. Over time, this lowers used car prices. Others with high-quality used cars leave the market, quality and prices fall further, and before you know it, only low-quality used cars are left on the market. This is what Aklerof calls "The Market for Lemons."[2] In the extreme case, the market collapses.

When the *Journal of Political Economy* rejected this paper, the editor informed Akerlof that "if this paper was correct, economics would be different."

It was, and economics is different.

Today we understand that information is the lubricant that makes markets work. Yet information asymmetries abound, especially in poor countries. Because of them, markets can fail. Surrounded by market failures, the prospects of poor people escaping from poverty are grim.

Food export markets provide a classic example of information asymmetries that make markets fail—for small producers, at least. Diversifying into high-value export crops is critical if poor countries wish to increase their foreign exchange and raise farm incomes. Some African countries, such as Ethiopia, Kenya and Uganda, are well positioned to supply crops year-round to developed countries, particularly in Europe. However, without the right information this trade cannot happen.

Take food safety, for example. High-income countries have stringent food safety standards. The United States inspects food imports to make sure they comply with food safety rules, even inspecting foreign food facilities.[3] The European Union, the world's biggest food importer, requires that all imported food meet the same level of food safety as food produced within the EU.[4]

Food safety concerns are understandable, of course. But even if a small African farmer can meet the EU's food safety requirements, how will she convince the EU that she has done so? The cost of many small producers complying with these requirements is likely to be significantly higher than the cost for a few big producers. Certifying food safety is a transaction cost of selling food to high-income countries. This can create major challenges when it comes to including small farmers in the export-supply chain (see box: "Selling Green Beans to Europe").

Another example involving certification is titling. It provides the security that the seller really owns the property being sold. Without it, a potential buyer would face risks that easily could kill the deal. Around the globe, governments keep public records of land and building titles and histories of sales permitting "title searches." In the United States, you cannot get a loan to buy a house without a title search; this information creates the credit. That's why land titling has been a focus of development projects by international development banks.

Selling Green Beans to Europe

If countries wish to export food to developed countries they have to meet food safety standards concerning pesticide residues, harvesting and packing operations, and a means to trace any food safety problems that do arise back to their source. A study by researchers at the International Food Policy Research Institute (IFPRI) investigated how these stringent food safety standards affect small farmers in Ethiopia, Kenya, and Zambia. The authors found that the standards "screened out smallholders in all these countries, excluding them from the green bean export chain." On a positive note, it uncovered some efforts to help smallholders work their way into the export supply chain, including some new public-private "farm-to-fork" partnerships and collective action by farmers to monitor their own food safety and assure buyers of traceability back to their farms. These actions have a single goal: to lower transaction costs by providing buyers with the information they need in order to meet importers' food safety standards.

Julius Juma Okell, Clare Narrod, and Devesh Roy, "Food Safety Requirements in African Green Bean Exports and Their Impact on Small Farmers," International Food Policy Research Institute Discussion Paper 00737, December 2007; http://www.ifpri.org/sites/default/files/publications/ifpridp00737.pdf

Information is critical to making other markets work. Without the certification that a fruit or vegetable was organically grown, who would be willing to pay the higher price to "buy organic?" Certification is the key to green, eco-friendly labeling. The same goes for any quality standard. The US Department of Agriculture enforces quality standards for agricultural products; no meat packing plant is without its USDA inspector or its inspection stamps. These activities not only protect consumer health but also create information vital to making markets work.

All the Apples in China

In March 2011, Apple Corp.'s CEO, Timothy Cook, head of the biggest corporation in the world, took an unprecedented step: He toured one of his main supplier's plants in China, Foxconn, to witness working conditions there. There is little danger that the market for Apple's products would collapse because consumers are worried about unfair labor practices in China, but the threat was real enough to catch Apple's eye. The Fair Labor Association, a non-profit consortium of universities, civil service organizations, and private companies, certifies that its member companies and their suppliers comply with national and international labor laws. Its monitoring includes independent and unannounced audits of factories abroad. Its efforts are not without controversy, but without independent monitoring and certification, the information needed to create a "market for fair labor practices" would not exist.

"Apple's Chief Visits iPhone Factory in China," by Kevin Drew, *The New York Times*, March 29, 2012; http://www.nytimes.com/2012/03/30/technology/apples-chief-timothy-cook-visits-foxconn-factory.html

---

In a striking example of the power of information and uncertainty, beef consumption in Japan fell 60% after the first case of mad cow disease was reported there in 2001. The vast majority of beef in Japan was free of the disease, of course, but without access to information about *which* meat was mad-cow free, the market reeled. The Japanese beef market recovered once the country began testing *all* of its cows.

Apple Inc. was so worried about labor certification that it sent its CEO to China (see box: "All the Apples in China").

Information asymmetries can easily shut small farmers out of domestic markets as well as international markets. Consider a poor farmer who can produce high-quality berries at a low price. In town, exporters are willing to pay 20 cents a basket for berries like the ones he can grow; however, poor roads and communications cut the farmer off from information about buyers: where to sell, when to sell, how to ensure quality, and the price the farmer might get once he transports his berries to the market. This makes marketing this perishable crop too expensive and risky. So the farmer produces a few baskets for his family's and maybe a few neighbors' consumption, and he spends the rest of his time doing low-wage work, when available, on a nearby ranch. A basket of berries costs him 10 cents to produce (including the cost of his time). Implicitly, then, this is his decision price, or the price at which he is willing to produce berries. If he could become part of the export supply chain, his decision price would increase to the market price. He could be more efficient, shifting some or all of his time from low wage work to berry production, and he would have an incentive to invest in his farm. Most importantly, he could generate badly needed cash for his family.

In this age of the supermarket revolution, getting small farmers into the Walmart supply chain can be the key to raising agricultural incomes and reducing poverty. But transaction costs can easily make Walmart shut its doors on small farmers (see box: "Walmart in Nicaragua").

Walmart in Nicaragua

Many people think of supermarkets as the rich world's place to shop, but the rapid rise of supermarkets is transforming agricultural supply chains in Africa, Asia and Latin America. The supermarket explosion leaves development economists with big new questions. Can poor farmers make their way into the supply chains of Walmart and other major supermarket players, given the exacting standards they face? Or will the supermarket revolution pass them by and possibly leave them more marginalized than they were before?

An economist at Columbia University's Earth Institute set out to answer these questions by asking what determines whether small farmers become suppliers of food to Walmart, Nicaragua. This is a tricky question, because like in program evaluation (Chapter 11), unobservable variables may determine whether farmers participate in the Walmart supply chain, and they can easily confound estimates of how other things affect participation. The study followed the same farmers over time. It found that only farmers with advantageous access to roads and water are likely to participate in the Walmart supply chain.

This study is important because it identifies obstacles to small-farmer participation in the Walmart supply chain, including factors related to transaction costs.

Hope C. Michelson, "Small Farmers, NGOs, and a Walmart World: Welfare Effects of Supermarkets Operating in Nicaragua."*American Journal of Agricultural Economics* (in press, 2013; advance access at http://ajae.oxfordjournals.org/content/early/2013/01/07/ajae.aas139.full).

We can use diagrams to illustrate the efficiency loss from high transaction costs. The right side of Figure 9.7 illustrates equilibrium in the regional berry market. It determines the regional price of berries, p_r. On the left side we see the village berry market. Its equilibrium price, p_v, is determined by village supply and demand. Here, $p_r > p_v$, so the farmer would like to sell into the regional market, getting p_r and producing Q_r.

In order to sell in the regional market, though, she'll have to incur a transaction cost equivalent to $t per unit sold. You can imagine the high cost of transporting the berries over bad roads, and before that, whatever costs in money and time she has to incur to travel to town, find out about prices there, and arrange the sale (a cell phone might help). Then there's always a risk that, once she delivers the berries to the market, the buyer will change his mind and decide not to buy (an enforceable contract would help). Market uncertainty adds what economists call a "risk premium" to t. You can think of it as the amount the farmer would be willing to pay to insure against the possibility of the sale falling through. When you talk to farmers in poor villages, these are the sorts of things they mention when explaining why they do not sell in outside markets.

Given these transaction costs, the farmer's net price will be $(1-t)p_r$. In our diagram, this is less than the village price. Faced by high transaction costs, then, the farmer is better off producing less (Q_v) and selling only in the village. In doing so, she loses profit (producer's surplus) equal to the shaded area A of the trapezoid in the next figure.

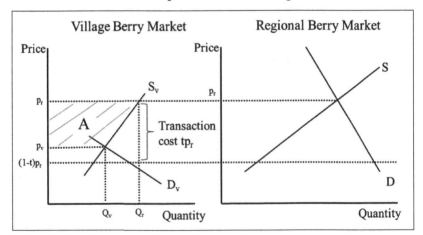

Figure 9.7: When transaction costs cut producers off from higher prices in outside markets, producer surplus falls (area A). Consumer surplus rises, but not by enough to compensate for the fall in producer surplus.

Microeconomics courses teach that firms optimize by producing where their marginal cost (MC) equals the output price, or equivalently, where each input is used at the point where its marginal value product just equals its price. Consumers do something similar by demanding goods at the level where their marginal rate of substitution (MRS, the slope of the indifference curve or ratio of marginal utilities any two goods create) just equals the ratio of prices.

If everyone bases their decisions on the same prices, things cannot be any more efficient. The MC will be the same for all producers (and equal to the output price). The marginal rate of substitution will be the same for all consumers (equal to the ratio of prices).

As you can see in the preceding diagram, though, when there are high transaction costs different producers face different prices and thus produce at different MCs. Recall that the supply curve *is* the marginal cost curve. The farmers who supply the regional market produce at a MC equal to p_r, whereas the village farmer produces at a MC equal to p_v. The same thing happens to consumers: they equate their marginal rates of substitution with the ratio of the prices they face, which may be very different from the prices others face.

When this happens, efficiency could be increased—dramatically, perhaps—by reducing or eliminating transaction costs, so that trade can equalize prices across markets. Remember this—it is the fundamental problem that high transaction costs create in poor economies: market failure occurs when economic actors are unable to get together to make efficiency-enhancing trades. Transaction costs resulting from imperfect information are a major reason why this happens. (Another is civil strife, like in the example from Tigray at the start of this chapter.)

When transaction costs cause prices to vary across space, a cell phone can literally keep food from rotting on the vine—or fish from rotting on the beach (see box: "Saving Fish with Cell Phones").

So can other innovative solutions aimed at lowering transaction costs. Here's one, inspired by the U.S. fast-food revolution:

 A Subway-inspired model to deliver healthcare in Kenya.

So far we've focused on the effects of transaction costs in output markets. Asymmetric information and high transaction costs can also shut farmers out of input markets. When a farmer cannot get fertilizer or hire labor at the times needed or be sure of input quality, less land may be sown, output may fall, and more productive technologies may not be adopted. Efficiency is critical, because even a small income gain can make a huge difference for an impoverished household.

Asymmetric Information in Labor Markets

Anyone who has taken microeconomics knows the solution to the labor-hiring problem: hire workers up to the point where their marginal value product (MVP) just equals the wage. The MVP is how much value (gross revenue) the last (marginal) worker will create. The wage is how much it will cost to hire him.

But how can we be sure that that last worker will really produce that MVP? Or the worker before him, for that matter? What if you hire him and he doesn't work hard, generating less revenue than the wage you have to pay him? This is called shirking, and it is a form of moral hazard. An employer can deal with this problem by monitoring the workers they hire, just like a bank can monitor borrowers, but that's expensive.

Saving Fish with Cell Phones

People need price information in order to trade efficiently. In Kerala, India, more than one million people fish. While at sea, fishermen can't observe prices at markets along the coast. Transportation costs are high, and fish are perishable. This keeps fishermen from moving from port to port looking for the best price once their boats are full. Thus, almost all fishermen sell their catch locally, and this can create a surplus of fish in some places—in fact, the price of fish can drop all the way to zero. When that happens, fish literally are left to rot. Meanwhile, just down the coast, people in other towns might be happy to pay a good price for this fish. If only the fishermen had known—they could have chosen to put in their boats down the coast, instead.

Between 1997 and 2001, mobile phone service was introduced in Kerala. Robert Jenson hypothesized that this could be very good for fishermen and consumers—not to mention the fish. He gathered data on the ups and downs of fish prices along the coast both before and after the introduction of cell phones. His analysis found that mobile phones dramatically reduced price variability and waste and raised fishermen's profits as well as consumers' welfare. Since improvements in market efficiency can benefit all market participants, even fishermen without cell phones were better off when some of their fellow fishermen started using them.

This study is a dramatic illustration of how the exchange of information via cell phones enabled fishermen to sell their catch where prices are high, leveling out price variability along the Kerala coast. Cell phones made the fish market work, and the market made people better off—while saving a whole lot of fish.

Robert Jensen, "The Digital Provide: Information (Technology), Market Performance, and Welfare in the South Indian Fisheries Sector," *The Quarterly Journal of Economics* CXXII(3), pp. 879-924, August, 2007.

There is also the possibility of adverse selection. Some workers are more productive than others. How do you know you'll end up with a "good" one—that is, a worker who produces a MVP higher than the wage? If the worker is a member of your own family, you'll have good information about him. If not, information may be asymmetric—the worker knows how good he is, but you do not. It might be possible to overcome adverse selection by offering a wage higher than the going market wage in order to attract more productive workers. But this, like monitoring, is costly.

The costs of monitoring and screening workers are transaction costs in labor markets. The true cost of hiring a worker is the wage plus these transaction costs. If the transaction costs are high enough, the labor market will fail: no workers will be hired. Then producers are forced to use their own labor. If you can hire workers, it doesn't matter how big your family's labor endowment is—you simply hire up to the point where the MVP equals the market wage. If you can't, then how much you produce depends on how much family labor you have.

In a labor-constrained household, the "family shadow wage," or opportunity cost of family time, is high. (The family shadow wage is the wage you would be willing to pay if you could hire workers.) In a labor-abundant household, the family wage is low; the market failure traps labor in the household. In that case, you would be willing to work for a relatively low wage, but no one will hire you because of the asymmetric information problem: employers are not sure how productive you'll be.

If my shadow wage is low and yours is high, we could both be better off if I worked for you. You'd pay a wage lower than your reservation wage, and I'd get a wage higher than my reservation wage. If transaction costs in the labor market are high, though, the labor exchange won't take place.

There is a simple solution to the adverse selection and moral hazard problems in labor markets: pay workers a piece rate. It is common in both poor and rich countries to pay farm workers a flat cash amount per unit harvested: box, kilo, bundle, etc. Harvest workers in Mexico often are paid a share of the corn crop. Fishermen often pay their crew a share of the catch. California farmers pay strawberry pickers a piece rate per 12-pint tray during peak harvest periods.[5]

Piece rates have advantages and disadvantages. From the producer's point of view, they have the advantage of shifting all the risk associated with adverse selection and moral hazard onto the workers. Farmers know exactly how much it will cost to pick, say, a ton of peaches if they pay a piece rate, but not if they pay a wage. Piece rates have the disadvantage of encouraging workers to focus on quantity, not quality, for example, to pick as many peaches as possible but not worry about bruising them. Employers who pay piece rates thus have to be extra careful about monitoring quality, for example, by checking the fruit and docking workers for poor quality.

The piece-rate system ensures that workers get paid according to their productivity. Pick fast and your day's pay will be higher. Pick too slow and you might not have enough food to eat. This is good news for highly productive workers, but it obviously is a disadvantage for less-productive ones. Less productive workers may not be able to pick enough to cover their subsistence (or the minimum wage, if there is one). In California, farmers are required by law to pay all workers at least the minimum wage, even if they are not productive enough to "pick" the minimum wage. This shifts some of the risk associated with adverse selection and moral hazard back onto employers. While some kinds of work lend themselves to piece rates, others do not. It's easy to pay a piece rate to strawberry pickers, but what about workers in soil preparation, planting, or weeding?

Other Inputs

When people fact transaction costs in input markets, the price they pay for their inputs includes the cost of making the transaction. Adverse selection and moral hazard are not so much problems in the case of purchased inputs; the quality of fertilizer usually is pretty much known by everyone, and fertilizer—unlike workers—does not have a mind of its own and need to be monitored.

Other problems can create transaction costs and make inputs markets fail, though. Foremost among them is timing. Not having an input at the time it is needed often is as bad as not having it at all. Seed, fertilizer, insecticides, and herbicides all must be applied at just the right time or the farmer will risk losing their crop. Input markets have to work efficiently to make sure this happens, yet often they do not.

Poorly functioning input markets can even keep people from adopting more productive technologies. Green revolution (high-yielding) seeds were engineered to give high yields as long as complementary inputs, particularly fertilizer, are applied in a timely fashion. If a farmer is unsure that he'll be able to buy fertilizer at the moment it has to be applied, he may be better off not planting the high-yielding variety.

People could take measures to ensure that they have the inputs they need at the time they need them. For example, instead of investing their scarce cash in more productive activities, they could use it to stockpile fertilizer when they can get it, then let the fertilizer sit there until the time comes to apply it. Or they could invest time and money into searching out sources of inputs, from distant cities if needed. By taking steps like these, farmers could make sure they have the inputs they need at the time they are needed, but obviously these steps are costly. In the end, the effective price of fertilizer is the market price plus the transaction cost the farmer incurs to make sure he has the fertilizer when he needs it. That transaction cost may make all the difference (see box: "Nudging Poor Farmers to Use Fertilizer").

Nudging Poor Farmers to Use Fertilizer

Poor farmers in Africa do not use nearly enough fertilizer. For example, fertilizer use in sub-Saharan Africa was only 8 kg/ha in 2002, compared with 101 kg/ha in South Asia. Such massive disparities in fertilizer use between Africa and the rest of the world suggest that there are structural impediments limiting fertilizer availability and demand. It is very unlikely that African farmers are applying fertilizer at a level that equates its marginal value product with the world price. They act as though the price of fertilizer is much higher than the price in the market. Why the disparity?

One possibility is that poor farmers simply don't have the cash. Three economists offered a different explanation: timing. Even poor farmers who are willing to pay the market price for fertilizer cannot be sure they'll be able to get the fertilizer they need when they need it.

In a clever experimental study in Kenya, some farmers were offered free fertilizer delivery early in the season and others not, while still others were offered a fertilizer subsidy. (Economic experiments like this one are the subject of Chapter 11.) The study found that offering delivery early was more effective at increasing fertilizer use than was a subsidy.

Esther Duflo, Michael Kremer and Jonathan Robinson, "Nudging Farmers to Use Fertilizer: Evidence from Kenya." *American Economic Review,* 101(6): 2350–90, 2011.

The Role of Government

We conclude this chapter with some thoughts about the role of government in a world of asymmetric information and market failures.

Economists almost uniformly agree that markets are crucial to people's welfare. Free-market economists believe that the free functioning of markets, without government intervention, leads to the greatest common good, often citing Adam Smith's reference to "an invisible hand." This belief is an underpinning of free-trade agreements and market reforms in LDCs. The fundamental theorem of welfare economics states that competitive markets lead to a "first best" allocation of resources that is *Pareto efficient*; that is, nobody can be made better off without someone else being made worse off.

The fundamental theorem does not necessarily hold when markets are incomplete or information is imperfect—two common features of LDC economies. We have seen that there are many cases in which there is no market, and we will see still others in the next chapter ("Credit and Risk"). In such an environment, there is no first-best outcome. A government hands-off or *laissez-faire* approach to markets is not likely to be optimal. The question is no longer whether governments should be involved in markets, but how much. As the Nobel laureate economist Joseph Stiglitz wrote:[6]

> Free markets, by themselves, often do not lead to what is best... the reason that the invisible hand often seems invisible is that it is often not there...The real debate today is about finding the right balance between the market and government.

One does not have to reject market economics to recognize situations in which governments should become involved in markets. One of these is the provision of information, which can lower transaction costs for everyone. Governments around the world have statistical bureaus that gather information and make it publically available.

There are other instances in which a strong case can be made for government intervention in markets:

- *Externalities:* when the actions of an individual have bad (or good) impacts on others for which the individual doesn't pay (or get compensated). Externalities are crucial in environmental economics. Markets, left to themselves, produce too much air and water pollution (which harms people who breathe the air or drink the water), too little research (which creates public benefits), too little education (my education can make other workers more productive), too few bee hives (bees pollinate peach orchards), too much global warming (how much carbon did you put into the atmosphere today?)—and yes, too little information. (How do you turn a profit selling information in a poor village?).

  Yet another negative externality is trash, which sadly is a pervasive feature of developing-country landscapes. How do you create a market for trash? India's ragpickers have an answer—with a little help from an NGO.

  Turning garbage into high fashion.

- *Public goods:* roads, marketing infrastructure, communications, police and fire fighting—these are public goods that create benefits for society that are difficult for private investors to capture; thus, there are not likely to be enough of them unless governments get involved. A classic case is firefighting. If fire departments were private, I might pay for fire protection but my neighbor might not. Yet if her house catches fire, the fire fighters will have to put it out in order to save my house—a classic free-rider problem.

- *Market power*: the welfare gains from markets depend on competition. When someone gains too much market power, either as a seller or buyer, the fundamental theorem breaks down. This is the justification for anti-trust legislation.

On the other hand, just because a market doesn't work well does not mean the government should fix it. There are many problems out there competing for scarce public funds. Is fixing a particular market failure the best use of scarce public resources?

Picture a poor isolated village facing high transaction costs. The government could build a new road there and put in a cell-phone tower, but the same money could be used to provide credit to poor farmers or schools or health care for their children. Policymakers, like poor people, often face cruel tradeoffs.

In addition to having access to inputs at the time and place needed, people need to have the cash to pay for them. This is especially important in agriculture, because farmers must purchase inputs months before the harvest. They also need a way to get food on the table if the crop fails.

That's where credit and risk come in. They are the subject of our next chapter.

Chapter Nine Notes

1. Akerlof, George A., "The Market for 'Lemons': Quality Uncertainty and the Market Mechanism." Quarterly Journal of Economics, 84(3), pp. 488-500, 1970.

2. George A. Akerlof, Writing the "The Market for 'Lemons'": A Personal and Interpretive Essay; http://www.nobelprize.org/nobel_prizes/economics/laureates/2001/akerlof-article.html

3. http://www.fda.gov/Food/InternationalActivities/ucm212024.htm

4. European Commission, "Health and Consumers," http://ec.europa.eu/food/food/chemicalsafety/residues/third_countries_en.htm.

5. "Labor: U.S. Fruits and Vegetables," *Rural Migration News*, January 2011 Volume 17 Number 1; http://migration.ucdavis.edu/rmn/more.php?id=1596_0_5_0.

6. Altman, Daniel. Managing Globalization. In: Q & Answers with Joseph E. Stiglitz, Columbia University and *The International Herald Tribune*, October 11, 2006.

10.

Credit and Risk

There is a good chance that you bought this book with a credit card, have a savings account, an ATM card, maybe a student loan. Yet well over half of the world's population does not participate in financial markets. Nearly all of the world's financially unserved adults live in Africa, Asia, or Latin America. In Kenya, Pakistan, and Nicaragua, fewer than one in five people use financial services of any kind, either as savers or borrowers.[1]

Without access to financial markets, people can still save, but they have to find ways to do it that don't involve banks or other financial institutions. For example, instead of putting their savings into an account that will give them a sure return, they might just have to buy a goat (see box: "Saving for a Rainless Day").

Saving for a Rainless Day

In the West African semi-arid tropics, poor households engage in rainfed agriculture in a drought-prone environment. Most lack access to credit or insurance to see them through when the rains don't come. Without other alternatives, animals are both the bank and the insurance company. In good years, households invest in animals, and in bad years they sell off animals in an effort to keep food on the table, like taking money out of the bank.

But a study by three development economists found that this is a far-from-perfect way of insuring against income shocks. The return to "livestock savings" is low if many people have to sell off animals at the same time to get through a drought. This study followed 631 Burkina Faso households over a period of four years that included a severe drought. It found that livestock sales play less of a consumption-smoothing role than expected. At most, sales of animals made up for fifteen to thirty percent of income shortfalls due to drought and other adverse shocks. Low prices from distress sales of livestock may make animals a poor way to save for a rainless day.

Marcel Fafchamps, Christopher Udry, and Katherine Czukas, "Drought and Saving in West Africa: Are Livestock a Buffer Stock?" *Journal of Development Economics* 55(2), April 1998, pp. 273–305.

Credit has three crucial roles in modern economies:

First, it allows you to get ahead (credit for investment). Borrowing money allows people with good ideas, skills, and other assets but who lack liquidity to make productive investments and raise income. Without credit, a farmer cannot purchase inputs ahead of the harvest (which she must do to get a good harvest), unless she has other sources of cash. A poor household cannot borrow to set up a small business—even if all this means is buying a sewing machine.

Second, it prevents you from falling behind (credit for consumption). Borrowing allows households that experience a negative income shock to maintain their consumption levels and assets, preserving their ability to produce income in the future. If the crop fails or a breadwinner becomes sick or injured, there is cash to see the family through. Credit is insurance, as anyone who has lost his job and used his credit cards to get through can attest.

Third, credit shifts risk from borrowers to lenders. Default clauses and liability rules define the conditions under which a borrower does not have to repay a loan. Because default is an option, loans shift risks from borrowers to lenders. Defaulting on a loan doesn't sound very nice, but actually default and bankruptcy play an important role in modern economies. By shifting risk from borrowers to lenders, credit can induce people to take out loans and make high-return, but risky, investments that they otherwise would not make. Any investor knows that high-return investments entail risk, and the higher the return, the more risk there is likely to be. Without risky investments, people are likely doomed to live in a low-return, low-income society.

Considering how important credit is, why don't more people have some? It's easy to buy a potato, but it's a lot harder to buy (most people would say "take out") a loan. The answer to this question comes right back to information. Credit is one of the most striking examples of how asymmetric information creates market failures.

Why Credit is Different from a Potato

When you buy a potato, the transaction is simultaneous: you pull the cash out of your purse or pocket, the vender hands you the potato. Usually, you and the seller agree on what you're getting. You can examine the potato to make sure it is fresh and firm. (As I write this I have just come back from the Berkeley farmer's market, where the peach venders offered samples just to make sure we knew how good they were!)

Credit is not like that, for several different reasons.

In a potato transaction, I pay and walk away with the potato, and after that, the vender and I can forget about each other. Credit involves an *inter-temporal* exchange. You loan me money today, I pay you back some time in the future. The lender gives up the use of the money in return for a promise to get the money back tomorrow. The borrower receives the money today in return for a promise to pay back the money tomorrow.

So, what's being transacted here? Promises, actually. The borrower is "selling" a promise that he will give the lender resources to use in the future. In return, he gets to use the resources today. The lender is "buying" this promise that the borrower will repay the loan in the future. In return, he gives up the use of the resources today.

If what's promised always happened, things would be simple and there would be a lot more credit in the world. In real life, though, repayment is uncertain. Borrowers face a variety of risks. Projects are risky: loans are used to up businesses that may or may not succeed or plant crops that fail if the rains don't come. A borrower may be unable to repay because of a variety of negative shocks—not only bad weather or a recession, but illness or injury that keeps him from turning the loan into the income he'll need in order to repay.

These kinds of uncertainties pose challenges to credit transactions, but they don't necessarily kill the deal. If lenders can correctly evaluate the risk of each borrower, they can cover for this risk by charging higher interest rates. High-risk borrowers would pay a higher interest rate than low-risk ones. The credit market could work just fine; borrowers, on average, could make a profit off their loans.

Credit and Asymmetric Information

Unfortunately, evaluating credit risk is hard to do.

Take you, for instance. There's a good chance you're reading this book because you're a student. Suppose you want to take out a student loan. You promise you'll pay it back once you're out of school and working. Should the bank say "take the money?"

Not so quick. From the bank's point of view, your repayment risk is uncertain because of things it cannot even see (maybe because you don't want it to!).

First, the risk depends on who you are, that is, your intrinsic characteristics. The bank can observe some of these. For example, it can verify that you're a student in good standing—a proof of enrollment and transcript will do. It can't see other things about you, though. How smart are you, really? And how driven to succeed? Making it to college is a good signal about your innate abilities, but how will that translate into labor market success, which is what you'll have to have in order to repay a student loan?

Strike 1 against getting a student loan.

Then there's the nature of the investment, itself. Your investment is in human capital. Is it a good investment? The bank would like to know that. It knows (from studies economists have done) that higher education translates into higher earnings for people in the workforce. (If you've ever taken an econometrics class, you may have estimated the economic returns to schooling, which usually come in at around a 7-percent earnings gain per year of additional schooling.)[2]

That's an average, though. Does it represent you? Maybe the field you decide to invest in won't be so marketable once you get out of school. In 2012, there was such a glut of lawyers that recent law grads sued their law schools for fraudulently marketing the profession as a secure source of employment. (The New York Supreme Court ruled that they couldn't.)[3]

Strike 2 against getting your loan.

Then there's the question of whether you'll behave or not. Your actions will determine the likelihood of paying back your loan. What choices will you make? Will you study hard and wisely use your loan to position yourself for labor-market success? And if there is life after graduation, will you choose to repay the loan when you are able? These are definitely concerns to lenders.

That's strike 3. You're out!

You're a lot like a poor farmer in this respect: who you are and what you do will shape your likelihood of repayment, and information about you is asymmetric. There are many intrinsic things about you that the bank *can't* see but you *can*, things that might well affect your ability to repay, positively or negatively. You probably know yourself pretty well, but the bank doesn't. You know more about your human capital investment project, too. And you can decide your own behavior, but the bank can't observe it until it might be too late.

Actually, the bank could get a lot of this information if it really wanted to. It could find out more about you, learn more about how your major and college are likely to affect your job prospects. It could even hire a private investigator to follow you around and make sure you study hard. Besides being kind of creepy, that would be expensive—so expensive that the bank would never do it. So the problem with asymmetric information is not that the bank can't get the information; it would simply cost a lot to get it. This is an example of a transaction cost: the cost of getting the information the bank requires before it will give you a loan. Transaction costs tend to be very high in credit markets (and even higher in insurance markets, as we'll see below).

If you've got a student loan, it's almost certainly government-guaranteed. That means the government has agreed to repay your loan if you fail to. That's what the banks demand in order to take on an investment as risky as you! If you didn't know before why student loans are government-backed, now you do.

Time, uncertainty, and information asymmetries imply that credit transactions require contracts—not necessarily written ones, as many villagers around the world know, but contracts nonetheless. You don't need a contract to buy a potato! Information flow is critical. So is legal enforcement of the contract. Without the ability to enforce the loan contract, the loan won't happen.

All this means that *institutions* play a *key* role in making credit markets work: the legal system, to enforce contracts; credit bureaus, to provide lenders with information about people's credit-worthiness, and property registries, to verify that the owners of property purchased with (or used to secure) credit are who they say they are.

In 2001, three economists—George Akerlof, Joseph Stiglitz, and Michael Spence—won the Nobel prize for their roles in creating the field of information economics. They and others have given us a powerful framework for understanding imperfections and failures in many markets where contracts are critical. Their work centers around two notions: adverse selection and moral hazard. Both are intimately related to asymmetric information. They explain why credit markets (and often other markets) don't work for most people in poor countries, and also why insurance markets are almost nonexistent. To understand why credit markets fail to meet the needs of poor people, we need to understand these notions of adverse selection and moral hazard.

Adverse Selection

Adverse selection is a situation in which "bad" outcomes happen because the seller has relevant information that the buyer lacks about some characteristic of the product being sold. In Akerlof's *Market for Lemons*, the seller is the used-car owner, and the relevant information is the car's quality. I've got a car I know is crummy, and I pretend it's a good car when I sell it to you. (Buyer, beware!)

The same thing can happen with crummy promises. In credit markets, the seller is the borrower; he sells the promise of repayment. He has better information about himself and his project—and thus his probability of default—than the lender does. The same problem arises in insurance markets: the insurer knows less than the insured. (That's why my insurance company gave me an EKG before it would issue me a life insurance policy. It wanted to be sure I wasn't hiding something!)

The borrower, or seller of the promise of future repayment, knows more about her own default probability than the lender does. Yet the quality of her promise depends on this default probability.

This has a huge implication for credit availability. If the demand for potatoes exceeds the supply, the vender raises the price of the potato. Everyone agrees there isn't enough credit out there to meet the demand—that's the big problem with credit in poor countries. You'd think banks would just raise the price of credit, the interest rate, and give out loans until the demand is met. Then there would be equilibrium in the credit market, and the equilibrium "price of promises" would be the interest rate.

Adverse selection keeps banks from doing this. By increasing the interest rate, lenders may adversely affect the quality of their applicant pool, and this would lower their profits. Think about it: suppose you're totally credit-worthy. You should be able to get a loan at a low interest rate, because your promise is good (that is, your risk of default is low). You are willing to take out a loan at a low interest rate, but not at a high one—those high-interest loans are for high-risk people, not you.

So what happens if banks raise their interest rate? High-quality borrowers like you "select themselves" out of the market. You're the seller of promises. If you've got good ones to sell, then having to pay a high interest rate means you're selling your promises too cheaply. It's just like owners of high-quality used cars leaving the market when the price of used cars goes down. Because of adverse selection, only low-quality cars are left in the used-car market. If the interest rate goes up high enough, only low-quality (high-risk) borrowers will be left in the credit market. You can see how the credit market, like the used car market, can easily fail when there is adverse selection.

Moral Hazard

The second big reason why credit markets fail is moral hazard. This is a situation in which the seller has relevant information that the buyer lacks about some *action* the seller takes that affects product quality.

In the Market for Lemons, knowing I'm going to sell my used car, I might not bother to take care of it, because it's unlikely the buyer will know. (That's why some people demand to see service records on the used cars they buy.)

In the world of credit, borrowers take actions that affect the quality of the promises they make, but the bank cannot see these actions. Credit shifts risk from borrowers to lenders. Consider this agricultural loan contract:

Repay if the harvest is successful, default (pay nothing) if the harvest fails.

This contract creates a disincentive for borrowers to take on "safe" projects, that is, ones with a high probability of success. A safe project might mean working hard and using seeds I'm pretty sure will give me a decent harvest, even if the weather is not great. An unsafe one might use a seed that *could* perform *really well* but only if the weather is perfect, which is unlikely in my village.

If my project fails, the worst that can happen to me is that I'll default on the loan, so I'll go for the unsafe project, knowing that if it does succeed I'll make a killing. The bank hopes a farmer who takes out a loan will buy seed, fertilizer and other inputs that (weather permitting) will enable her to repay the loan after the harvest. But it knows the farmer *could* gamble on a risky seed. She could even use the money for something else, like play the lottery. (You could do that with your student loan, too.)

The higher the interest rate, the more of a gain I'll have to make to cover the loan and come out ahead, so the more likely I'll go for the high-risk, high-payoff investment. Thus, moral hazard, like adverse selection, can make lenders unwilling to raise interest rates and make loans even if there is excess demand for credit.

In short, borrowers have greater information than lenders—information that affects the probability of involuntary as well as voluntary default. Borrowers know themselves, their projects, and the actions they take. If lenders raise the interest rate, they cause good types of borrowers to drop out of the market (adverse selection). They also can cause borrowers to take actions that the lender doesn't like, for example, choosing a risky technique (moral hazard). Lenders would have to charge a high interest rate to cover the risks of default caused by adverse selection and moral hazard, but if the interest rate is too high, the market collapses.

In economics we're accustomed to thinking that the quantity of a product depends on its price. When it comes to credit, though, the quality of customers and their actions depends on the price (the interest rate), too.

When credit markets fail, profitable investments don't happen, and poor people stay poor. Research by development economists documents how big a difference credit can make (see box: "Credit and Productivity in Peru").

Solving Adverse Selection and Moral Hazard

History provides frightening examples of illegitimate measures taken to overcome the problems of moral hazard and adverse selection, as anyone who has seen the Hollywood film "The Godfather" knows. (Even today, mafias and loan sharks have effective ways to make borrowers pay back their loans.)

There are two kinds of *legitimate* mechanisms that lenders can use to try to resolve the problems of adverse selection and moral hazard: indirect mechanisms involving the terms of contracts, and direct mechanisms, or actions that address information asymmetries.

Indirect Mechanisms

Credit contracts can include many different terms. The most obvious one is the interest rate. We've already seen that if lenders set the interest rate too high they may lose quality borrowers and encourage borrowers to take riskier actions. By carefully adjusting the interest rate, a lender can partially control both adverse selection and moral hazard.

A second indirect mechanism involves the loan size. A lender could start out by offering a borrower a small loan. If it is repaid, he can offer the borrower larger and larger loans—like when the bank raises the limit on your credit card. This is called progressive lending. It addresses adverse selection by enabling the lender to cheaply identify really bad types (they default on the small loans). It addresses moral hazard because the promise of larger future loans gives the borrower an incentive to behave well (repay). An obvious problem here is that the larger the loan, the greater the incentive to misbehave (moral hazard). A bad guy could behave well, maximize his credit line, then "cash out" by defaulting.

Credit and Productivity in Peru

Estimating how credit affects production is tricky, because the kinds of people who get credit are different from the people who do not. For example, more productive farmers are probably more likely to succeed in getting credit. So if we find that farmers with credit are more productive, is it because of the credit or because productive farmers are the ones who get credit in the first place?

There are two main ways to get at this question using econometrics: first, control for the characteristics that determine whether farmers are credit constrained or not, and second, track the same farmers over time. Catherine Guirkinger and Steve Boucher did both, using what is called "switching regression" and data from a survey of farmers they carried out in Northern Peru. Their analysis found that credit constraints lowered the value of agricultural output in the study area by 26 percent. This study was important because it documented the importance of credit for productivity while controlling for who gets credit and who doesn't.

Catherine Guirkinger and Stephen R. Boucher, Credit Constraints and Productivity in Peruvian Agriculture, *Agricultural Economics* 39 (3), pp. 295-308, November 2008.

Indirect mechanism number three is the threat of termination. If a borrower defaults, the bank denies future access to loans. This addresses moral hazard, by providing incentives for borrowers to behave well or else risk termination. A problem with this mechanism is that you probably do not have access to information from other lenders who may have terminated someone who applies for a loan from you. That's why credit agencies were created: to provide lenders with credit information about you before they give you a loan. You won't find many of them in poor rural areas, though. Another problem is that default may be legitimate: even quality borrowers make investments that fail sometimes. That's what business bankruptcy laws were created for, but you will not find this institutional development in most parts of the world, either.

A fourth loan-contract term to make credit markets work is collateral; that is, requiring borrowers to secure the loan with personal property like land or a house, which the lender can foreclose upon in the event of default. Collateral addresses adverse selection: risky types won't apply for a loan because the probability of losing their collateral will be too high. It addresses moral hazard: the threat of foreclosure creates incentives for borrowers to behave well so they can repay their loans and keep their house.

Collateral requirements create other problems, though, particularly in poor societies. Many people do not have the collateral required to secure a loan. Institutions and laws may not make it feasible for lenders to foreclose on lenders who default. For example, many small farmers do not have formal title to their land. For collateral to work, property rights must be well defined and easily transferable. Titled land, a house, a business, jewelry, machines, vehicles, or a standing crop (harvest) are good candidates for use as collateral. The value of the collateral must not be subject to moral hazard. (I could trash my house or run off with my jewels before the bank takes them.) The property must be immobile (like a house) or else really small, so that the lender can hold it (a diamond ring). Collateral also creates risk rationing: people with good projects may not undertake them because collateral-based contracts force them to bear too much risk. I want to invest in a business, but I won't risk my house for it.

Collateral requirements are generally not a good way to get credit to poor people, who do not have many assets. The assets poor people have may be unacceptable to banks. The transaction costs of posting collateral are high. Even if they have some assets that banks accept, poor people may be unwilling to risk using them as collateral.

Collateral requirements affect the demand for credit as well as the supply. A poor person may not have credit because she tried to get it but was denied (supply rationing), she was unwilling to pay the high interest rate (price rationing), or she didn't apply because she was unwilling to put her collateral at risk (demand rationing).

Direct Mechanisms

Contractual terms to deal with adverse selection and moral hazard are what we call indirect mechanisms. They are indirect because they try to influence what kinds of people apply for loans (selection) and their behavior once they get a loan (moral hazard). Lenders can also try to deal with adverse selection and moral hazard directly, by screening applicants ex-ante and monitoring them ex-post. Direct mechanisms, like indirect ones, can take many forms.

Ex-ante, loan officers can require would-be borrowers to fill out loan application forms, documenting their income and assets and providing other information critical to screening. They can require loan applicants to submit investment plans showing the project for which the loan will be used is viable. They can directly inspect applicants' farms, businesses, and assets to make sure they are good enough to use as collateral. A loan officer might interview family members and neighbors to learn about the applicant's personal integrity, work ethic, reliability, and other characteristics that otherwise would be invisible to the lender. If a credit bureau exists, the loan officer almost certainly will buy information about the applicant's credit history. This last step can be crucial, because it provides information on the applicant's performance on loans from other lenders, which almost certainly would not be known otherwise.

This all sounds like a lot of snooping around, and it is. But borrowers put up with this sort of thing all the time in order to get a loan. Lenders incur the costs of screening in order to get the best applicants.

These ex-ante measures deal mostly with the adverse selection problem. However, they also can address moral hazard, for example, by screening out the applicants most likely to shirk or misbehave once they have a loan.

Ex-post, lenders can take direct actions to increase the likelihood of repayment. They can visit borrowers and their farms or businesses to make sure the loan funds are being used properly and check on the progress of the project. Is the business being run efficiently? Are the fields being carefully tended? If the loan is for crop production, a loan officer might well show up just before the harvest—not a bad strategy given that the loan repayment is sitting out in the field! (Pretending you have a smaller harvest than you do to avoid repayment is a great example of moral hazard.)

Direct and indirect measures like these can go a long way towards resolving the problems of adverse selection and moral hazard. However, they are costly; information is not free. The value of the time loan officers invest in screening applicants and monitoring borrowers can add considerably to the cost of loans. These are classic examples of transaction costs, not unlike the transaction costs of marketing green beans to Europe (see box in Chapter 9). They make the transaction more expensive, and if high enough, they keep the transaction from happening. Without them, though, information asymmetries may shut down the market altogether.

Given the high transaction costs of overcoming information problems in credit markets, it is little wonder that formal lenders do not serve poor people or, for that matter, farmers or entrepreneurs who are not poor but small. If you're a lender, and you have to incur these transaction costs no matter who you lend to, clearly you're better off making a few big loans than many little ones.

The Micro-credit Revolution

That's where micro-credit comes in. Micro-credit is the provision of very small (micro) loans, typically less than US$100, by lending institutions. Micro-credit institutions focus on people near or below the poverty line who have been excluded from the formal credit market (that is, banks). They also lend to micro-entrepreneurs, people with small-scale (typically informal) businesses. Micro-loans usually are made without collateral.

Wait a minute, you might say. Isn't this a set-up for failure? Banks don't loan to poor people and small businesses because of the high transaction costs of overcoming adverse selection and moral hazard. Demanding collateral is a critical tool to ensure repayment. Why would a micro-credit institution think it could pull off something that well-staffed banks—not to mention well-funded government credit programs—have failed miserably at?

Actually, making small loans to low-income people and micro businesses is not new. Informal village moneylenders have been doing it profitably for centuries, usually at very high interest rates. What do they know that we don't?

Seeing local moneylenders thrive in villages that banks will not touch seems puzzling. But clearly there's a lesson here, and in the past couple of decades economists, micro-credit instions, and governments have begun to catch on. If banks won't make small loans to poor people, the transaction costs of doing so must be high for banks. If local moneylenders *do* make small loans to poor people, they must have figured out a way to overcome the problems of adverse selection and moral hazard, and at a low enough cost to turn a profit.

In 1976, the Bangladeshi Muhammed Yunnis, third of nine children and son of a jeweler, began working with poor women who made bamboo furniture with usurious loans in the village of Jobra, near the university where he lectured in economics. Three decades later, in 2006, he (together with the Grammeen Bank he founded) received the Nobel Peace Prize. The Nobel Committee declared:

> Muhammad Yunus… managed to translate visions into practical action for the benefit of millions of people, not only in Bangladesh, but also in many other countries. Loans to poor people without any financial security had appeared to be an impossible idea. From modest beginnings three decades ago, Yunus has, first and foremost through Grameen Bank, developed micro-credit into an ever more important instrument in the struggle against poverty.

Yunus figured out how to solve the asymmetric-information problem (see box).

By 2010 the Grameen Bank had a total loan portfolio of $939 million, 8.3 million active borrowers with an average loan of $113. The vast majority of its borrowers are women. Repayment rates are claimed to be 95 percent.

The Grameen Bank's methodology has been replicated and spread throughout the world, including the United States. Yunus became an international micro-credit phenomenon, appearing on *The Daily Show with Jon Stewart* (2006), the *Oprah Winfrey Show* (2006), the *Colbert Report* (2008), and *The Simpsons* (2010). Texas named a holiday after him. The United Nations declared 2005 as the "International Year of Microcredit."

 One rural Bangladeshi woman's Grameen Bank story.

Muhamad Yunus and the Grameen Bank

The Bangladeshi economist Muhamad Yunus had an answer: Design a system in which local information and monitoring could make loans viable. While visiting some of the poorest village households in India, he realized that very small loans could make a big difference. In the village of Jobra, women made bamboo furniture but had to pay usurious interest rates on loans to buy bamboo. Yunus' first loan, out of his own pocket in 1976, was for US$27, but it wasn't to a single individual; it was to 42 women!

What was Yunus' secret to solving the moral hazard and adverse selection problems?

Informal groups of women apply for loans. They know each other. The group's members act as co-guarantors of repayment. If one member fails to do what she needs to do to pay back her part of the loan, the rest of the group has to pay or else loses the chance to get loans in the future. The group, therefore, has a vested interest in seeing to it that every member of the group succeeds. That means monitoring and supporting one another—just what is needed to overcome moral hazard. What about adverse selection? Well, who would *you* choose to have in your group?

Yunus turned micro-credit into a viable business model, which has spread around the world. That's why the Nobel Committee recognized his contribution to humanity by awarding him the Peace Prize in 2006.

Micro-credit in Theory and Practice

Grameen-style micro-credit addresses asymmetric-information problems in two ways.

First, through self-selection into borrower groups. To take out a Grameen loan, people have to get together and form a borrower group. The loan goes to the borrower group then is dispersed to individuals within the group. Loan repayments are made jointly, by the group, and with high frequency. If one member does not repay, the entire group is denied access to loans in the future. This is called *joint liability*. Thus, the group has to make sure each of its members pays back her loan—or else cover for members who do not repay.

Who, then, would you have in your group? Clearly, you should admit only good types of borrowers into your group. Since you live in the same village, you probably have pretty good information about who those people are. This addresses the adverse-selection problem. Group monitoring, to make sure each member repays, addresses the moral hazard problem. Together, they make the group loan a low-risk investment for the micro-credit institution, which thus can charge an interest rate low enough to keep the good types in the market. Micro-credit solves the adverse selection and moral hazard problems by taking advantage of borrowers' information about each other, and also by designing contracts to give borrowers incentives to overcome the asymmetric information problems that banks cannot overcome.

Development is not easy, and there are plenty of challenges and critiques when it comes to micro-credit which make some observers feel that the promise of micro-credit is overblown.

First, it's hard to implement a successful micro-credit scheme. For every Grameen-style success, there are ten failures! A lack of human capital, administrative expertise to build a micro-finance institution, and corruption all are major obstacles to successful micro-credit programs.

Second, it's expensive. Average interest rates on micro-credit loans are in the 30 to 40 percent range.

Third, most successful micro-credit programs have had subsidies—sometimes large ones—to help them get started. The cost of these subsidies often is not factored in when people gage the success of micro-credit programs. This raises the question: Is micro-credit the best use of scarce public money?

Fourth, micro-credit programs are vulnerable to *covariate shocks*, which are unexpected events affecting many people in a locality at the same time. An example is a drought or flood, which affects everyone in a locale, as opposed, say, to a health shock that affects a single individual. When covariate shocks negatively affect many group members at the same time, it is unlikely that the group will be able to repay its loan. Large banks and insurance companies cover themselves for multivariate shocks by making loans over a large geographic area instead of focusing on individual locations. Even so, covariate risks can kill a deal even in rich economies, as anyone who's tried to get earthquake insurance in California can attest!

Fifth, micro-credit programs have a built-in problem of borrower "graduation." Good types of borrowers often don't need micro-credit anymore once they've succeed in "getting ahead." This tends to drain credit groups of their lowest-risk members over time, which can make it hard for groups to remain viable and repay future loans.

Finally, as with any development project, there is the big question of whether micro-credit is the best way to use scare resources, including the money and efforts of international development agencies and local governments. Does it address the deeper, structural causes of poverty? Inequality, lack of infrastructure, poor educational systems, poor health care systems—these are all critical issues that need to be addressed by development policies. Micro-credit obviously is not a cure-all for these problems, but it has become an essential part of the development economist's toolkit.

Asymmetric Information in Other Markets

Output and credit markets provide many instances in which information problems can lead to market failure. We conclude this chapter by summarizing how asymmetric information can shut down insurance markets, and how this can lead to efficiency losses that keep poor people poor.

Insurance

There is nothing more important to poor people than the security of having food on the table. Without any way to smooth consumption, income shocks would translate directly into consumption shocks. We illustrate this in Figure 10.1 by graphing the hypothetical ups and downs of a family's income and consumption. You can see that the variation in income around its mean is high. In many years (six, to be exact), income is lower than the subsistence minimum needed for the family to survive. If consumption followed income exactly, this family would be in trouble.

How can a household decouple its consumption from its income enough to keep from falling below the subsistence minimum? Decoupling consumption from income is called *consumption smoothing*. There are two ways to smooth consumption: ex-ante and ex-post.

Ex-ante, a household can take steps to smooth out its income. For example, instead of specializing in a single source of income (say, a single cash crop), it can diversify its activities. It can put some land in cash crops, some in staples; some labor in crop production, some in wage work or migration. Ex-ante risk coping tries to compress the income profile in this figure, pulling the troughs up, but in the process almost certainly pushing the spikes downward (see box: "Why Poor People Pay a High Price for (Ex-ante) Insurance").

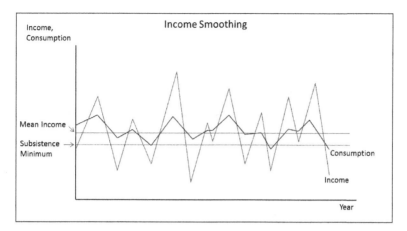

Figure 10.1. Consumption smoothing seeks to break the connection between consumption and income and keep households above their subsistence minimum even in bad years.

Why Poor People Pay a High Price for (Ex-ante) Insurance

A study of rural Indian households by Mark Rosenzweig and Hans Binswanger found that, in order to protect themselves against income uncertainty, poor households diversify their activities more than rich households. That way, for example, if the rains don't come and the crop fails, they'll have other activities to fall back upon. The authors found that in places with high climate risk, poor households diversify more. By diversifying, though, poor households forfeit the income gains from specializing in what they do best. The authors concluded that access to insurance could bring substantial economic benefits to rural households, especially the poor. A crop insurance policy guarantees that poor families will have food on their table even if the rains don't come, and this should make them more willing to plant crops, if that's what they do best.

Rosenzweig, Mark, and Hans Binswanger, "Wealth, Weather Risk, and the Consumption and Profitability of Agricultural Investments," *The Economic Journal* 103:56-78, 1994.

Ex-post, households can try to smooth their consumption given income swings like the ones shown in the figure. If households had access to formal insurance, this would be easy. They'd pay a premium (the price one pays to buy an insurance contract), which would bring down their income in good years. However, in bad years the policy would pay out, providing cash for consumption. Formal income insurance is virtually nonexistent in poor societies, though, for reasons we'll look at below.

How else can you smooth your consumption when income is so volatile? I use my credit card, but that isn't an option for a poor household in rural Malawi. We just saw why credit is so hard to come by. Poor people could save in good years and dis-save in bad ones, but that's harder said than done when there is no access to savings institutions.

In ancient times there were no banks, and people kept their savings for a rainy day in silver and gold coins, hidden away in a metal box. This was called "hoarding." Today ancient coin hoards are still found from time to time around the Mediterranean Sea. Behind every one of these uncovered hoards is a story, long lost, that no doubt would illustrate why hoarding is not a very good insurance strategy.

Without markets, households could use their money in good times to buy things they can sell off in hard times. Many poor people in rural areas use livestock as a bank. Distress sales of animals are a common feature of people trying to make it through an adverse shock, for example, a severe drought.

There are problems with selling off assets, though. One is the price: if you're selling because of a drought, there's a good chance other people are, too, so the price is likely to be low at just the wrong time. In a poor economy facing high transaction costs, cut off from outside markets, there's the question of whom to sell your assets to. The biggest problem is that once you sell off your assets you've lost the chance to use them to recover from the shock. Knowing that makes it hard to sell off that last animal (see box: "Holding on to the Last Cow (or Two)")

Credit and insurance often come up in the same breath when we talk about risk. The possibility of using credit or savings ("borrowing from yourself") to get through hard times makes credit and insurance close relatives when it comes to survival in poor societies.

Why Insurance Markets Fail

The same problems of adverse selection and moral hazard that constrain credit markets virtually prevent the formation of insurance markets in poor areas.

Adverse Selection

When a person takes out life or crop insurance, he buys a promise from the insurance company to "pay off" if he dies or the crop fails. He pays the insurance company the price of the policy (the policy premium) in return for this promise. The insurance company sells him the policy if his risk of death (or crop failure) is low enough that, on average, the company will make a profit. The higher the risk of death (or crop failure), the higher the premiums the insurance company will have to charge.

Holding on to the Last Cow (or Two)

When a covariate shock (for example, drought) or an idiosyncratic one (illness) strikes, one way to pull through is to sell off some assets—say, your animals—to keep up your consumption. That's called *consumption smoothing*, and it's what some households in the Sahel of Burkina Faso did in the 1984 drought. But what if you're down to your last couple animals—your breeding stock? Two UC Davis economists hypothesized that poor people may go to extremes to avoid selling off their last few assets. In other words, at some point they become *asset smoothers* instead of *consumption smoothers*.

Using panel data from Burkina Faso, Michael Carter and Travis Lybbert discovered that during the drought, people sold off their assets to keep food on the table—but only up to a point. People with few assets left were significantly less likely to sell. By holding on to their last few assets, poor people cling to the chance of being able to recover from the drought instead of falling into an "asset poverty trap" they might not be able to get out of. (We learned about poverty traps in Chapter 4.)

But there's a big catch. If holding onto those last assets means your family doesn't have enough food to eat, you may be trading off future human capital (the bodies and brains of your children, who cannot develop properly without food and thus may be less productive in the future) in order to hold onto your last remaining physical capital. A lack of insurance to protect assets leaves poor households with this cruel inter-temporal choice.

Michael R. Carter and Travis Lybbert, "Consumption Versus Asset Smoothing: Testing the Implications of Poverty Trap Theory in Burkina Faso," *Journal of Development Economics*, 99(2):255–264, 2012.

That's where adverse selection and moral hazard come in. People with a high risk of death or crop failure have more of an incentive to get insurance than people with a low risk. Often, the high-risk people know who they are, but the insurer does not. If I have a terminal disease, I will want life insurance. If I farm in a risky environment, I will want crop insurance. There's no reason to buy earthquake insurance on your house if you live in Kansas, but a big reason to if you live in San Francisco. In short, the kinds of people with the greatest incentive to get insurance are the worst bets for the insurance company. This drives the price of insurance upward. But as the insurance premium rises, low-risk people no longer find it advantageous to buy insurance. Only the high-risk types stay in the market.

Adverse selection is a big reason why insurance markets fail. They also explain why insurance companies test people and look at their medical records before selling them a life insurance policy, and why private health insurance is hard to get and often has exclusion clauses for "pre-existing conditions" (a practice not permitted under the new U.S. health reform law).

Moral Hazard

Once a person gets insurance, the moral hazard problem comes in. Knowing the insurer will pay off in the case of my crop failure, what incentive do I have to work hard in my field? Armed with a good life and health insurance policy, am I more inclined to take on risky behavior, like smoking or flying over the Himalayas in a hot-air balloon? With a good theft policy, I could sell my bike, declare it stolen, collect on insurance, and double my money (and hope no one catches me!).

As in the case of credit, insurers could invest in screening (getting information about how risky I am) and monitoring (making sure I work hard on my land); however, this is expensive. Screening and monitoring are part of the transaction cost of insurance. The rarity of insurance suggests that this cost is simply too high for formal insurance markets to form in most parts of the world.

Index Insurance

There is, in theory, a simple solution to both adverse selection and moral hazard in insurance: design the insurance policy so that its payout is completely independent of who demands insurance and how he behaves. That's what *index insurance* does. An index insurance policy pays out if some trigger goes off that has nothing to do with what the insured people do.

An example of an index trigger is a drop in your neighbors' yields, in the water level in the local irrigation reservoir, or in rainfall measured at a local weather station. Even if you choose a risky action or fail to work hard, you won't affect any of these indices, so your riskiness to the insurance company will not depend on who you are or what you do. If your yields tend to move up and down with the yields of others around you, though, index insurance can be valuable to you. It can also be profitable for an insurance company: knowing what the probability of the trigger event is, the company can price its product to make a profit, on average.

Access to index insurance might enable farmers to get bank credit and achieve higher crop yields. Imagine two farmers soliciting a loan, both farmers identical except that one has index insurance and the other does not. Which one would you give the loan to if you were the bank?

A trick is coming up with a good index. Satellites can help (see box: "Insuring with Satellites").

Insuring with Satellites

A big challenge in index insurance is how to come up with a good index. If there is no irrigation, you can't draw a line on the side of the irrigation reservoir. You could base the index on local rainfall data, but crop yields depend on when the rains come as well as how much rain there is. Ideally, the index would be based on whether overall yields, say, in a valley, drop enough to trigger an index insurance payout. But that would require annual yield surveys in the valley, which would be costly.

That's where satellites can help.

Satellite pictures provide a way to measure vegetation density, using the Normalized Difference Vegetation Index (NDVI). Every ten days NDVI is measured and freely available on the Family Early Warning System Network website, at a resolution of 8x8 kilometers. Rachid Laajaj and Michael Carter showed that the NDVI can be used to make an effective insurance index. In the region they studied in Burkina Faso, they showed that a satellite-based index captured 89 percent of the variance of village yields—much better than an index based on rainfall.

Rachid Laajaj and Michael Carter, 2009 "Using Satellite Imagery as the Basis for Index Insurance Contracts in West Africa," http://i4.ucdavis.edu/projects/contracts/files/laajaj-using-satelliteimagery.pdf

Government, Credit, and Risk

In light of the problems of adverse selection and moral hazard we have looked at in this chapter, it is little wonder that governments have had a poor record of solving credit market failures. India gives us a striking example: In 2008, the Finance Ministry had to forgive government loans to 40 million small and marginal farmers, at a cost of over US$15 billion. What went wrong? Asymmetric information. The government did not know the people it was lending to. This resulted in both moral hazard and adverse selection. By trying to address a credit market failure, India had a big-time policy failure on its hands.

That doesn't mean there isn't anything governments can do to address credit and insurance market failures. We have seen the importance of public goods to the functioning of credit markets, including titling of collateral, legal institutions to enforce credit contracts, and credit market information. These are likely to fall into the domain of the public sector. So is investment in public education to increase "financial human capital," including poor people's awareness of, and ability to use, financial institutions.

There may also be a role for subsidies to give poor people better access to financial institutions, particularly in rural areas. In Mexico, a relatively high-income developing country, 74 percent of all counties (*municipios*) had no bank branches in them at all in 2007. Not surprisingly, these are mostly rural counties, in which the transaction costs of offering banking services tend to be high.[4]

Public provision of weather and other geographic information system (GIS) information, not to mention satellite imagery, are critical to the functioning of index insurance schemes. Providing critical public goods can have positive repercussions that go well beyond credit and insurance markets.

Whatever policies are considered to provide credit and income security to poor people, it is important to keep in mind that the same problems that make markets fail in the first place are likely to hamper government efforts to correct market failures. This leaves us with the question: "What works and what doesn't?" It is the subject of our next chapter.

Chapter Ten Notes

1. Alberto Chaia, Aparna Dalal, Tony Goland, Maria Jose Gonzalez, Jonathan Morduch, and Robert Schiff, "Half the World is Unbanked," Financial Access Initiative Framing Note, October 2009; http://financialaccess.org/sites/default/files/110109%20HalfUnbanked_0.pdf

2. You can see a cool example in *Rebeltext: Essentials of Econometrics*, Chapter 7; rebeltext.org.

3. *Businessweek*, "Glut Leads Lawyers to (Surprise) Sued Law Schools," March 23, 2012, http://www.businessweek.com/articles/2012-03-23/glut-leads-lawyers-to-surprise-sue-law-schools.

4. J. Edward Taylor, Antonio Yúnez-Naude, and Alfredo González C., "Informe Consolidado: Estudios sobre Políticas Públicas para el Sector Rural en México," Report prepared for the Inter-American Development Bank and the Mexican government's Secretaría de Hacienda y Crédito Público, August 28, 2007.

11.

What Works and What Doesn't?

I've got allergies. Not the dangerous kind some people have from peanuts or bee stings, but the hay fever kind: sneezing, itchy eyes, congestion, and on bad pollen days, a grueling sinus headache now and then. Fortunately, there is a spray I can shoot up my nose that really helps. I'm sure of it. Well, I think so. Maybe. Alright, there are days when I use it and still feel pretty messed up, and other days when I don't use it but feel just fine.

The problem is, on spring days when puffballs of pollen float through the air like in a Fellini film, I don't know what *would* have happened if I *hadn't* sniffed the stuff. Those are the days I almost always use it. When I forget to, I can't be sure what would have happened if I *had* taken it.

To complicate matters, once I use that spray, I act differently. I feel like I can take on any allergen out there! I bicycle through the Davis countryside with the crops are in bloom. I sneeze from time to time, but that's because I'm really putting the sniffer to the test and it isn't supposed to work all the time. Right?

In 2011, international development agencies spent at least an estimated $US147.74 billion to solve problems far more serious than my allergies.[1] Trying to evaluate whether or not development programs work is a lot like figuring out whether my allergy medication works. Development programs are a treatment, and the problems they try to solve are like my allergic reaction to pollen.

Donors must have better ways of knowing whether their programs work than I have for nose spray, right?

Sadly, until fairly recently they did not. Development agencies' shelves and hard disks are filled with final reports concluding that the projects they funded were successful (usually) at achieving their stated goals. But it can be extremely difficult to show whether a treatment is successful or unsuccessful. That is, unless you've got an experiment.

The people who made my nose spray know all about experiments. That's what drug trials are all about. Before they can market a new drug, they have to perform a *randomized control trial*, or RCT. The formula to do a RCT is simple: (1) Devise a treatment; (2) Identify your target population and from it randomly select a sample to run your experiment on; (3) split the sample randomly into two groups: a treatment group and a control group; (4) give the treatment group the treatment and the control group a "placebo" that looks like the treatment but isn't; (5) after enough time has elapsed for the treatment to take effect, gather new information on your treatment and control groups; (6) compare outcomes of interest between the treatment and control groups.

In 1997, Mexico did something similar to a drug experiment, but it was to test a different kind of treatment: a new kind of welfare program. The PROGRESA program was designed to combat rural poverty from two angles. First, it gave cash to poor people. A number of studies have shown that women are more likely than men to spend income on food and other goods likely to benefit their families, so women were the target of the program. Second, in order to get the cash, a poor woman had to follow some rules to improve nutrition, health, and education. Kids had to be enrolled in school and in the local clinic. These behavioral requirements made PROGRESA what is called a "conditional cash-transfer program" or "CCT."

The theory behind this CCT was simple. In the short run, cash is what poor people need most in order to feed and clothe their families and satisfy their basic needs and wants. In the long run, the best way to break the inter-generational transfer of poverty is to give kids the human capital they need to lead productive lives; hence the two "Cs."

So far, we've got the most of the first two elements of an RCT: the treatment (the CCT) and a target population (poor rural women). Mexico had to figure out who was in this target population, so it carried out a nation-wide survey. It identified 2.6 million families in 50,000 rural communities who were eligible to receive PROGRESA benefits. That's about forty percent of all rural families. The plan was to give the PRO-CAMPO treatment to all eligible women.

If all eligible women get the treatment, how can we test whether the treatment works? We could compare everyone before and after the program starts. But if we saw differences, say, in school attendance or family nutrition, could we be sure it was because of PROGRESA? Many other things were happening in Mexico at the same time as PROGRESA. NAFTA (the North American Free Trade Agreement) had just gone into effect. In Mexico like many other countries, the mid-1990s saw far-reaching agricultural reforms that included eliminating subsidies for small farmers, with big impacts on rural incomes. New rural schools were being built. People were migrating. The weather was changing. There was lots of pollen in the air.

If you give everyone an allergy spray, they might still sneeze if the pollen count rises—or they might not sneeze at all if it doesn't. When you can't control for everything else, you can't figure out whether your treatment worked. Something else might have changed. This has been the curse of development-program evaluations over the years. We need a control group of randomly chosen people who did *not* get the treatment but experienced, on average, the same changes in all those other variables that the treated households did. If treatment and control groups go into the pollen together, we should be able to figure out whether the drug worked.

Whether by design or by luck, Mexico gave us a random control group to evaluate PROGRESA. There was no way to roll out the program to all eligible families in rural Mexico at the same time, so the government had to choose which poor villages to "treat" first. It could have gone for the villages closest to Mexico City, near where powerful politicians lived, or where poverty was highest, but it didn't. Instead, it rolled out the program randomly. All eligible women in randomly chosen villages got PROGRESA payments the first year of the program. They were the treatment group. In the rest of the villages, none of the eligible women got PROGRESA right away. They were the control group.

Randomization ensured that the treatment and control villages, households, and women, on average, were identical except for the treatment, just like the treatment and control groups in a drug trial. Researchers could compare any outcome they wanted—school attendance, nutrition, whatever—between the eligible households in these two groups of villages. All you had to do was compare averages. The difference could be attributed to PROGRESA.

Within three years, all 2.6 million eligible families were getting PROGRESA, so the experiment vanished. But for a short period of time, Mexico had given the world the gift of a randomized "social experiment" in the form of an RCT (see box: "Progressing with PROGRESA"). PROGRESA became the model for both designing and evaluating antipoverty programs in many other developing countries and even in New York City.[2]

Randomization and the Selection Problem

Over the years I've noticed that people who use nose sprays sneeze more than people who don't. Could it be that nose spray *makes* you sneeze?

That's a silly question, you say. People who use nose spray sneeze more because they had more allergies to begin with; that's why they chose the nose spray treatment. That's probably true, but you can see the problem here. We cannot determine whether the nose spray is effective by comparing people who use it with people who don't. If we do that, we might well conclude the drug makes people sneeze! This is what experimentalists call *selection bias*.

Progressing with PROGRESA

Mexico's PROGRESA data has spawned more development economics research (not to mention Ph.D student theses) than almost any other data set in the world. Here are some key findings on PROGRESA's impacts, all made possible by the way in which the program was randomly implemented across rural Mexico:

Nutrition: PROGRESA improved both calorie consumption and the quality of beneficiaries' diets. Eligible households in treatment localities consumed 6.4% more calories than comparable households in the control localities. When it comes to nutrition, the quality of calories also matters. The study found that PROGRESA's biggest impact was on calories from vegetable and animal products. PROGRESA made people eat not only more, but better.

Hoddinott, J. and E. Skoufias (2004) "The Impact of *Progresa* on Food Consumption", *Economic Development and Cultural Change*, October: 37-61.

Schooling: PROGRESA had a significant positive effect on school enrollment. Many kids drop out of school after grade 6, when often they must leave their village to continue on in school. The largest difference between PROGRESA and control households was for kids who had already completed grade 6; the PROGRESA kids' enrollment rate was 11.1 percentage points higher, reaching 69%, and the program's impact was disproportionately concentrated among girls. Exposure to PROGRESA for 8 years, starting at age 6, increases children's educational attainment by an average of 0.7 years, and 21% more children would attend secondary school.

Schultz, T. Paul (2004): "School Subsidies for the Poor: Evaluating the Mexican Progresa Poverty Program," *Journal of Development Economics*, 74:2, 199-250.

Behrman, Jere R., Piyali Sengupta and Petra Todd (2005): "Progressing through PROGRESA: An Impact Assessment of a School Subsidy Experiment," *Economic Development and Cultural Change*, 54:1, 237–275.

Health: PROGRESA significantly increased preventive care including prenatal care, child nutrition monitoring, and adult checkups. It reduced inpatient hospitalizations, suggesting a positive effect on major illness. PROGRESA children 0-5 had a 12 percent lower incidence of illness, and prime age adults (18-50) had 19 percent fewer days of difficulty due to illness than non-PROGRESA individuals.

Paul Guertler. 2002. Final Report: The Impact of PROGRESA on Health. Washington, DC: International Food Policy Research Institute (IFPRI); http://www.ifpri.org/sites/default/files/publications/gertler_health.pdf

Selection bias confounds all sorts of studies. Here are three illustrations:

The economists Jushua Angrist and Jörn-Steffen Pischke took people who were hospitalized (the treatment group) and people who were not (the control group) and compared their health status a year later. The people who had been hospitalized were less healthy. Do hospitals make people sick?

Governments around the world offer job training programs. Many studies find that a year or two later the people who choose to be in these programs are more likely to be employed than the people who chose not to do the job training. Are job training programs successful, then, or is it the kind of person who chooses to go for job training?

Economic studies consistently show that people with more education have higher earnings. Is this because schools make people more productive, or do higher-ability people choose to go to school?

In these (and countless other) cases, the outcomes we see after the treatment reflect two things: first, who chooses to get the treatment (the selection effect), and second, the effect of the treatment, itself. Because of this, simply comparing outcomes for people who did and did not get a treatment may tell us nothing at all about whether the treatment was effective. We've got to untangle the two.

What we'd really like to do is compare the same person's outcome with and without the treatment. We can't do that, though, because once a person gets treated, we can't see what would have happened to her without the treatment. And if the person does not get the treatment, we'll never know what would have happened if she had been treated.

The selection problem is that things that determine whether or not someone gets treated are correlated with the outcome we want to measure. Sick people (whether they go to hospital or not) are likely to be less healthy in the future. Motivated people choose to participate in a training program, but they are more likely to get a job with or without the program. High-ability people are more likely to have higher earnings, regardless of how much more productive schools make them.

Randomization solves the selection problem. By randomly choosing who gets the treatment and who does not, RCTs create a treatment and control group that on average are the same except for the treatment. Any differences we observe between the two, then, must be the result of the treatment.

Theoretically, in a perfectly designed experiment, we could test whether or not the treatment is successful simply by comparing outcomes between treatment and control groups. Randomization would ensure that everything but the treatment is identical, on average, between the two groups. Real life rarely gives us something approaching perfect randomization, though. Thus, we usually need baseline (pre-treatment) information to make sure the treatment and control groups really are the same except for the treatment. Baseline surveys are costly, but tests showing there are no significant differences between the treatment and control group prior to the treatment are important to validate RCTs.

Baseline surveys are important for other reasons. We saw previously that Mexico's PROGRESA program had to carry out a baseline survey in order to figure out who would be in its target population, that is, which women met the criteria for receiving PROGRESA payments.

Baseline information can help researchers control for other variables that affect the outcome of interest. For example, while treatments are carried out, other things in the economy are changing, like the weather, macro-economic policies, and recessions. With good baseline data, we can compare changes in outcomes for the treated and control groups before and after the treatment. For example, we might hope that cash transfers raise crop production in poor households. Meanwhile, if the economy is growing, poor households might increase their crop production with or without the program. If the transfers really do increase crop production, though, the change in crop production should be larger in the households that got transfers. Instead of comparing crop production between treated and non-treated households, then, we can learn more about the program's impacts if we compare *differences* in crop production between the two groups. This is called the "difference in difference" method. We first calculate the difference in the outcome variable (crop production) before and after the treatment for both the treatment and control groups. Then we calculate the difference between these differences. If it's positive, we conclude that the treatment had a positive effect on the outcome. This useful method requires having data on the treated and control groups before as well as after the treatment.

The Experimental Revolution in Development Economics

Development economists have moved to the forefront of bringing experimental methods to bear on important questions. Esther Duflo co-founded the Poverty Action Lab (J-PAL), which is dedicated to the use of RCTs.[3] She writes:

> Creating a culture in which rigorous randomized evaluations are promoted, encouraged, and financed has the potential to revolutionize social policy during the 21st century, just as randomized trials revolutionized medicine during the 20th.

The J-PAL website states:

> Randomized evaluations are often deemed the gold standard of impact evaluation, because they consistently produce the most accurate results...to determine whether a program has an impact, and more specifically, to quantify how large that impact is.[4]

Today, RCTs are being used to evaluate a wide array of development programs, from a new generation of cash transfer programs in sub-Saharan Africa to microcredit, HIV/AIDS prevention, immunization, and even "hope." Here are a few examples of the kinds of questions RCTs address.

Esther Duflo explains testing solutions with randomized trials.

Africa RCTs

African countries are different from Mexico in ways that could shape the outcome of cash transfer programs. They are poorer and characterized by a greater level of risk and vulnerability. HIV/AIDS has its global epicenter in Southern Africa. The region has less developed markets and greater political instability. People's livelihoods and ability to escape from poverty are more linked to small holder agriculture and the informal economy than to the formal wage economy. Public institutions tend to be weaker, governments have fewer resources to invest in poverty programs, and thus international donors play a much more significant role in financing social programs in sub-Saharan Africa. Competing donors often have conflicting ideas as to the types of social protection interventions to pursue. There is a lack of consensus among governments, too, along with a weaker capacity to implement and evaluate programs and fewer complementary services like health, education, and nutrition. All these considerations make sub-Saharan Africa both an important laboratory for impact evaluation and a challenging place to do it.[5]

Another fundamental difference between the African and Mexican programs is that, for the most part, the African ones are not conditional. Often, behavioral changes like better nutritional practices and keeping kids in school are encouraged, but with few exceptions they are not required as a condition of getting the transfer. These programs are often referred to as social cash transfer (SCT) instead of CCT programs. Is conditionality really needed, or given the cash and information, will people choose to do the right thing? These questions loom in the debate and evaluation of SCTs in sub-Saharan Africa. There are exceptions. Ethiopia's Productive Safety Net Program pays people from eligible households in chronically food-insecure *woredas* (districts) to work on labor-intensive projects. It is conditional in the sense that people have to work in order to get benefits. The idea behind this project is to give cash and food to the poor while building up the country's infrastructure, particularly irrigation, via work projects in which the beneficiaries participate.

A number of evaluations have come out of pilot programs designed to test the effectiveness of SCTs before the programs are "scaled up" to the larger population. The box below ("Impacts of SCTs in Sub-Saharan Africa") summarizes what some of the key African SCT evaluations have been finding. As we'll see in the next section, randomization of the "SCT treatment" is the key to being able to make statements of causality. In the following section we'll look at what can go wrong in RCTs and what the limits of this approach are.

Impacts of SCTs in Sub-Saharan Africa

An evaluation of a pilot SCT program in Malawi showed a significant reduction in child morbidity, gains in school enrolment, and increases in food consumption and diet diversity. Agricultural investments increased. The SCT reduced child labor outside the home.

Miller, C., Tsoka, M., and Reichert, K., 2010. Impacts on children of cash transfers in Malawi. *In*: S. Handa, S. Devereux and D. Webb, eds. *Social protection for Africa's children*. London: Routledge Press, pp. 96–116.

Katia Covarrubias, Benjamin Davis and Paul Winters, "From protection to production: productive impacts of the Malawi Social Cash Transfer scheme," *Journal of Development Effectiveness*, 4:1, 50-77, 2012.

Ethiopia's Productive Safety Net Program caused an increase in school attendance for some groups, particularly younger children, and a reduction in child labor for some activities among boys but an increase in girls' labor time.

Hoddinott, J., Gilligan, D.O. and Taffesse, A.S., 2011. The impact of Ethiopia's productive safety net program on schooling and child labor. *In*: S. Handa, S. Devereux and D. Webb, eds. *Social protection for Africa's children*. New York: Routledge, 71–95.

South Africa's Child Support Grant increased school attendance and decreased hunger among children receiving the grant, increased access to cell-phone use, and supported the sustainability of agricultural activities in households with children receiving the grant.

Samson, M., *et al.*, 2010. Impacts of South Africa's child support grants. *In*: S. Handa, S. Devereux and D. Webb, eds. *Social protection for Africa's children*. London: Routledge Press, pp. 117–145.

Kenya's Cash Transfers for Orphans and Vulnerable Children (CT-OVC) increased children's secondary enrollment on par with what has been found from *conditional* cash transfer programs in other parts of the world. Participating households had significantly higher expenditures than control households in food, health, and clothing and significantly less spending on alcohol and tobacco. They shifted from tubers to cereals, meat and fish, and dairy.

The Kenya CT-OVC Evaluation Team, "The impact of Kenya's Cash Transfer for Orphans and Vulnerable Children on human capital," *Journal of Development Effectiveness*, 4:1, 38-49, 2012.

_____. "The impact of the Kenya Cash Transfer Program for Orphans and Vulnerable Children on household spending," *Journal of Development Effectiveness*, 4:1, 9-37, 2012.

Credit

Access to credit is vital to people in poor as well as rich countries, as we saw in Chapter 9. There is strong theoretical reason to think that people will invest in new activities and technologies when they get access to credit. But how big is the impact? Do micro-credit projects really make people more productive, and if so, how much?

Testing the effect of credit on investments and other outcomes is difficult, because the kinds of people who get loans (both apply and are accepted) are different than the kinds that do not, so we cannot simply compare the two. How can you make an experiment out of credit?

Dean Karlan and Jonathan Zinman figured out a way. They convinced a lender in South Africa to grant loans to a random sample of applicants with low credit scores. These were people who applied for credit but had been deemed not credit-worthy. By randomly giving credit to people in this group, Karlan and Zinman avoided the problem that more credit-worthy people get the loans and might have done well with or without them. It was an RCT because only some randomly chosen people with low credit scores were given loans, while others were not.

The researchers compared those who got credit to those who did not in terms of "economic self-sufficiency" (employment and income), food consumption, and other outcomes six to twelve months after the treatment. They found that economic self-sufficiency and food consumption were higher for the treated group. They also found that depression and stress were higher for the people who won the loan lottery, perhaps due to anxiety from being in debt.[6]

People didn't randomly incur debt in the RCT that Suresh de Mel, David McKenzie, and Christopher Woodruff did in Sri Lanka—they just got money or machines.[7] The entrepreneurs who got chosen for this Santa Claus treatment ended up with a significantly larger capital stock, which is not so surprising for the ones that got the machines but not predictable for the ones that got the cash. However, the effect of this treatment on the profitability of enterprises was small or insignificant. These results suggest that some businesses are constrained by a lack of capital while others are not.

Insurance

Evaluating how insurance affects poor households is challenging because almost no rural households have access to insurance, and those that do have insurance tend to be very different from those that do not. Characteristics of households that are correlated with whether or not they have insurance are also likely to explain outcomes like crop production, income, or nutrition. Because of this selection problem, comparing outcomes between households that get insurance and those that do not generally tells us little.

We know from past research (see Chapter 10) that poor households diversify their activities more than rich households and by doing so forfeit the income gains from specializing in what they do best. Access to insurance could bring substantial economic benefits to rural households, especially the poor, by increasing their access to credit and enabling them to specialize. To test this, though, we need a treatment group of households that have access to insurance and a control group that does not. We also need to avoid the problems of adverse selection and moral hazard; otherwise, insurance companies will not be willing to offer insurance to small farmers. Where can we find all of this?

Michael Carter and Sarah Janzen figured out a way. They offered a new kind of insurance to a random group of pastoralists in the Marsabit District of northern Kenya: index-based livestock insurance (IBLI). Satellite measures of vegetative cover are used to predict average livestock mortality from drought in local communities. The payout households get from this insurance has nothing to do with their behavior; this insurance pays if the average livestock mortality predicted from satellite images reaches 15%. This avoids the problem of moral hazard (people changing their behavior once they have insurance; see Chapter 10). Carter and Janzen convinced an insurance company in Kenya to make this insurance randomly available to some small farmers but not others. This helped solve the problem of adverse selection (higher-risk people taking out insurance; see Chapter 9).

A drought hit in 2011, after the insurance was made available. Insured households got an average payout of $150. It is too soon to tell what impact this insurance will have, but we can ask what people *think* it will have. Carter and Janzen asked both the insured and uninsured households how they plan to deal with the drought. The percentage saying they'll eat fewer meals was 22 percentage points lower for the households with insurance. The number who anticipated selling additional livestock to cope with the drought was 50% lower for the insured households. The insured households also said they will rely less on food aid and assistance from others.

If what households end up doing is anything like what they say they'll do, this project will have succeeded in helping pastoralists deal with drought risk and avoid some of the worst impacts of drought, while demonstrating the importance of insurance in risky environments.

Hope and Optimism

Most people care about their future. But what if, when they look there, what they see are dim economic prospects? Psychologists call the uncomfortable tension people feel from simultaneously holding conflicting thoughts "cognitive dissonance." Could it be that the poor, by closing their eyes on the future, reduce their psychological distress at the cost of worsening their future economic wellbeing? If poor people close their eyes on the future, they will have no reason to save and invest for it. This can create a "psychological poverty trap."

In November-December 2010, a team of researchers in Mozambique ran a lottery in which the winners got a free input subsidy for 70% of the cost of a seed and fertilizer package.[8] Winners of this lottery could expect to get a larger harvest. In April-May 2011 both the winners and losers of the lottery were asked the question "How much time ahead do you plan your future expenditures?" On average, winning the lottery increased an individual's time horizon by more than a month, from 198 days to 235 days. It seems that the farmers who won the lottery became more forward looking.

Another RCT, in India, found evidence that helping desperately poor people invest gave far better results than expected, consistent with breaking out of a psychological poverty trap (see box: "Hope").

Hope

In the Indian state of West Bengal, a microfinance institution, BRAC, tried something different. Instead of giving loans to extremely poor people, who they thought would be unlikely to repay, they gave out assets: a few chickens, a cow, a pair of goats. They also taught people in this treatment group how to take care of their animals and manage their households. Just to make sure they wouldn't eat the animals right away, they also gave them a little cash to spend.

The theory behind this RCT was that people would learn how to manage their finances better and make a little income selling the products their farm animals would provide. To test the results of this project, researchers compared these treated households with a random control group of poor households, which did not get any of these things.

The results? The treatment worked better than anyone had hoped for. Long after the treatment ended, the treated households ate 15% more, earned 20% more, and skipped meals less often than households in the control group. They were savings more, too. The improvements were far too big to be explained by the direct effects of the grants. That is, the treated households could not have sold enough eggs, milk, or meat to explain these big outcomes.

The project gave the treated households more than it had expected. The research team, headed by economist Esther Duflo, called it hope. The project gave people a reason to work harder—28% more hours, to be precise. The incidence of depression fell. In addition to a few animals and a bit of advice, it seemed, BRAC had succeeded in administering a healthy dose of optimism. Could it be that the hope for escaping from poverty traps is hope, itself?

"Hope springs a trap: An absence of optimism plays a large role in keeping people trapped in poverty," *The Economist*, Free Exchange, May 12, 2012 (http://www.economist.com/node/21554506)

HIV-AIDS

In 2010 an estimated 22.9 million people in Sub-Saharan Africa were living with HIV and 1.2 million died of AIDS, leaving 16.6 million children orphaned. Rates of HIV infection among adults 15-49 years old were 17.8% in South Africa, where 5.6 million adults were infected, and reached as high as 23.6% in Lesotho, 24.8% in Botswana, 25.9% in Swaziland.[9] Besides being a human tragedy of epic proportions, AIDS can have a major impact on countries' economic prospects because it strikes at the heart of the working-age population and thus takes a particularly heavy toll on human capital. A study in Mozambique concluded that the disease reduced total economic growth by as much as 1% per year. Estimates for other sub-Saharan African countries range from 0.56 to 1.47% lost income growth per year, and these estimates may be low.[10]

RCTs are giving us important insights into how to fight HIV-AIDS in poor countries. Lack of education and economic dependence on men ("transactional sex") are believed to be important causes of HIV infection among young women. An RCT tested whether cash transfers to young women reduced infections among school-age girls in Malawi, where 11% of the adult population has HIV-AIDS. It found strong evidence that they did, provided that they target young unmarried women still in school (see box).

A Cash Transfer Program for AIDS

In the Malawi AIDS study, 1,289 females aged 13-22 years who were never married and enrolled in school were randomly assigned to get cash payments (treatment group) or nothing (control group). Women in the treatment group were randomly divided into two sub-groups, one getting the cash unconditionally, the other conditional upon school attendance. The payments ranged from US$1 to $5 monthly, and the women's parents were given $4 to $10 per month. After 18 months, 1.2% of the treatment group and 3.0% of the control group tested positive for HIV. The study found no significant effect of conditioning payments on school attendance among the treatment group. It also included 417 women in the same age group who already had dropped out of school before the experiment. Among these women, the cash transfer had no significant effect at all.

Sarah J Baird, Richard S Garfein, Craig T McIntosh, and Berk Özler, "Impact of a cash transfer program for schooling on prevalence of HIV and HSV-2 in Malawi: a cluster randomized trial," *The Lancet*, Volume 379, Issue 9823, Pages 1320 – 1329, 7 April 2012 (http://www.thelancet.com/journals/lancet/article/PIIS0140-6736%2811%2961709-1/abstract)

Immunizations

Immunizations are one of the most effective ways to save lives, yet the World Health Organization reports that 27 million children don't get essential immunizations each year. Immunizations are a centerpiece of work by the wealthiest foundation in the world (Gates), and governments as well as donors invest considerable resources in them. So why do so many poor children not get immunized? Is it that parents do not believe in immunizations, or is it something else?

It could be what Ester Duflo calls "the last mile." Parents procrastinate, health centers usually are a good walk away, and once people get there, lines are long and the health center is certainly understaffed and maybe not open. The cost (including time) of getting to immunization centers and unreliable service create disincentives for parents to get their children immunized. Researchers at J-PAL designed an RCT to test this (see box: "The Last Mile?").

The Last Mile?

Researchers hypothesized that eliminating these disincentives would make the difference between children getting or not getting immunized. In Udaipur, Rajasthan, India, researchers set up monthly "vaccination camps" in randomly selected treatment villages. These camps were well publicized and sure to be open rain or shine. The idea was to replicate an ideal health-delivery system. They also gave some randomly chosen people an extra incentive: a kilo of lentils. Then they compared immunization rates between these treated villages and random control villages, where there were no camps.

The percentage of vaccinated kids tripled, from 6% to 18%, in the villages with camps. When lentils were thrown in, they rose by a factor of more than six, to 39%. An unexpected benefit of the program was that the cost of immunizations fell by half, as the same number of nurses were able to immunize many children.

This project's research contribution was not so much to show that economic incentives work, because we already knew that from PROGRESA and other CCT programs. It was to demonstrate that a small incentives, like a few lentils, can have a big effect on people's demand for crucial health services like immunization.

Abhijit Banerjee and Esther Duflo, "A new look at an old problem: Why do so many poor children miss out on essential immunizations?" UNICEF, Child Poverty Insights, June 2011 (http://www.povertyactionlab.org/sites/default/files/ChildPovertyInsights_June2011_EN%281%29.pdf)

When Experiments Can Go Awry

For all their promise, RCTs have many pitfalls. We have highlighted a collection of well-executed experiments above, but in practice, the ideal experiment is exceedingly hard to find. In general, the best designed and executed experiments are those in which the question asked lends itself neatly to experimental methods and the researchers have control over how the experiment is designed and executed. This usually is not the case with large-scale government programs, in which many things can go wrong, from politics to poor administration of treatments and research. Anyone reading about or especially designing RCTs had better be aware of these pitfalls. Here are some of the major things that can go wrong in experiments:

Creating Treatment and Control Groups

A RCT requires treating one randomly-selected group and denying treatment to another. Before we can conduct an experiment, we need to have a valid treatment and control group.

Sometimes it simply is not possible to create a control group. Take tourism, for example. Eco-tourism development projects are among the fastest-growing parts of development bank loan portfolios. Many countries see tourism as a way to stimulate economic growth and fight poverty. Suppose we are interested in quantifying the impacts of a tourism-development project. The treatment is the project. The treatment group is effectively the entire population at the tourist destination, and the control group is the same population without the project. It is not possible to make this project happen for one group of people but not others at the tourist destination. One might argue that the project could be implemented at some randomly chosen tourist sites but not others. However, almost by definition tourist destinations are unique (hence the reasons tourists want to go there). This makes it difficult to come up with reasonable alternative locations as a control, that is, sites identical to the "treated" site except without the treatment. They simply do not represent the region without the project. There is no counter-factual for the Galápagos Islands.

There are many other cases in which problems arise when constructing treatment and control groups. Irrigation and other infrastructure projects create public goods that potentially affect everyone in the zone in which the projects are carried out. Staple price supports frequently have been used as a mechanism to transfer income to farmers (with dubious welfare benefits). However, it is generally not feasible to offer a high price to some randomly selected farmers but not others.

It may be politically infeasible to randomly create a treatment group, or it may be considered unethical to deny benefits to a control group (see "The Ethics of Experiments," below). In theory, input subsidies could be implemented randomly through targeted vouchers. In practice, though, it may not be politically feasible to deny benefits to a control group while offering them to a treatment group.[11] Even in a country like Malawi, where fertilizer vouchers targeted poor farmers, they were not given out randomly. If subsidies are given to all qualifying farmers, there is no control group.[12] It is not uncommon for researchers to be called upon to conduct impact evaluations after a project has already been implemented. In this case, we can see who got the treatment and who did not, but we might not have the pre-treatment data we need to do a clean RCT, and there might be concerns over whether the creation of the treatment and control groups was truly random.

Control Group Contamination

Measuring a project's impact on the treated requires isolating the control group from the project's effects. This is often not so easy to do in practice. Even in a medical experiment it may be difficult to isolate the control group from the treatment, for example, if the treatment involves curing a communicable disease. The effects of treatments on control groups frequently confound experimental research in the social sciences. A well-known RCT in Kenya illustrates this point. It was designed to treat school children with worms in an effort to keep them in school. But by treating kids in some schools, the incidence of worms among kids in control schools went down (see box: "Worms"). When the treatment affects the control group as well as the treatment group, it can be difficult or impossible to reliably estimate the impact of the treatment, because both groups change. We call this problem "control group contamination."

Worms

Worms are bad (unless they're the garden variety). Hookworm and roundworm each infect approximately 1.3 billion people around the world; whipworm affects 900 million, and 200 million are infected with schistosomiasi. Intense worm infections keep kids from going to school and reduce their educational achievement. Could it be that the key to literacy is (getting rid of) worms?

Edward Miguel and Michael Kremer analyzed a RCT experiment to raise school attendance in Kenya by treating children for worms. A clearly defined treatment for worms was administered to children in a randomly selected sample of schools (the treatment group) but not in other schools (the control group). It had a simple and easily measured outcome: school attendance. The ex-post research question was whether or not children in the treated schools were more likely to attend school after the treatment.

It seemed to be a squeaky clean experimental design. What could go wrong with it?

Actually, something went too right, from an analytical point of view. The treated schools treated the control schools. Maybe treated kids played with control kids after school or had contact with others who, in turn, had contact with control kids. The study could not tell us why, but for whatever reason, kids in the control schools got better, too.

Miguel and Kremer call this an externality of the treatment. In experimental jargon, it is called control group contamination. Really, it is a linkage—in this case, an epidemiological one—that transmitted the benefits of the project from those directly affected (the kids in the treatment school) to others in the project's zone of influence. Not surprisingly, the effect was weaker the farther away the control schools were from the treated schools.

Since kids in control schools got better, it was hard to find a positive effect on school attendance by comparing the treatment and control groups. It is ironic that a treatment potentially can be so successful that you cannot show it has any effect at all.

Edward Miguel and Michael Kremer, "Worms: Identifying Impacts on Education and Health in the Presence of Treatment Externalities," *Econometrica* 72(1, January):159-217, 2004.

Economic linkages can transmit impacts from treatment groups to others inside and outside the local economy. Take a cash transfer program. The household that gets the cash spends it. In the process, it transmits the impacts of the program to others inside and outside the village. I spoke with a shopkeeper in an Ethiopian village who loved the cash transfer program there. "You get transfers?" I asked. "No, but those that do come here to spend!" he answered.

This shopkeeper was not eligible for the treatment, but he benefited from it just the same. If treated households buy more food, local farmers can benefit. If they fix up their house, so can the local bricklayer. These people, in turn, may hire more workers and buy more inputs. It can lead to a village version of Keynesian economics, in which the infusion of new cash into the economy has a multiplier effect on village income.[13] If we only look at the treated households, we may underestimate the overall effects of the treatment.

Economic spillovers do not necessarily result in control group contamination, but they may. If the control households are in another village, economic linkages from the treated villages might not reach them. However, all around Africa, periodic markets bring people together from many different villages to buy and sell. If households from treated and control villages interact in these markets, the result can easily be control group contamination.

Treatment spillover effects raise challenges for RCTs, and they can be good or bad for people. If the treatment positively affects the control group, we might conclude that the treatment was not effective when in fact it was—both the treatment and control group benefit from it. It is also possible that the spillover is negative. For example, some villagers complain that cash transfers push up food prices. Giving cash to people might lead them to work less, in which cases wages could go up. This creates a cost for those who hire workers. If a project negatively affects the control group, we run the risk of concluding that the treatment was effective when really it was not: the treatment appears to make the treated better off when really it makes the control group worse off.

Under ideal circumstances, randomization can ensure that the expected outcome for the control households equals the expected outcome of the treated households had they not gotten the treatment. As it turns out, this rarely is the case, particularly in large-scale government programs. Perfect randomized experiments are few and far between.

This ideal randomization relies in fact on two conditions. The first is having a "clean" control group that is isolated from the treatment. That is, it must be absolutely unaffected by the presence or absence of the treatment (on the treated households). The second is that the control group needs to be so similar to the treatment group on average that, had there been no treatment, the two groups would have displayed the same outcome.

Beyond Experiments: Local Economy-wide Impacts of Development Programs

Suppose we wish to evaluate the impact of an income transfer program on rural poverty. Poor households receive the transfer, which might entail some sort of conditionality (for example, PROGRESA's require-ment that children attend school) or not (almost all of the SCT programs in Africa). Figure 11.1 illustrates the pathways by which this project might impact a local economy.

Arrow (a) represents the transfer's direct effect on the income of a recipient (poor) household. This is equal to the amount of the transfer. With higher income, the household's demand for normal goods and services increases. The transfer can affect other household activities in a number of different ways. By raising the household's income, it can stimulate consumption demand, including the demand for leisure and subsistence goods produced by the household. Both could affect the household's production activities when there are nontradables (see Chapter 9).[14]

For example, an increased demand for food could encourage a subsistence household to grow more food crops, while an increased demand for leisure could do the opposite, depending on how well integrated the household is with food and labor markets. If leisure demand increases, wage labor supply could decrease, negatively impacting income. The transfer also could loosen liquidity constraints on crop production, enabling the household to purchase more fertilizer and other inputs or shift into cash crops.[15] Finally, it could reduce income risk, and this might encourage the household to invest more of its scanty resources in risky activities. Conditionality could create still other effects. For example, the requirement that children attend school could decrease the family's labor available for crop production. Arrows (b) depict these myriad indirect effects of the transfer on the treated household's income from production and labor activities. Experimental methods, when feasible and carefully executed, can provide insights into the net influences represented by arrows (a) and (b).

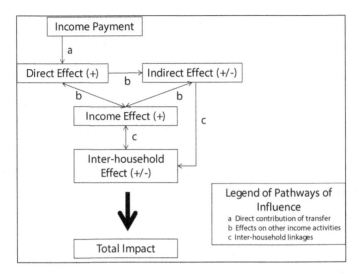

Figure 11.1: An income transfer project creates both direct and indirect income effects in the treated economy.

As the recipient households demand more consumption goods and change their allocation of resources to production and wage activities, others in the local economy invariably are affected. Local markets transmit impacts of the transfer from the recipient to non-recipient households. Households and businesses supplying goods and services to the recipient households benefit. If the transfer alters the recipient household's wage labor supply, this could drive up wages, or as consumption demand rises, so might local prices. These will affect non-recipient households in other (possibly negative) ways. As local activities adjust, a new round of changes in input demands, incomes, and household expenditures follows, creating still more rounds of changes in incomes and expenditures. Given income leakages, successive rounds of impacts become smaller and smaller, and the total (direct plus indirect) effect of the program eventually converges to an income multiplier. To the extent the goods demanded by the recipient households are supplied locally, the income transfer could create a multiplier considerably greater than one. On the other hand, if the recipient households purchase goods from outside the local economy, some or perhaps most of the multiplier will go elsewhere. Clearly, the behavior of the households that get the transfer to begin with is critical in shaping the impacts that result from the program, but so is the behavior of the nontreated groups and the structure of the local markets connecting them with each other.

The economic linkages which transmit impacts through economies are called general-equilibrium feedback effects. In a few cases, RCTs have collected data on ineligible households and found evidence that they are affected by treatments. One such study was done on the effects of Mexico's PROGRESA program on the households that did not get PROGRESA transfers. The impact was found to be positive, implying that only focusing on the treated underestimates the program's impact.

To understand the ways in which a treatment affects both treated and non-treated households, we generally have to go beyond RCTs and try to model economic linkages. As the diagram above illustrates, the direct and indirect impacts of an intervention are shaped by how households change their supply and demand decisions and by the structure of local markets, which in turn reflect various constraints (technology, transaction costs, liquidity, risk). Performing project evaluations in such environments may require integrating models of heterogeneous households into a general equilibrium model of the zone of interest. General-equilibrium models for the economy targeted by the project (village, region, rural sector) provide a laboratory in which the project is designed and its impacts assessed, using a simulation approach.

There are fundamental differences—some might call these philosophical differences—between RCTs and simulation models. An RCT, we've seen, is like a drug experiment; it can tell us whether something works, but not why. An advantage of experiments is that statistical significance can be attached to RCT findings; for example, "with 95% certainty we can say that the transfer increased food consumption by between $10 and $15 per month." The validity of an RCT depends on getting the experiment right; otherwise, the findings, however significant statistically, may be biased. At conferences where researchers present studies using RCTs, much of the discussion typically centers around what might have gone wrong in the experiment and how this might have affected the results. This illustrates how much more difficult it can be to run "clean" economic experiments than drug trials. Often, one is left with questions about why a treatment had the effect that it did on those who got the treatment.

Simulation models try to answer the question "why" while capturing complex interactions that shape project outcomes, in ways that often are beyond the reach of experiments. The validity of a simulation model depends on getting the model right. Imagine a flight simulator. Pilots do not have to be taught to fly by being hit with dangerous real-world situations mid-air. They can step into a flight simulator. The simulator is programed with equations representing the physics of flight. It becomes a laboratory in which flight experiments are conducted. If you've ever played a computer game, you know what simulations are all about. If the flight simulator is programed wrong, well, you won't want to fly with that pilot!

A simulation approach to project impact evaluation highlights the interactions within the local economy that transmit impacts, good or bad, from directly affected actors to others in the economy. We can construct simulation models using data from the same surveys that are used to do RCT research. If our simulation model represents the way in which the local economy works, it can be a valuable tool to understand the full, economy-wide impacts of cash transfers and many other programs and policies.

There are two main knocks against simulation models. One is that they depend on getting the model right, especially how agents behave and how markets transmit impacts from one agent to another (like getting the flight simulator right). Another is that it is more difficult (though not impossible) to attach statistical significance to simulation results.

A new method, called Local Economy-wide Impact Evaluation (LEWIE), uses data from the same surveys carried out for RCTs to estimate simulation models and construct confidence bounds around their results. This is a step in the direction of bringing together the best of RCT and GE simulation methods.

A LEWIE simulation model was used to evaluate the local GE effects of a cash transfer program in the southern African country of Lesotho. It uncovered import spillover effects, including on the households that did not get the transfer (see box, "Impacts of Treatments on the Nontreated in Lesotho").

The Invariance Assumption

Experiments, in order to be valid, must satisfy the "invariance assumption," which states that the actual program will act like the experimental version of the program. Often, the purpose of RCTs is to test interventions which, if deemed successful, will be scaled up to a larger—or perhaps the entire—population. Will the large-scale program have the same kinds of impacts as the small-scale RCT? Or is there something about ramping up a project that creates new impacts not captured in experiments?

Actually, there is. Once the program gets scaled up, the control group disappears. Linkages transmit impacts of the program through the whole economy. Now everyone is likely to be affected, directly or indirectly, by the treatment. We call the total effect on the economy the "general equilibrium (GE) effect." GE effects are a major reason why the invariance assumption may be violated. An intervention does not have to be particularly large in order to unleash general-equilibrium effects; it only has to be important relative to the size of the economy in which it happens. In a poor region, a small project can have a large general-equilibrium impact.

Impacts of a Treatment on the Nontreated in Lesotho

When poor people get cash transfers, they spend them. This transmits impacts of cash transfer programs from treated to nontreated households. New impact simulation models are being used to evaluate how treatments affect the nontreated. Lesotho's Child Grants Program (CGP) seeks to improve the living conditions, nutrition, health, and schooling of orphans and vulnerable children. The CGP seeks to accomplish this via an unconditional cash transfer targeted to poor and vulnerable households. The Program's immediate impact is to raise the purchasing power of the households that are eligible for the program. As the eligible households spend their cash, the impacts of the transfer immediately spread to ineligible households in the same villages as well as to other villages. The overall impact on the local economy depends on whether the local supply of goods and services expands to meet the new demand.

The results of a local economy-wide impact evaluation (LEWIE) simulation suggest that experiments comparing treated and control households may significantly understate the program's full impact. The study finds that each $1 of transfer raises total income in the treated villages by $2.23, with a 90% confidence interval (CI) of $2.08 to $2.44. Even though all of the transfers go to eligible households, nearly half of the benefits they create ($1.18) go to ineligible households.

The transfer also affects local prices, and this raises consumption costs for everyone in the local economy. Because of higher prices, the multiplier is lower in real terms: price inflation results in a real income multiplier of $1.36 (CI: $1.25-$1.45). The study found that loosening capital constraints, say, through effective micro-credit programs, is key to avoiding inflation and raising the real transfer multiplier. If capital investment expands to meet the new demand, the real income multiplier rises from \$1.36 to \$1.59 (CI: \$1.53-\$1.65).

This study is important because it reveals potential impacts of cash transfer programs unlikely to be picked up by RCTs, including on households that do not get the treatment.

J. Edward Taylor, Mateusz Filipski, and Karen Thome. Evaluating General Equilibrium Impacts of Lesotho's Child Grants Program. UN Food and Agricultural Organization (FAO) and UNICEF-ESARO, Rev. June 2012.

Multiple Treatments and Interrelated Outcomes

In the worms experiment there was a clearly defined treatment and outcome of interest: children's school attendance. Often, programs have multiple instruments (e.g., a transfer plus conditionality and eligibility requirements, or multiple transfer instruments) and interrelated outcomes, and it quickly becomes difficult to connect specific components of the program with specific outcomes of interest.

Consider Tigray, Ethiopia's, social cash transfer (SCT) program initiated in 2011. Many of the households eligible to receive the SCT already participated in a different transfer program: The Productive Safety Net Program (PSNP) had been offering them the opportunity to work a limited number of days on public projects in return for food or cash. When a household gets the SCT treatment, it stops getting the PSNP one. The new program crowds out the old, and both coexist within the same (treatment and control) localities. Disentangling the effects of these two programs is essential if we wish to evaluate the SCT's impacts. Some of the best experiments involve multiple treatments, but when there are many different interventions happening simultaneously, RCTs may not be up to the task of sorting out the impacts.

The impacts of most projects and policies are almost certain to be heterogeneous, with both winners and losers. Few experimental studies consider the ways in which these outcomes are interrelated.

"Whether," "Why," and "How"

A common rap against experimental methods is that they are good at testing whether a treatment has an effect but not at explaining why. The economist Angus Deaton wrote:

> In ideal circumstances, randomized evaluations of projects are useful for obtaining a convincing estimate of the average effect of a program or project. The price for this success is a focus that is too narrow to tell us "what works" in development, to design policy, or to advance scientific knowledge about development processes.[16]

Designing good policies depends on understanding "why" as well as "whether." It also requires focusing our research on the highest-priority questions.

The best experimental studies not only test program impacts but also try to offer glimpses into the structural reasons why a treatment produces the outcomes it does. For example, in a clever experimental study in Kenya, some farmers were offered free fertilizer delivery early in the season and others not, while still others were offered a fertilizer subsidy. The study found that offering delivery early was more effective at increasing fertilizer use than was a subsidy.[17]

In general, though, it is far more difficult to answer the question why a treatment has the effect it does than to test whether or not the treatment's effect is significant.

Opportunity Costs

So, what if a RCT finds that a program is effective at achieving its goals? Should the program be scaled up? The answer implicit in most experimental studies seems to be "yes." But is it the best way? Economists often talk about "opportunity costs." The opportunity cost of doing something is the value of what you could have done instead. When doing RCTs, it is easy to forget that every project and every way of carrying out a project has an opportunity cost. Finding that a treatment has a significant effect on an outcome of interest does not necessarily imply that the treatment is the best use of scarce public resources. A cash transfer, output price support, technology policy, or fertilizer voucher all may raise incomes in the beneficiary households, but they are unlikely to be equally effective at transforming a dollar of public expenditure into an increase in income in the treatment (or non-treatment) households.

The Ethics of Experiments

Experimenting on people raises ethical considerations. History gives us extreme and frightening examples of incidents in which people have been harmed by research, particularly in the medical and psychological areas. They include deliberate infection with serious diseases, exposure to biological or chemical weapons, human radiation, and many other atrocities. Some are less obviously harmful. A Stanford University study funded by the U.S. Office of Naval Research in 1971 used students as guinea pigs to investigate the causes of conflict between military guards and prisoners. Students participated voluntarily for $15 per day. They were randomly assigned to play the roles of prisoners and guards in a mock prison in the basement of the psychology building, but they internalized their roles too well. By the time the experiment was terminated, the guards were subjecting their prisoners to physical and psychological abuse. The Stanford Prison Experiment often is held up as an example of unethical scientific research.

Today, any time human subjects are part of research, careful measures are required. Institutional review boards (IRBs) have to approve, monitor and review biomedical as well as behavioral research involving humans. IRB approval is even required in order to carry out most kinds of economic surveys. It is important to remember this anytime you engage in social science research involving people. Guidance on complying with human subjects requirements is available at most universities and from the U.S. Department of Health and Human Services (HHS; http://www. hhs.gov/ohrp/archive/irb/irb_guidebook.htm).

Despite IRB reviews, as RCTs have become a dominant methodology in development economics, they have raised considerable controversy, including with regard to ethics. Economists Chris Barrett and Michael Carter point out four classes of ethical considerations that arise in experiments by development economists. They are:

Adverse consequences of experiments. The first rule in studies involving humans is the "do no harm" principal. Experiments manipulate people's environment in an effort to learn about their behavior. If in doing so they harm people, they are unethical and should not be implemented. This is the primary focus of IRBs.

Often, adverse effects of experiments are predictable and clear-cut. For example, if a RCT would encourage people to do something illegal or would put them in harm's way, it clearly is not ethical. A RCT in India created incentives for people to get drivers licenses without successfully completing the required training and testing, obviously putting innocent people at risk on the roads.

Other experiments are less blatant but still raise concerns. For example, researchers in China studied the impact of treating kids for iron deficiency (anemia) on school performance. Some children known to have anemia were given iron pills, and others were not. This study would not be approved in the United States, because withholding treatment for something like anemia would not be considered ethical.

Chris Barrett and Michael Carter listed a number of cases in which experiments are likely to produce adverse consequences.[18] One experiment tested whether large grants of money to women's organizations changes them in ways that lead to the exclusion of poor women, potentially harming poor women. The study's finding that it did lead to exclusion seems to confirm that poor women may have been harmed by the experiment.

Think about the credit experiment we looked at previously, in which some people with low credit scores were given loans. Does it comply with the "do no harm" rule? Fannie Mae (the Federal National Mortgage Association), a U.S. government-sponsored enterprise, made home loans to people who should not have gotten them. This was a major cause of the "Great Recession" beginning in 2008. Needless to say, it was not a good thing for the people who shouldn't have gotten loans and ended up going into default. Giving loans to people who do not qualify for them can put their property and reputation at risk.

It is hard to imagine doing any harm by giving people good stuff like goats, chickens, or cash. Yet as we have seen, cash transfer programs can potentially harm some non-participants, for example, by pushing up local prices for food and other items they buy. This is not to say that these programs should not be implemented—they almost certainly do considerably more good than harm. Nevertheless, when we implement experiments or other programs, we have a responbsibility to anticipate possible negative impacts on participants or nonparticipants and do whatever we can to mitigate them. This is part of the "do no harm by doing good" maxim.

Informed Consent. There is a difference between people being willful participants in experiments and people as subjects manipulated for research ends. The right of informed consent is well-accepted; everyone who participates in a drug trial does so voluntarily. In RCTs, people often are unaware that they are (or are not) part of an experiment.

Blindedness. Medical research uses a placebo to "blind" individuals as to whether they are in the treatment or control group. Very few RCTs do this. This raises a "do no harm" question: do the people who know they are in a control group suffer emotional distress, knowing they are not getting the benefits of the treatment? Imagine that you are desperately poor and malnourished. Could there be adverse emotional, psychological, even health consequences of knowing that you have been excluded from a treatment that could significantly improve your situation? This could raise not only ethical but research concerns. If you know you're in the control group and lose hope as a result, you could end up doing worse than you would have without the experiment. Thus, the treatment group might look better-off compared to you, making it seem like the treatment worked better than it did.

Medical research can use placebos, but in economic experiments, it seems impossible to keep people from knowing whether they are or aren't getting a treatment. A study based at a Dutch university came up with a way, though (see box: "What? An Economic Placebo?"). Their findings raise a new question: even if you can give people in the control group an "economic placebo," does this make any sense?

What? An Economic Placebo?

Using a placebo is basic in medical research: the treatment and control groups both take an identical pill, but no one (except the researcher) knows which pill has the real thing in it. That's important, because if you know you are (or aren't) getting the treatment, the experiment is likely to get contaminated; for example, your behavior might change (like me riding off into the pollen on my bicycle).

Economic RCTs are different, though. For example, people know whether or not they're getting a cash transfer. It's impossible to give people an "economic placebo."

...or is it? Four researchers ran a RCT in which farmers didn't know whether or not they were getting the real treatment. In randomly-chosen treatment villages, farmers got a modern high-yielding variety of cowpea seed. In control villages, they got the placebo: a traditional variety (TV). None of the farmers knew which seed they were planting. The result? Yields were the same between the treatment and control groups.

In another set of treatment villages, the farmers ran a normal RCT: the farmers knew they were getting the HYV. When the farmers knew they were planting the new seed, their yields were significantly higher.

If this were a medical experiment, we would say that there's only a placebo effect. When people know they're getting the real treatment, their behavior changes, and that's what accounts for the different outcome between treatment and control farmers, not the treatment.

But economics is different. High-yielding seeds are designed to produce more when given the right combination of inputs: fertilizer, water, etc. To reap the benefits from HYVs, farmers plant them on their best soils and give them the other inputs they need. If you don't know whether you've got a HYV, will you still do that? In this study, the farmers who didn't know whether they had the HYV did not. They knew that if you plant on your best soil and invest in all those inputs but the seed turns out to be a TV instead of a HYV, you lose.

In short, this economic placebo does not make any sense, because farmers *have to* adjust their inputs in order to get the benefits of this economic treatment.

Erwin Bulte, Lei Pan, Joseph Hella, Gonne Beekman and Salvatore di Falco, "Pseudo-Placebo Effects in Randomized Controlled Trials for Development: Evidence from a Double-Blind Field Experiment in Tanzania," Development Economics Group, Wageningen University, Netherlands (https://editorialexpress.com/cgi-bin/conference/download.cgi?db_name=CSAE2012&paper_id=251).

Targeting. Development organizations and governments have scarce resources to carry out development projects. It might seem logical (and ethical), then, to efficiently target these resources. Community knowledge can be used to make sure help goes to those most in need. RCTs routinely treat individuals who are not most in need of the treatment, while denying treatment to those who are. Strict randomization thus is viewed by many as being both wasteful and unfair. This can—rightly—be a stumbling block to convincing governments and communities to participate in RCTs.

Can Development Be Studied Like a Pill?

Chapter 6 ("Growth") ended with a debate between two leading development economists: William Easterly, who argues that incentives are the key to creating a self-sustaining development dynamic, and Jeffrey Sachs, who claims that major infusions of aid are needed to get poor economies moving. Neither of these economists bases his position on RCTs. Even though the Millennium Village Project is a grand social experiment, it was not set up as an RCT. This limits the project's impact, in the minds of many development economists. In response, Sachs says, "Millennium Villages don't advance the way that one tests a new pill."

RCTs are a major—perhaps the major—focus of development economics today. It is hard to find a development student Ph.D thesis that does not include some kind of randomized treatment. The strongest proponents of RCTs argue that randomized evaluations are "the gold standard of impact evaluation, because they consistently produce the most accurate results…to determine whether a program has an impact, and more specifically, to quantify *how large* that impact is."[19] A big lesson from RCTs is that there is no single solution or explanation for underdevelopment. Different kinds of action are needed in different settings.

Others, we have seen, question whether RCTs are the end-all tool they claim to be and whether the most pressing development questions can be answered using a randomized experiment. What do you think?

When There Is No Experiment

Some famous movie scenes with villains have a hall of mirrors. Every time the villain moves, so does his reflection in a bunch of different mirrors. That's what happened to James Bond in "The Man with the Golden Gun." This is a classic identification problem. You see the outcome (all those bad guys raising their guns in the mirrors), but you don't know the cause (which one is the real bad guy?).

That's how it often is with identifying cause and effect in economics. We see the outcome, but usually we don't have a neat RCT, so we need more information to figure out the cause. For example, if the villain coughs or steps on a twig, James can isolate him and take him down. The sound lets him separate the villain from his reflection. Basically, that's the strategy we have to follow in order to figure out cause and effect in economics when we don't have a RCT.

Here's an example. Indonesia launched a huge school-building campaign between 1973 and 1978, adding more than 61,000 new schools. What effect did this have on educational attainment and earnings? This is a hard question to answer, because the number of schools increased for *everyone* in Indonesia. It's like the refection in all those mirrors; we can't figure out cause and effect. To figure out the effect of the new schools, we'd need a treatment group of people who got more schools and a control group that didn't. But we don't have that, right?

Actually, we do. It occurred to economist Esther Duflo that new schools wouldn't have much effect on schooling for people who were too old to go to school, but they would have an effect on kids who were just the right age to benefit from them. She took children 2 to 6 years old in in 1974 and found they got significantly more schooling than people who were older at the time the new schools were built. It's pretty random how old a person was at the time of the school-building craze. That's what made it possible to isolate cause and effect. Duflo also found that the new schools had a big effect on wages.[20]

James Bond found a more straightforward solution to his identification problem. He broke all the mirrors until the only image left was the bad guy, Francisco Scaramanga!

Economists are always on the lookout for variables that are correlated with treatments but not with the outcomes they study. These are called instrumental variables. An example is the age of children at the time of Indonesia's school construction campaign. Many of the most important development economics questions cannot be studied with the aid of well-designed RCTs. Econometric methods are then used, along with carefully chosen instruments, in an effort to isolate cause and effect.

Chapter Eleven Notes

1. This is the amount reported by the 24 members of the OECD's Development Assistance Committee for 2011 (http://stats.oecd.org/Index.aspx?DatasetCode=ODA_DONOR). About 80-85% of developmental aid comes from government sources as official development assistance (ODA). The remaining 15-20% comes from private organisations such as "Non-governmental organisations" (NGOs), foundations and other development charities (e.g. Oxfam).

2. Opportunity NYC, an experimental CCT, was launched in New York City with support from The Rockefeller Foundation, Robin Hood Foundation, the Open Society Institute, Starr Foundation, AIG, and Mayor Bloomberg's personal foundation. It ended on August 31, 2010.

3. Now called the Abdul Latif Jameel Poverty Action Lab (J-PAL).

4. Poverty Action Lab, "What Is Randomization?" http://www.povertyactionlab.org/methodology/what-randomization

5. For an excellent discussion see Benjamin Davis, Marie Gaarder, Sudhanshu Handa, and Jenn Yablonski, "Evaluating the Impact of Cash

Transfer Programmes in Sub-Saharan Africa: An Introduction to the Special Issue," Journal of Development Effectiveness 4(1):1-8.

6. Karlan, Dean, and Jonathan Zinman, "Expanding Credit Access: Using Randomized Supply Decisions to Estimate the Impacts," *Review of Financial Studies*, 2009, doi:10.1093/rfs/hhp092

7. de Mel, Suresh, David McKenzie, and Christopher Woodruff, "Returns to Capital in Microenterprises: Evidence from a Field Experiment. Quarterly Journal of Economics 123(4): 1329–1372, 2008.

8. Rachid Laajaj, "Closing the Eyes on a Gloomy Future: Psychological Causes and Economic Consequences," University of Wisconsin, Madison and Paris School of Economics, December 7, 2011 (http://agecon. ucdavis.edu/research/seminars/files/laajaj-closing-the-eyes-on-a-gloomy-future.pdf).

9. These statistics are from the United Nations: "UNAIDS report on the global AIDS epidemic," 2010 and "World AIDS Day Report 2011."

10. Bell C, Devarajan S, Gersbach H (2003) (PDF). *The Long-run Economic Costs of AIDS: Theory and an Application to South Africa*. World Bank Policy Research Working Paper No. 3152. Retrieved 2012-04-17.

11. An excellent discussion appears in Christopher B. Barrett and Michael R. Carter, "The Power and Pitfalls of Experiments in Development Economics: Some Non-random Reflections," *Applied Economic Perspectives and Policy*, volume 32, number 4, pp. 515–548, 2010.

12. A next-best strategy could be to use the same farmers prior to the subsidy as a control group, provided that before-and-after data are available. This effectively is what Sadoulet, de Janvry and Davis (2001) did in their fixed-effects analysis of the income effects of Mexico's PRO-CAMPO crop subsidy program. This strategy can be confounded by the inability to adequately control for time-varying variables, however. For example, changes in the economy at large might coincide with the timing of the transfers and affect the outcomes of interest.

13. In Keynesian economics, government spending can increase income by more than the amount of the spending. This is the idea behind economic stimulus programs in the U.S. and other countries in response to the economic crisis beginning in 2007-08.

14. Benjamin, Dwayne, "Household Composition, Labor Markets and Labor Demand: Testing for Separation in Agricultural Household Models." *Econometrica*, March 1992; Jacoby, H. 1993. "Shadow Wages and Peasant Family Labor Supply: An Econometric Application to the Peruvian Sierra." *Review of Economic Studies* 60: 903-921; de Janvry, A., M. Fafchamps, and E. Sadoulet. "Peasant Household Behavior with Missing Markets: Some Paradoxes Explained." *The Economic Journal*, 101:14001417, 1991.

15. Sadoulet, E., A. de Janvry and B. Davis. "Cash Transfer Programs with Income Multipliers: PROCAMPO in Mexico." *World Development* 29(6):1043-1056, 2001.

16. Angus S. Deaton, "Instruments of Development: Randomization in the Tropics, and the Search for the Elusive Keys to Economic Development," National Bureau of Economic Research Working Paper 14690, January 2009 (http://www.nber.org/papers/w14690).

17. "Nudging Farmers to Use Fertilizer: Evidence from Kenya" (Esther Duflo, Michael Kremer and Jonathan Robinson). *American Economic Review*, forthcoming (also see NBER Working Paper No. 15131, 2009).

18. Christopher B. Barrett and Michael R. Carter, "The Power and Pitfalls of Experiments in Development Economics: Some Non-random Reflections, Applied Economic Perspectives and Policy, Volume 32, No. 4, pp. 515-548, 2010.

19. Poverty Action Lab, "What Is Randomization?" (http://www.poverty-actionlab.org/methodology/what-randomization).

20. Esther Duflo, "Schooling and Labor Market Consequences of School Construction in Indonesia: Evidence from an Unusual Policy Experiment," National Bureau of Economic Research Working Paper 7860, August 2000 (http://www.nber.org/papers/w7860).